Contents

Italian

Vocabulary

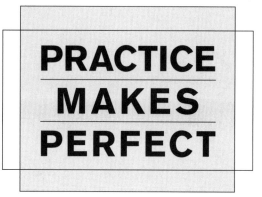

PRACTICE
MAKES
PERFECT

Italian Vocabulary

Daniela Gobetti

New York   Chicago   San Francisco   Lisbon   London   Madrid   Mexico City
Milan   New Delhi   San Juan   Seoul   Singapore   Sydney   Toronto

1 2 3 4 5 6 7 8 9 10 11 12 13 14 15 16 17 18 19 20 21   QPD/QPD   0 9 8 7

ISBN 978-0-07-148286-8
MHID   0-07-148286-5
Library of Congress control number 2006931667

McGraw-Hill books are available at special quantity discounts to use as premiums
and sales promotions, or for use in corporate training programs. For more information,
please write to the Director of Special Sales, Professional Publishing, McGraw-Hill, Two
Penn Plaza, New York, NY 10121-2298. Or contact your local bookstore.

This book is printed on acid-free paper.

Introduction

This book provides readers with basic Italian words in a variety of fields, and with exercises to practice how those words are used. It is divided into sixteen units corresponding to as many themes. In each unit words are clustered according to sub-themes, but within each sub-theme I have chosen to list nouns separate from verbs, pronouns, and so forth, rather than list them thematically.

Italian is a rule-based, rather than a pattern-based language. Familiarity with grammar rules is therefore indispensable even at the elementary level. While doing the exercises, users are encouraged to keep a grammar book, a verb book, and a dictionary at hand to clarify their doubts. Here I wish to provide just a few reminders.

- ◆ I have clustered together adjectives, adverbs, and phrases that are used to qualify nouns or verbs, because it often happens that a qualifier conveyed by an adjective in English is conveyed by an adverb or phrase in Italian, and vice versa. Adjectives and phrases composed of an adjective and a preposition, such as **bello** *(beautiful)*, **grande** *(large, great)*, **piccolo** *(small, little)*, **solo** *(alone)* and **da solo** *(alone)*, **da piccolo** *(as a kid/young boy)*, **da grande** *(as an adult)*, etc., must be coordinated in gender and number with the noun to which they refer. Adverbs such as **bene** *(well)*, **velocemente** *(fast)*, etc., are unchangeable, as are the complements **a disagio** *(not at ease, uneasy)* and **di corsa** *(in a hurry)*, which are formed of a noun and a preposition.
- ◆ Italian is rich in compound nouns, which can be formed by an adjective and a noun or a noun followed by a phrase (called a "complement" in Italian) that changes its basic meaning: **la malattia tropicale** *(tropical disease)*, **la barca a vela** *(sailing boat)*, **la tazza da tè** *(teacup)*. Only when compound nouns are formed by adding an adjective do the rules of coordination apply: **la guida turistica** *(tourist guide)*, **le guide turistiche** *(tourist guides)*.

  When the context is clear, the adjective or complement used as a qualifier can be dropped. I have listed in square brackets the word that can be omitted: **i [pomodori] pelati** *(peeled tomatoes)*; **le patatine [fritte]** *(potato chips)*.

  In general, square brackets are used to indicate that the word or words in question can be omitted.
- ◆ I have listed nouns in the masculine, unless the noun happens to be feminine: **la guida** *(guide)*, **la persona** *(person)*. The notation (m. and f. / f. and m.) (masculine and feminine / feminine and masculine) means that the

word in question can refer to either gender, even if the gender of the word is only masculine or feminine.

Since the masculine is the default gender in Italian, the masculine plural of nouns ending in -a can be used for women as well: l(o)'alpinista (*male mountain climber*), l(a)'alpinista (*female mountain climber*) → gli alpinisti (*male, female, or male and female mountain climbers*). But nowadays you can assume that, in everyday language, when the singular takes the feminine article, the plural will do so as well: la pediatra → le pediatre (*female pediatricians*), la fisioterapista → le fisioterapiste (*female physical therapists*).

I have not given the plural of nouns, but for exceptions such as l'uovo → le uova (*egg → eggs*), some compound nouns (il lavapiatti, le lavapiatti), and nouns ending in -o in the singular and -a in the plural (il dito, le dita).

I have added the notations (sing.) or (pl.) to some nouns to indicate that the noun only has the singular or the plural, or that in the context in which it is introduced it is used mostly in the singular or in the plural.

◆ Italian verbs in compound tenses can take as auxiliary either avere (*to have*) or essere (*to be*). The reflexive and passive forms require the auxiliary essere. When verbs are in the active form, transitive verbs always take avere. We call transitive those verbs whose action falls directly on an object. Intransitive verbs, which only take an indirect object introduced by a preposition, usually take essere. Since there are, however, a good number of intransitive verbs that take avere, and some verbs that can take either avere or essere, I have given the auxiliary or auxiliaries after these verbs.

As readers know, Italian has many irregular verbs. I have not dwelled on this point in the text. Consult a book listing all conjugations if you are in doubt.

◆ I have given only basic information about how to use pronouns and prepositions. For details, I wish to refer readers to *Practice Makes Perfect: Italian Pronouns and Prepositions*.

◆ I have not devoted specific sections of this book to coordinating and subordinating conjunctions, but I have listed "question words," and used some conjunctions in exercises: e (*and*), ma (*but*), o (*or*); quando (*when*), perché (*because*), se (*if/whether*), etc.

◆ Italian is rich in words taken from other languages: Latin, French, Arabic, German, etc., and now English above all. Pronunciation of these words is often "Italianized." And non-Italian words will always follow the rules of Italian grammar when it comes to placement in a sentence.

Words taken from other languages used to be considered all masculine and unchangeable, but that rule is often disregarded. When a noun refers to a human being, the masculine form can be used to refer to a man or a woman, il leader, il partner, but you will also find the feminine used: la leader, la partner. Nouns that refer to objects take the article of the corresponding Italian words, when there is one: la star del cinema (f. and m.) (*movie star*), because in Italian we can say la stella del cinema. In the plural, you may find the English plural used: il film, i films.

To conclude, I have chosen words that are widely used, and I have given their idiomatic equivalents in Italian: the literal translation of the English word *projects* is i progetti, but used in reference to housing it corresponds to le case popolari / l'edilizia agevolata. You will find *project* translated as il progetto in another part of the book.

Buon lavoro!

Family

A typical Italian family is composed of father, mother, and often just one child, because Italy is one of the countries in the world with the lowest birthrate. Since most Italians live with their parents until they get married, and reside in or near the town where they were born, family relations remain strong. However, the rate of divorce has been growing, especially among people with young children, as have unconventional families.

It is still common for elderly parents who are no longer independent to join their children's household. Whey they cannot, the alternative to a retirement home is to remain at home assisted by a **badante** (*caretaker*), usually an immigrant woman from eastern or central Europe, South America, or the Philippines.

il bambino; il figlio	*child*
la famiglia	*family*
la figlia	*daughter*
il figlio	*son*
i fratelli [e/o le sorelle] (pl.)	*siblings*
il fratello	*brother*
i genitori (pl.)	*parents*
la madre	*mother*
la mamma	*mom*
il padre	*father*
il papà	*dad*
la sorella	*sister*
l(a)'unità famigliare; la famiglia	*household*

I miei figli sono già grandi.	*My children are grown up.*
Sono in cinque tra fratelli e sorelle.	*They are five siblings.*

Close relatives

la cognata	*sister-in-law*
il cognato	*brother-in-law*
il cugino	*cousin*
il gemello	*twin*
il genero	*son-in-law*
il nipote	*grandson; nephew*
la nipote	*granddaughter; niece*
i nipotini (pl.)	*grandchildren*
la nonna	*grandmother*
il nonno	*grandfather*
i nonni	*grandparents*

la nuora	daughter-in-law
il, la parente	relative
la suocera	mother-in-law
il suocero	father-in-law
la zia	aunt
lo zio	uncle

Vedi quella ragazza? È mia nipote.	See that girl? She's my niece.
Vedi quella ragazza? È mia nipote.	See that girl? She's my granddaughter.
Carlo frequenta poco i suoi parenti.	Carlo doesn't see his relatives much.

The list below includes several members of the family. For each, give the complementary person.

EXAMPLE   il fratello la sorella

1. il cognato _____

2. il fratello _____

3. il genero _____

4. il papà _____

5. il suocero _____

6. la cugina _____

7. la figlia _____

8. la nipote _____

9. lo zio _____

Engagements and weddings

la coppia	couple
la fidanzata	fiancée
il fidanzato	fiancé
il marito	husband
la moglie	wife
la sposa	bride
lo sposo	groom
lo sposo; il, la consorte	spouse
il testimone	best man
la testimone	bridesmaid

| Sono una bella coppia. | They are a nice couple. |
| Oggi sposi! | Just married! |

Complete the following sentences with the most appropriate noun, choosing from the ones suggested after each sentence.

1. Non è sua moglie, è la sua _____.
   a. testimone   b. coppia   c. fidanzata

2. Lo sposo ha baciato la _____.
   a. fidanzata   b. sposa   c. moglie

3. La _____ è andata in luna di miele alle isole Maldive.
   a. coppia   b. testimone   c. fidanzata

4. Non è il cugino di Laura, è suo _____.
   a. testimone   b. marito   c. moglie

Other relationships

l(o, a)'amante	*lover*
il compagno; il, la partner	*companion; partner*
la figliastra (derogatory, rarely used)	*stepdaughter*
il figliastro (derogatory, rarely used)	*stepson*
il figlio adottivo	*adopted son*
la matrigna (derogatory, rarely used)	*stepmother*
il patrigno (derogatory, rarely used)	*stepfather*
la mia, tua, sua, etc. **ragazza**	*my, your, his, etc., girlfriend*
il mio, tuo, suo, etc. **ragazzo**	*my, your, her, etc., boyfriend*
il, la single	*single man/woman*
la vedova	*widow*
il vedovo	*widower*

Sono molto attaccata ai figli di mio marito.	*I'm very attached to my stepchildren.*
Le single sono in aumento.	*The number of single women is growing.*

Used in the plural, a masculine noun indicates a group of males and a group of males *and* females: **i figli**, *sons* or *sons and daughters*; **le figlie** means *daughters*. Some nouns are gender specific in the singular and the plural:

il fratello / la sorella	*brother/sister*
il genero / la nuora	*son-in-law/daughter-in-law*
il marito / la moglie	*husband/wife*
il maschio / la femmina	*male/female*
il padre; il papà / la madre; la mamma	*father; dad / mother; mom*
l'uomo / la donna	*man/woman*

Provide the masculine singular of the following nouns. Remember that some nouns differ completely in the two genders.

1. le amanti _____

2. le cognate _____

3. le fidanzate _____

4. le madri _____

5. le mogli _____

6. le nipoti _____

7. le nuore _____

8. le parenti _____

9. le spose _____

10. le zie _____

Give the Italian version of the nouns listed below. Use the masculine plural when two nouns are listed in English.

1. aunt and uncle _____

2. bride and groom _____

3. brother-in-law and sister-in-law _____

4. cousins _____

5. fiancé and fiancée _____

6. grandchildren _____

7. father-in-law and mother-in-law _____

8. nephew and niece _____

Articles

In Italian the definite articles are: **il, lo, l(o)', i, gli, la, l(a)', le**; the indefinite articles: **un, uno, una/ un'** (*a, an*). We can also use indefinite qualifiers such as **un po' di** (*a little of; some*), **molto** (*very;*

much; a lot of), **poco** (*too little*), **tanto** (*so much*), and the **preposizione articolata** (*preposition +
article*) **del, dello** (**dell'**), and **della** (**dell'**, *some*).

With uncountable nouns, Italian uses the definite article and indefinite quantifiers, but not
the indefinite article **un, uno**, etc. We can convey indefinite quantities of countable nouns in the
plural with **alcuni** (*some; any; a few*), **qualche** (*some,* followed by the singular, but conveying a
plural meaning), **molte** (*many; a lot*), **poche** (*few*), **tante** (*so many*), and **dei, degli,** and **delle**
(*some*):

l(o)'affetto (*countable and uncountable*)	*affection; care*
l(o)'amore (*countable and uncountable*)	*love; love affair*
l(o)'anello di fidanzamento	*engagement ring*
l(o)'anniversario	*anniversary*
la bugia	*lie*
il divorzio	*divorce*
la fede [nuziale]	*wedding ring*
la fiducia (*uncountable*)	*trust; faith*
il litigio	*argument*
la luna di miele	*honeymoon*
il matrimonio	*marriage; wedding*
le nozze (pl.)	*wedding*
la promessa	*promise*
la relazione [extraconiugale]	*(love) affair*
la separazione	*separation*
il tradimento	*betrayal*

Provo un grande affetto per te.	*I feel great affection for you.*
Casanova è famoso per i suoi amori.	*Casanova is famous for his love affairs.*

ESERCIZIO

1·5

Translate the following expressions into English.

1. un po' di affetto _____

2. l'anello di fidanzamento _____

3. un anniversario _____

4. delle bugie _____

5. poca fiducia _____

6. la luna di miele _____

7. un matrimonio _____

8. un amore _____

Possessive adjectives carry the article. They do not when they refer to family members in the
singular form (note, however, that the possessive adjective **loro** always carries the article): **mia
madre** (*my mother*); **suo marito** (*her husband*); **nostro figlio** (*our son*), unless a qualifier, including a possessive adjective, accompanies the noun: **la mia mamma** (*my mom*); **il figlio più grande**

(*the older son*). Possessives are coordinated in gender with the person (or thing) to which they refer, and in number with the owner and with the "thing" owned.

la zia mia e di mia sorella → nostra zia	*our aunt*
lo zio di Pietro → suo zio	*his uncle*
il gatto di Gianna → il suo gatto	*her cat*
le gatte di Gianna → le sue gatte	*her cats*

Possessive pronouns *always* carry the article. And **i miei, i suoi**, used by themselves, mean: *my parents, relatives,* etc. We do not use it for the third person plural: **i loro**.

Possessive adjectives and pronouns

il mio, la mia, i miei, le mie	*my; mine*
il tuo, la tua, i tuoi, le tue	*your; yours*
il suo, la sua, i suoi, le sue	*his; her; hers; its*
il Suo, la Sua, i Suoi, le Sue	*your; yours (you formal, sing.)*
il nostro, la nostra, i nostri, le nostre	*our; ours*
il vostro, la vostra, i vostri, le vostre	*your; yours*
il loro, la loro, i loro, le loro	*theirs*
il Loro, la Loro, i Loro, le Loro	*your; yours (you formal, pl.)*

ESERCIZIO
1·6

Add the appropriate possessive to the following sentences.

1. I fratelli di vostro padre sono i _____ zii.

2. Il figlio di mio fratello è _____ nipote.

3. Il padre del loro papà è il _____ nonno.

4. Il padre di suo marito è _____ suocero.

5. La figlia di mia sorella è _____ nipote.

6. La sorella di tua madre è _____ zia.

7. Le cugine di nostra sorella sono anche le _____ cugine.

Verbs

abbracciare	*to embrace; to hug*
abitare (con) (aux. avere); vivere (con) (aux. **avere/essere**)	*to live (with)*
aiutare	*to help*
amare	*to love*
andare d'accordo (con)	*to get along well (with)*
corteggiare	*to court*
divorziare (da) (aux. avere)	*to divorce (from)*
fare l'amore (con)	*to make love (with)*
fidanzarsi (con)	*to get engaged (with)*

fidarsi (di)	*to trust*
innamorarsi (di)	*to fall in love (with)*
lasciare	*to leave*
litigare (con) (aux. **avere**)	*to argue (with)*
odiare; detestare	*to hate*
perdonare	*to forgive*
piacere (a)	*to like; to be pleasing to*
promettere (a) (aux. **avere**)	*to promise (to)*
rimproverare	*to scold*
sposare	*to marry*
tradire	*to betray*
viziare	*to spoil (a person)*
voler bene (a) (aux. **avere**)	*to care for; to love*

Le piacciono i bambini.	*She likes children.*
Mio nonno ha vissuto bene e a lungo.	*My grandfather had a good and long life.*
Bianca è vissuta per molti anni in Brasile.	*Bianca lived many years in Brazil.*

ESERCIZIO
1·7

Complete the following sentences with one of the verbs listed below each of them.

1. I suoi genitori _____ dopo trent'anni di matrimonio.
   a. sposano   b. amano   c. divorziano

2. Lui dice che _____ sua moglie, ma continua a vivere con lei.
   a. perdona   b. ama   c. odia

3. Mio marito mi _____ con la mia migliore amica.
   a. vive   b. tradisce   c. corteggia

4. Non puoi _____ Luigi? Ti ha tradito, ma ti ama ancora.
   a. perdonare   b. viziare   c. abbracciare

5. Se lo _____ davvero, aiutalo a fare quello che desidera.
   a. ami   b. odi   c. rimproveri

In the infinitive, Italian verbs end in **-are**, **-ere**, or **-ire**: **am-are** (*to love*), **promett-ere** (*to promise*), **pun-ire** (*to punish*). In the reflexive form, they end in **-arsi**: **sposarsi** (*to get married*), **-ersi**: **prendersi cura di** (*to take care of*), and **-irsi**: **sentirsi** (*to feel*) (aux. **essere**). The reflexive form also indicates a reciprocal action, conveyed in English with the phrases *one another, each other, mutually*, etc.

Si è comportata male.	*She misbehaved. / She behaved badly.*
Elena e Vincenzo si amano.	*Elena and Vincenzo love each other.*
Giovanna e Filippo si odiano.	*Giovanna and Filippo hate each other.*

Reflexive pronouns

mi	*myself*
ti	*yourself*
si	*himself/herself; oneself; itself*
Si	*yourself* (you formal, sing.)
ci	*ourselves*
vi	*yourselves*
si	*themselves*
Si	*yourselves* (you formal, pl.)

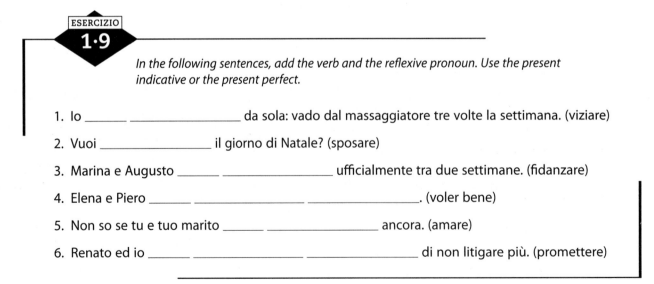

ESERCIZIO
1·8

Turn the following verbs into reflexive verbs.

1. abbracciare _____

2. aiutare _____

3. amare _____

4. perdonare _____

5. sposare _____

6. tradire _____

7. promettere _____

8. voler bene _____

ESERCIZIO
1·9

In the following sentences, add the verb and the reflexive pronoun. Use the present indicative or the present perfect.

1. Io _____ _____ da sola: vado dal massaggiatore tre volte la settimana. (viziare)

2. Vuoi _____ il giorno di Natale? (sposare)

3. Marina e Augusto _____ _____ ufficialmente tra due settimane. (fidanzare)

4. Elena e Piero _____ _____ _____. (voler bene)

5. Non so se tu e tuo marito _____ _____ ancora. (amare)

6. Renato ed io _____ _____ _____ di non litigare più. (promettere)

The pronoun **si** also means *one, people, we, you, they,* etc. **Si** is used as an impersonal subject which may or may not include the speaker.

Si va al cinema stasera?   *Are we going to the movies tonight?*
Si dice in giro che la sua ditta stia fallendo.   *People say that his firm is going bankrupt.*

Used impersonally, **si** can be followed by the third person singular or plural.

Si apre il negozio alle 9.   *The store opens at 9 A.M.*
Si aprono le porte del teatro alle 9.   *The theater's doors open at 9 P.M.*

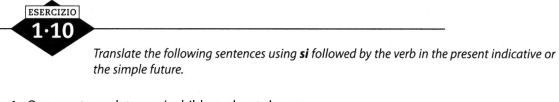

ESERCIZIO
1·10

*Translate the following sentences using **si** followed by the verb in the present indicative or the simple future.*

1. One must speak to one's children about drugs.

   _____

2. You help your own relatives.

   _____

3. They say Elena and Giorgio will get a divorce.

   _____

4. We are going to the restaurant tonight.

   _____

Describing family relationships

affettuoso	*affectionate*
affezionato (a)	*attached (to)*
amato	*loved*
divorziato	*divorced*
fidanzato	*engaged*
innamorato (di)	*in love (with)*
intimo	*intimate*
materno	*motherly; maternal*
paterno	*fatherly; paternal*
perdonato	*forgiven*
promesso	*promised*
sposato (a/con)	*married (to/with)*
tradito	*betrayed*
vedovo	*widowed*

Elsa è una bambina affettuosa.   *Elsa is an affectionate child.*
Mio fratello è affezionato al suo cane.   *My brother is attached to his dog.*

Give adjectives that correspond to the following definitions.

1. Formally engaged to get married. _____

2. Hidden in one's own self; secret. _____

3. Legally separated from one's spouse. _____

4. Legally united to another person in marriage. _____

5. Someone deeply in love with someone else. _____

6. Someone who survives one's deceased spouse. _____

Pronouns

When we refer to someone whom we have already mentioned, we can use subject, direct object, or indirect object pronouns.

Subject pronouns

io	*I*
tu	*you*
lui/lei	*he/she* (including pets)
esso/essa	*it*
noi	*we*
voi	*you*
loro; essi/esse	*they*

Replace the name or noun referring to a person in parentheses with the appropriate subject pronoun, or add the pronoun when it has been omitted.

1. (I miei cugini) _____ comprano una casa.

2. (I serpenti) _____ non sono pericolosi.

3. (Il serpente) _____ non è pericoloso.

4. (La nostra gatta) _____ ha avuto dieci gattini.

5. (Mario, Gianna ed io) _____ andiamo al cinema.

6. (Suo padre) _____ non sta bene.

7. _____ vai al mare?

8. _____ volete cambiare la prenotazione?

Direct object pronouns

ATTACHED TO OR BEFORE THE VERB	AFTER THE VERB	
mi	me	*me*
ti	te	*you*
lo/la	—	*him/her; it*
—	lui/lei	*him/her* (persons and pets only)
ci	noi	*us*
vi	voi	*you*
li/le	—	*them* (persons and things)
—	loro	*them* (persons only)

ESERCIZIO
1·13

Replace the name or noun referring to a person with the appropriate direct object pronoun, or add the pronoun when it has been omitted. Use the pronouns that can be placed before the verb.

1. Accogliamo gli ospiti. _____ accogliamo.

2. Ascoltano te? _____ ascoltano?

3 Hai comprato le patate? _____ hai comprate?

4. Hai pagato i muratori? _____ hai pagati?

5. Amano molto me e mia sorella. _____ amano molto.

6. Amano molto te e i tuoi fratelli. _____ amano molto.

7. Incontro sua sorella a teatro. _____ incontro a teatro.

8. Mangio la torta. _____ mangio.

Indirect object pronouns

ATTACHED TO OR BEFORE THE VERB		AFTER THE VERB	
mi	*me*	a/per me	*to me*
ti	*you*	a/per te	*to you*
gli	*him/her*	a/per lui/lei	*to him/her* (persons and pets)
—		a/per esso/essa	*to it* (things)
ci	*us*	a/per noi	*to us*
vi	*you*	a/per voi	*to you*
gli	*them*	a/per loro; loro	*to them* (persons and pets)
—		a/per essi/esse	*to them* (things)

Replace the names, nouns, or pronouns with the appropriate indirect object pronoun placed before the verb.

1. Ha comprato una pelliccia per me. _____ ha comprato una pelliccia.

2. Hanno lasciato un messaggio per voi. _____ hanno lasciato un messaggio.

3. Lascio qualcosa da mangiare per il cane. _____ lascio qualcosa da mangiare.

4. Lascio un messaggio per i nostri inquilini. _____ lascio un messaggio.

5. Offri un bicchiere di vino alla signora? _____ offri un bicchiere di vino?

6. Raccontate la storia a noi? _____ raccontate la storia?

7. Servi il cognac a tuo zio? _____ servi il cognac?

8. Vendo a te quel quadro. _____ vendo quel quadro.

People

Italians spend their leisure time with friends as much as with family members. Limited geographical mobility enables people to maintain friendships made even in their childhood or teenage years. People become friends with their peers in college, or through sports, political parties, religious functions, and participation in the countless volunteer organizations existing in Italy, more than through their work environment.

il carattere	*character*
il cognome	*last name*
la donna	*woman*
l(o)'essere umano (m. and f.)	*human being*
la gente (collective sing.) / **le persone;**	*people; peoples*
le genti / i popoli	
l(o)'individuo (m. and f.)	*individual; person*
il nome (proprio)	*(given) name*
la persona (f. and m.)	*person*
la personalità	*personality*
la ragazza	*girl*
il ragazzo	*boy*
il tipo / la tipa	*kind of person; guy; character*
l(o)'umore	*mood*
l(o)'uomo, gli uomini	*man*

Olga è un bel tipo!	*Olga is quite a character!*
Sei di cattivo umore?	*Are you in a bad mood?*

ESERCIZIO

2·1

Complete the sentences on the left with the appropriate noun from those listed on the right.

1. Che _____ hanno dato al bambino? a. carattere

2. È una donna con una forte _____. b. cognome

3. Elena ha un buon _____. c. nome

4. Franco è un _____ un po' strano. d. personalità

5. Hanno lo stesso _____, ma non sono parenti. e. persone

6. I suoi vicini sono _____ simpatiche. f. tipo

Describing personalities

aggressivo	*aggressive*
antipatico	*off-putting*
buono; bravo	*good*
cattivo	*bad*
curioso	*curious*
debole	*weak; fickle*
dolce	*sweet*
forte	*strong*
furbo	*cunning*
generoso	*generous*
normale	*ordinary; normal*
paziente	*patient*
prepotente	*overbearing*
profondo	*profound*
saggio	*wise*
serio	*serious*
severo	*strict*
sicuro di sé	*confident*
simpatico	*nice*
superficiale	*superficial*
timido	*shy*
vivace	*lively; vivacious*

Vittorio è davvero antipatico.   *Vittorio is really off-putting.*
Tuo figlio è molto prepotente.   *Your son is very overbearing.*

ESERCIZIO
2·2

Complete the following sentences, choosing from the adjectives listed below each of them.

1. Sua figlia ha letto tutte le lettere di sua sorella. È una bambina molto _____.
   a. vivace   b. curiosa   c. furba

2. Passa ore e ore nel suo studio a meditare. È un uomo _____.
   a. normale   b. paziente   c. profondo

3. Corre dietro a suo figlio tutto il giorno. È un bambino _____.
   a. vivace   b. prepotente   c. curioso

4. Amministrano bene il suo patrimonio. Sono molto _____.
   a. seri   b. severi   c. pazienti

Personality traits

la bontà	*goodness*
la curiosità	*curiosity*
la debolezza	*weakness*
la forza	*strength*
la furbizia	*cunning*

la generosità	generosity
la normalità	normality
la saggezza	wisdom
la serietà	seriousness
la stima; il rispetto	respect

Gandhi è un esempio di saggezza.	Gandhi is an example of wisdom.
La bambina prende tutto con serietà.	The little girl takes everything seriously.

We can derive nouns from adjectives that describe personality traits by adding various endings. One of the most common ending is **-ità** (English *-ity*, as in *curios-ity*), which is added to an adjective by dropping the end-vowel, and sometimes modifying it.

curioso	**curios*ità***	*curious*	*curiosity*
serio	**ser*ietà***	*serious*	*seriousness*
buono	**bontà**	*good*	*goodness*

In Italian most of these nouns are feminine and uncountable, take the definite article, and cannot be used in the plural. We can convey single instances through a periphrasis: **un atto di bontà** (*a good deed*), **(degli) atti di bontà** (*good deeds*), **un atto di generosità** (*an act of generosity*), **(degli) atti di generosità** (*acts of generosity*), etc.

ESERCIZIO
2·3

Turn the adjectives listed below into the corresponding nouns, add the article, and translate them into English. Consult a dictionary if you are not sure of the spelling.

1. aggressivo _____

2. normale _____

3. profondo _____

4. severo _____

5. superficiale _____

6. vivace _____

ESERCIZIO
2·4

Give the noun conveying the characteristic evoked by the situation or event which is described in the following sentences.

1. «Cosa cerchi nella sua scrivania»?! «La lettera della sua prima moglie». _____

2. È una persona che cambia opinione ogni cinque minuti. _____

3. Dopo la guerra, siamo tornati alla solita vita. _____

4. Urlava e minacciava. Che reazione esagerata per quello stupido incidente! _____

5. Ma tuo padre ti sgrida sempre tanto? _____

Adverbs

Adverbs enable us to add important qualifications to situations, actions, and descriptions, by modifying verbs, adjectives, nouns, other adverbs, and entire sentences. With a few exceptions, they change neither gender nor number.

Parla **normalmente**.	She speaks **normally**.
La sua gamba è **molto** debole.	Her leg is **very** weak.
Sei arrivato **troppo** tardi.	You arrived **too** late.

bene	*well; good*
curiosamente	*curiously*
debolmente	*weakly*
dolcemente	*sweetly*
forte; fortemente	*strongly; with great energy*
generosamente	*generously*
male	*badly*
normalmente	*normally*
seriamente	*seriously*

In Italian most adverbs derive from adjectives. Adverbs that emphasize how something is, happens, or is done, are formed usually by adding **-mente** (*-ly, -ily*) to the feminine singular of adjectives in **-o**: **aggressiv-o → aggressiv-a → aggressiva-mente** (*aggressively*); or to the singular of adjectives in **-e**: **dolce → dolce-mente** (*sweetly*). When the last syllable of adjectives in **-e** ends in **-le** or **-re**, the final vowel is omitted: **umil-e → umilmente** (*humbly*).

ESERCIZIO
2·5

Turn the following adjectives into adverbs.

1. affettuoso _____

2. intimo _____

3. paziente _____

4. saggio _____

5. severo _____

6. timido _____

7. vivace _____

ESERCIZIO
2·6

Combine the sentence listed in the left column with the appropriate adverb chosen from the right column.

1. A due anni, suo figlio parla già _____.   a. bene

2. Mi ha chiesto _____ un favore.   b. curiosamente

3. Osservava la ragazza _____, come se
fosse un'extraterrestre.

   c. generosamente

4. Il preside ci ha puniti _____.

   d. severamente

5. Li hai ricompensati anche troppo _____.

   e. timidamente

Essere

We can add an adjective to the verb **essere** (*to be*) to talk about a state of affairs or a situation. The verb does not take any subject and is always in the singular. It can be followed by the present or the past infinitive, or by a declarative dependent clause introduced by **che**, when we wish to emphasize who is or should be performing an action. When the main clause conveys possibility, uncertainty, or a subjective opinion or feeling, the verb of the dependent clause will be in the subjunctive.

È importante vederla.	*It's important to see her.*
È certo che Adriana è partita.	*It's certain that Adriana left.*
È commovente che tu lo abbia perdonato.	*It's moving that you forgave him.*

Here follows a list of common adjectives used with the verb **essere**.

carino; bello	*nice*
certo; sicuro	*certain*
commovente	*moving*
curioso	*curious*
difficile	*hard; difficult*
facile	*easy*
giusto	*right; fair*
importante	*important*
normale	*normal*
sbagliato	*wrong*
strano	*strange; weird*

ESERCIZIO
2·7

Match the main clause on the left with the appropriate conclusion among those listed on the right.

1. È giusto che loro _____

   a. abbiate invitato mio fratello.

2. È stato piacevole _____

   b. hanno divorziato.

3. È probabile che Luisa _____

   c. passare il Natale in famiglia.

4. È carino che voi _____

   d. sposi Roberto.

5. È certo che Giancarlo e Sandra _____

   e. dicano la verità alla madre.

Social relationships

l(a)'amicizia	*friendship*
l(o)'amico	*friend*
la compagnia	*company*
il complimento	*compliment*
la conoscenza (f. and m.)	*acquaintance*
la conversazione	*conversation*
l(o)'estraneo; lo sconosciuto	*stranger*
il flirt	*flirt; flirtation*
il giovanotto	*young man*
il pettegolezzo	*(piece of) gossip*
il regalo	*gift*
la richiesta	*request*
lo scherzo	*joke*
(la) signora	*lady; Madam; Ms.*
(il) signore	*gentleman; Sir*
(la) signorina	*young lady; Ms.; Miss*
il silenzio	*silence*
la solitudine	*loneliness; solitude*
il vicino [di casa]	*neighbor*
la visita	*visit*

«Hai avuto una storia»? «No, solo un flirt».	*"Did you have an affair?" "No, just a flirtation."*
Sono solo pettegolezzi.	*It's just gossip.*

ESERCIZIO
2·8

Match the first half of the sentences listed on the left with their complementary part among those listed on the right.

1. A mia madre piace _____

2. Enrico non sta bene. _____

3. I due amici fanno _____

4. I nostri vicini di casa _____

5. Le hanno fatto molti _____

6. Quando sei al giardinetto, non parlare _____

a. Andiamo a fargli visita?

b. complimenti per la nuova casa.

c. con gli estranei.

d. la compagnia dei suoi cugini.

e. sono molto gentili.

f. una lunga chiacchierata.

Keeping company and socializing

accompagnare	*to accompany; to go with*
annoiare	*to bore*
aspettare; attendere	*to wait (for)*
aspettarsi (da)	*to expect (from)*
chiamare; telefonare (a)	*to call*

chiamarsi	*to be called; to be named*
comportarsi	*to behave*
conoscere (aux. **avere**); **sapere** (aux. **avere**)	*to know*

Note that **conoscere** means *to be acquainted with*; whereas **sapere** means *to know something, to know how + infinitive.*

Conosci mio fratello?	*Do you know my brother?*
Sapete la poesia a memoria?	*Do you know the poem by heart?*
Sapete come fare ad arrivare a casa?	*Do you know how to get home?*

dare/darsi del Lei	*to be on formal terms*
dare/darsi del tu	*to be on familiar terms*
dire (a)	*to say (to)*
domandare (a); chiedere (a)	*to ask*
fare una domanda (a)	*to ask a question*
frequentare	*to frequent*
importare (a)	*to mind; to matter (to)*
mettersi in contatto (con)	*to get in touch (with)*
offendere	*to offend*
parlare (a/con) (aux. avere)	*to speak (to/with); to talk (to/with)*
passare (da)	*to stop by*
ringraziare	*to thank*
rispondere (a); rispondere al telefono	*to answer; to answer the phone*
salutare	*to greet*
scrivere (a)	*to write (to)*
scusare; chiedere scusa (a); chiedere permesso (a)	*to excuse*
scusarsi (con)	*to apologize (with)*
spettegolare (aux. avere)	*to gossip*
stare zitto	*to be quiet*
toccare a qualcuno (in coda)	*to be someone's turn (in line)*
uscire (con qualcuno)	*to go out (with someone)*
vedere; andare a vedere; andare a trovare	*to visit*

Ti dispiace se abbasso la radio?	*Do you mind if I turn down the radio?*
Tocca a me, adesso.	*It's my turn.*

ESERCIZIO

2·9

Among the verbs listed above, choose those that describe the following actions. Use the infinitive.

1. A man with a sorry look on his face tries to placate an angry woman. _____

2. A woman is standing outside a movie theater, checking her watch every five seconds. _____

3. Someone with a map stops a passerby for directions. _____

4. You're trying to reach a colleague by phone. _____

5. You've decided to pay a friend an unannounced visit. _____

When we wish to convey how something is done we can use an adverb, or a complement introduced by **con** (*with*) + *noun*, **in maniera** + *feminine adjective* (*in a _____ manner*), or **in modo** + *masculine adjective* (*in a _____ way*). Experience and context will tell you when it is idiomatically more appropriate to use the adverb, and when to use the complement **con** + *noun*, or **in modo / maniera** + *adjective*.

Li ha rimproverati severamente. → Li ha rimproverati con severità.   *He reproached them severely / with great severity.*
Parlava curiosamente. → Parlava in maniera curiosa / modo curioso.   *She was speaking curiously / in a curious manner/way.*

ESERCIZIO
2·10

*In the following sentences, replace the adverb in parentheses with the corresponding complement. Use either **con** + noun or **in modo** + masculine adjective as indicated.*

1. Ascolta tuo nonno (pazientemente) con _____.

2. Conosciamo i nostri vicini di casa (superficialmente) in modo _____.

3. I nostri fratelli ci hanno ringraziato (affettuosamente) con _____.

4. I suoi genitori parlano del loro figlio medico (orgogliosamente) con _____.

5. Il suo direttore lo tratta (famigliarmente) in modo _____.

6. La bambina ha salutato (timidamente) con _____.

Sharing events with others

accettare	to accept
augurare	to wish
brindare (a)	to toast
celebrare; festeggiare	to celebrate
dare il benvenuto (a)	to welcome
invitare	to invite
offrire (a)	to offer (to)
ospitare	to host
portare	to bring
prendere; portare	to take
presentare (a)	to introduce (to)
regalare	to give
ricevere	to receive; to have someone over
rifiutare	to refuse

Posso presentarla al nostro vescovo?   *May I introduce you to our bishop?*
Ricevono molto.   *They have people over quite often.*

On the board of a college dormitory students have posted notes seeking people for their weekend activities. Match them with the answers left by interested students.

1. Ragazzi, se venite allo stadio, portate i buoni per la pizza. _____

2. Cerchiamo tre rematori per la regata di domenica. _____

3. Diamo il benvenuto alla classe del 2007! Grande festa alla piscina comunale! _____

4. I miei vanno via questo fine settimana. Posso ospitare quattro ragazzi a casa mia! _____

5. Isabella, perché non mi presenti alla tua amica? _____

6. Vendo biglietti per il concerto di Bruce Springsteen. 100 euro l'uno. _____

   a. Accettiamo volentieri, ma non abbiamo i remi.
   b. I buoni per la pizza sono finiti. Portiamo i buoni per McDonald's.
   c. Grazie dell'invito a casa dei tuoi, ma io rifiuto.
   d. Io non sono della classe del 2007. Posso venire lo stesso?
   e. La mia amica è già fidanzata!
   f. Sono senza soldi. Posso offrire sei biglietti per il concerto delle Dixie Chicks.

Social occasions

l(o)'appuntamento	*appointment*
la buona educazione (sing.); le buone maniere (pl.)	*good manners*
la cattiva educazione (sing.); la maleducazione (sing.); le cattive maniere (pl.)	*bad manners*
il compleanno	*birthday*
il comportamento	*behavior*
la domanda	*question*
il favore; il piacere	*favor*
la festa / il party	*party*
la gentilezza	*kindness*
l(o)'invito	*invitation*
il numero di telefono / telefonico	*telephone number*
l(o, a)'ospite; l(o)'invitato	*guest*
l(o, a)'ospite; il padrone / la padrona di casa	*host; hostess*
i ringraziamenti (pl.)	*thanks*
la risposta	*answer*

Puoi farmi un favore?	*Could you do me a favor?*
Mamma mia, che maleducazione!	*Good gracious, what bad manners!*

Donatella and her sister-in-law, Marianna, are inviting people to a surprise party for Donatella's husband's birthday. Complete the dialogue using words listed in Units 1 and 2.

1. «_____, Marianna, sono Donatella. Come va»?

2. «Va benissimo. Mi _____ a organizzare la festa? Vorrei invitare non più di venti _____».

3. «Vuoi che telefoni agli ospiti o vuoi mandare degli _____»?

4. «Puoi mandarli tu? Ma non voglio _____ Anselmo».

5. «Non lo vuoi invitare, dici? Perché no? È un _____ brillante».

6. «L'ultima volta il suo _____ è stato orribile. Ha delle _____ pessime».

7. «Come vuoi tu. Questa è la tua _____."

Responses

As Donatella and Marianna's conversation shows, adverbs, nouns, adjectives, names, and verbs can be used as interjections, invariable parts of speech which can express emotions on the part of the speaker—*Ouch!*—or carry specific meanings—*Hello!*

Rosanna non viene. Peccato!	*Rosanna's not coming. Pity!*
Mamma, ho fame!	*Mom, I'm hungry!*
arrivederci (informal); **arrivederla** (formal)	*good-bye*
buona fortuna	*good luck*
ciao (informal); **pronto** (when answering the phone)	*hello*
cin cin; **salute**	*cheers* (when toasting)
congratulazioni; **complimenti**	*congratulations*
di niente	*not at all*
forse	*maybe*
grazie	*thank you*
mi scusi; **scusi**	*excuse me; sorry*
no	*no*
per favore	*please*
prego	*you're welcome*
sì	*yes*
Pronto, chi parla?	*Hello, who's speaking?*
Ciao, Carla, come stai?	*Hello, Carla, how are you?*

Match the sentences or interjections listed on the left with their appropriate counterparts among those listed on the right.

1. Prego, _____   a. Buona fortuna!

2. Pronto?! Pronto?! Ma chi parla?! _____   b. ecco la vostra cantante preferita!

3. Ragazzina, devi essere _____   c. Guardi che chiamo la polizia!

4. Signore e Signori, _____   d. passi prima lei, Signor Salvi.

5. Vai sul Monte Everest?! _____   e. un po' più rispettosa con il nonno.

Describing social situations

da solo	*(all) alone; by oneself*
gentile	*kind*
(molto) impegnato; occupato	*busy*
insieme	*together*
libero	*free*
malvolentieri	*reluctantly*
personale	*personal*
(in) pochi	*few (people)*
pronto	*ready*
scortese; sgarbato	*impolite*
solo	*alone*
(in) tanti	*a lot of (people)*
volentieri; con piacere	*gladly*

Ha pitturato il garage da sola.	*She painted the garage herself.*
Siamo in tanti!	*There are so many of us!*

Give the qualifiers that correspond to the following definitions.

1. Doing something gladly. _____

2. Doing something reluctantly. _____

3. Doing things by oneself. _____

4. A small group of people. _____

5. Someone who is very busy. _____

Questions

When talking to people, we often ask questions. The main question words are:

Che? Quale?	*What? Which?*
Che cosa? Cosa?	*What?*
Chi?	*Who? Whom?*
Come?	*How?*
Di chi?	*Whose?*
Dove?	*Where?*
Perché?	*Why?*
Quando?	*When?*
Quanto? Quanta? Quanti? Quante?	*How much? How many?*

Question words can be used both in direct and indirect questions.

Chi viene a cena?	*Who's coming for dinner?*
Indovina chi viene a cena.	*Guess who's coming for dinner.*

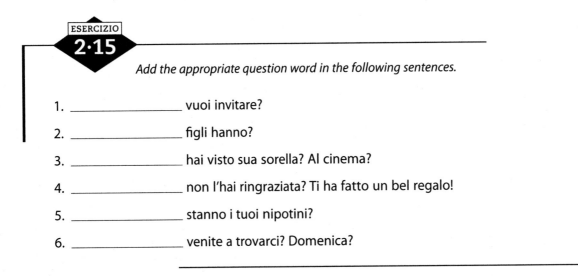

ESERCIZIO
2·15

Add the appropriate question word in the following sentences.

1. _____ vuoi invitare?

2. _____ figli hanno?

3. _____ hai visto sua sorella? Al cinema?

4. _____ non l'hai ringraziata? Ti ha fatto un bel regalo!

5. _____ stanno i tuoi nipotini?

6. _____ venite a trovarci? Domenica?

The body and the senses

In today's society thin, tall, and beautiful people are at an advantage over fat, short, and unattractive ones. Italians attach great importance to posture. They buy leather shoes even for babies, though many teenagers have joined the flip-flop and sneaker-footed tribe. Americans don't gesticulate much, but often convey through facial mimicry what Italians convey with their hands.

la bocca	*mouth*
il braccio, le braccia	*arm*
il capello, i capelli	*a single hair (on the head); hair (on the head, collective sing.)*
il collo	*neck*
il corpo	*body*
il dente	*tooth*
il dito, le dita	*finger; toe*
la faccia / il viso	*face*
la gamba	*leg*
il ginocchio, le ginocchia	*knee*
la gola	*throat*
il gomito	*elbow*
il labbro, le labbra	*lip*
la lingua	*tongue*
la mano, le mani	*hand*
il naso	*nose*
l(o)'occhio	*eye*
l(o)'orecchio, le orecchie	*ear*
la pelle (sing.)	*skin; hide*
il pelo	*(body) hair*
il petto	*bosom*
il piede	*foot*
la schiena	*back*
il sedere	*bottom*
il seno	*breast*
la spalla	*shoulder*
la testa	*head*
la vita	*waist*

Anna ha avuto una vita molto interessante. — *Anna's had a very interesting life.*

Maria ha la vita stretta. — *Maria has a narrow waist.*

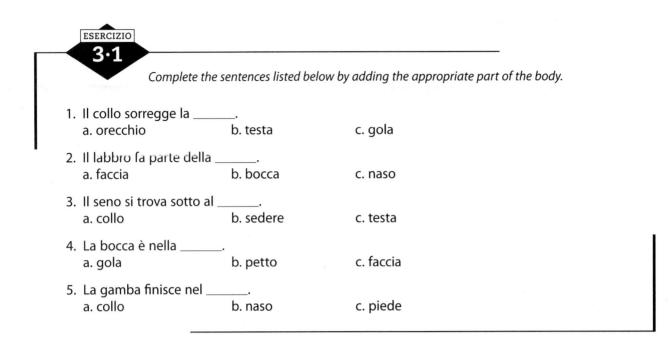

Complete the sentences listed below by adding the appropriate part of the body.

1. Il collo sorregge la _____.
   a. orecchio   b. testa   c. gola

2. Il labbro fa parte della _____.
   a. faccia   b. bocca   c. naso

3. Il seno si trova sotto al _____.
   a. collo   b. sedere   c. testa

4. La bocca è nella _____.
   a. gola   b. petto   c. faccia

5. La gamba finisce nel _____.
   a. collo   b. naso   c. piede

Internal organs and body parts

l(a)'arteria	*artery*
la carne (sing.)	*flesh, meat*
il cervello	*brain*
il cuore	*heart*
il fegato	*liver*
l(o)'intestino	*intestine*
il muscolo	*muscle*
il nervo	*nerve*
l(o)'organo	*organ*
l(o)'osso, le ossa (human); gli ossi (animal)	*bone; bones*
il polmone	*lung*
il sangue	*blood*
lo stomaco / la pancia	*stomach*
la vena	*vein*

Mamma, ho mal di pancia!	*Mom, my tummy hurts!*
Soffre di mal di fegato.	*She has liver problems.*

When we wish to convey what happens to one's own body and its parts, in Italian we use the definite or the indefinite article, depending on whether we are talking about our liver, body, head, etc., or about one or more of our many arteries, nerves, etc.

Ha avuto problemi **al cuore**.	*He's had **heart** problems.*
Mi sono rotta **una** mano.	*I broke **one of my** hands.*

In talking about the body, we can use verbs followed by a direct object: **rompersi qualcosa** (*to break something / a part of one's body*), or verbs that take an indirect object: **farsi male** (*to hurt oneself*) and **sentire male a** (*to feel pain in*), **soffrire di** (*to suffer from*), and **avere dolore/male a/di** (*to feel pain in/at*).

Complete the following sentences by choosing the appropriate article, following the examples mentioned above.

1. Mi sono rotta _____ braccio.

2. Mi sono fatta male _____ testa. (**a**)

3. Sua sorella si è presa una storta _____ piede. (**a**)

4. Ha un'aritmia _____ cuore. (**a**)

5. Ti hanno tolto _____ rene?

6. Si è scottata _____ lingua.

7. Ha perso sensibilità _____ nervo. (**a**)

Describing the body

arterioso	*arterial*
cardiaco	*cardiac*
corporeo	*corporeal; bodily*
facciale	*facial*
intestinale	*intestinal*
mentale	*mental*
muscolare; **muscoloso**	*muscular*
nervoso	*nervous*

Mio figlio ha un sistema nervoso fragile.	*My son has a fragile nervous system.*
Gianni è molto muscoloso.	*Gianni is very muscular.*

Choose the appropriate adjective to convey the part of the body indicated in parentheses.

1. Ha avuto dei problemi _____. (al cuore)

2. Giorgio va in palestra perché vuole diventare più _____. (forte di muscoli)

3. Dopo l'incidente ha dovuto fare una chirurgia plastica _____. (alla faccia)

4. Ha un sistema _____ molto fragile. (dei nervi)

Other adjectives

There is broad latitude in the choice of qualifiers, especially when they are used metaphorically. We can say that eyes are large, deep, beautiful, mean, insincere, etc. Here follow some adjectives used to talk about the body and its features.

alto	*tall*
attraente (women)	*attractive; nice-looking*
bello	*beautiful*
brutto	*ugly*
carino (women and the very young)	*pretty*
destro	*right*
grosso	*big*
lungo	*long*
nudo	*naked*
pallido	*pale*
piccolo (**di statura**); **basso** (height); **corto** (length)	*short; small*
prestante (men)	*handsome*
sinistro	*left*

È una ragazza carina.	*She's a pretty girl.*
Di solito la mano destra è più forte della sinistra.	*Usually the right hand is stronger than the left.*

ESERCIZIO 3·4

*Decide whether the following statements are True (**T**) or False (**F**).*

1. La maggior parte delle persone usa di più la mano destra. _____

2. La ragazza più brutta vincerà il concorso di bellezza. _____

3. Giovanna è molto pallida perché non sta bene. _____

4. La statua del David di Michelangelo rappresenta un uomo nudo. _____

5. Di solito, i giocatori di pallacanestro sono piccoli. _____

Italian uses suffixes to modify nouns, adjectives, and even adverbs. Suffixes can convey emotional tones absent from the basic word: endings in **-etto**, **-etta** and **-ino**, **-ina** are diminutives which carry a sense of endearment. Magnifiers in **-one** and **-ona**, can be used in both positive and negative ways. The ending **-accio/-accia** carries negative overtones.

Identify the nouns from which the following diminutives derive. Add the article.

1. braccetto _____

2. ginocchietto _____

3. linguetta _____

4. muscoletto _____

Identify the nouns from which the following diminutives derive. Add the article.

1. bocchina _____

2. braccino _____

3. dentino _____

4. ditino _____

Identify the nouns from which the following magnifiers derive. Add the article.

1. dentone _____

2. ditone _____

3. manona _____

4. nasone _____

Verbs for moving

alzarsi [in piedi]	to stand up
camminare (aux. avere)	to walk
correre (aux. avere)	to run
lasciar(e) cadere	to drop
piegare; piegarsi	to bend
sdraiarsi	to lie (down)
sedersi; accomodarsi	to sit down
sollevare; alzare	to lift
spingere	to push
stringere/stringersi la mano	to shake hands
tenere	to hold; to keep
tirare	to pull

Signora, le è caduto il portafoglio.	Madam, you dropped your wallet.
Prego, si accomodi.	Please, have a seat.

ESERCIZIO
3·8

Complete the following sentences with the appropriate verb.

1. Si usano le mani per _____.
   a. alzarsi   b. piegarsi   c. spingere

2. Per raccogliere qualcosa da terra, bisogna _____ la schiena.
   a. piegare   b. sedersi   c. sdraiarsi

3. Per salutare una persona, _____ la mano.
   a. stringiamo   b. teniamo   c. solleviamo

4. Usiamo le gambe per _____.
   a. sollevare   b. camminare   c. sedersi

Verbs for bodily functions

battere	to beat
bere	to drink
digerire	to digest
inghiottire; deglutire	to swallow
mangiare	to eat
masticare	to chew
respirare (aux. avere)	to breathe
sputare	to spit

Decide which organ or part of the body performs the following functions.

1. _____ batte.
   a. Il cuore   b. Il polmone   c. L'intestino

2. _____ digerisce.
   a. La testa   b. Il muscolo   c. Lo stomaco

3. _____ respirano.
   a. Gli intestini   b. I polmoni   c. Il corpo

4. _____ masticano.
   a. I denti   b. La bocca   c. La lingua

5. _____ inghiotte.
   a. La lingua   b. La testa   c. La gola

The senses

la cecità	*blindness*
il colore	*color*
il gusto	*taste*
il mutismo	*mutism; dumbness*
l(o)'odorato	*(sense of) smell*
l(o)'odore	*odor; smell*
le papille gustative	*taste buds*
la pelle	*skin*
il profumo	*perfume; scent*
il sapore	*flavor; taste*
la sensazione	*sensation*
il senso (di)	*sense (of)*
la sordità	*deafness*
il suono	*sound*
il tatto	*touch*
l(o)'udito	*hearing*
la vista	*sight; vision*

Il nonno ha perso il senso del gusto.   *Our grandpa has lost his sense of taste.*
L'organo del tatto è la pelle.   *The organ of touch is the skin.*

Use the words listed in this unit to complete the following sentences.

1. L'organo della vista sono _____, che si trovano nella _____.

2. L'organo dell'udito sono _____, che si trovano ai lati del _____.

3. L'organo del gusto sono _____, che si trovano nella _____.

4. L'organo del tatto è _____, che copre tutto il _____.

5. L'organo dell'odorato è _____, che si trova sopra la _____.

Describing sensations

acido	*sour*
alto; troppo alto	*loud*
amaro	*bitter*
basso	*low*
cieco	*blind*
dolce	*sweet*
freddo	*cold*
gustoso; buono	*tasty*
miope	*near-sighted*
morbido	*soft*
muto	*mute; dumb*
presbite	*far-sighted*
salato; (troppo) salato	*savory; (too) salty*
sordo	*deaf*

Ai bambini non piacciono le cose amare.	*Kids don't like bitter things.*
Il latte è diventato acido.	*The milk went sour.*

Complete the following sentences by choosing from the options listed below.

1. Gli occhi vedono _____.
   a. i gusti b. i profumi c. i colori

2. Il naso sente _____.
   a. gli odori b. i colori c. i suoni

3. La lingua sente _____.
   a. i gusti b. i suoni c. gli odori

4. La pelle sente _____ e _____.
   a. il dolce; il salato b. il caldo; il freddo c. l'alto; il basso

5. Le orecchie sentono _____.
   a. i suoni b. i sapori c. i colori

Nouns can be formed by adding the suffix **-ezza** (*-ness* in English) to adjectives conveying physical qualities or psychological states of mind: **bello → la bellezza** (*beauty*), and **brutto → la bruttezza** (*ugliness*). These nouns are always feminine. At times they take the plural.

Mia madre ha sopportato grandi amarezze.	*My mother has endured great sorrows.*
Mi ha accolto con grande freddezza.	*He greeted me with great coldness.*

ESERCIZIO
3·12

*Translate the following adjectives into Italian, turn them into nouns by adding **-ezza**, then translate the nouns into English. Add the article.*

1. beautiful _____

2. bitter _____

3. cold _____

4. soft _____

5. sweet _____

ESERCIZIO
3·13

Identify the quality or characteristic which is implied in the situation or event described in each of the following sentences.

1. Gianni ha il naso storto, la fronte bassa e gli occhi sporgenti. _____

2. Ha perso il marito a trent'anni e suo figlio a trentacinque. _____

3. Ha vinto il concorso di Miss Universo. _____

4. Il nuovo direttore è corretto, ma non è certo cordiale. _____

Verbs of sensation

annusare	*to sniff*
ascoltare	*to listen to*
assaggiare	*to taste*
guardare	*to look at; to watch*
osservare	*to observe*
sentire (gli odori)	*to smell (odors)*
sentire; udire	*to hear*
toccare	*to touch*
vedere	*to see*

Hai guardato le Olimpiadi?	*Did you watch the Olympic games?*
Senti che odore strano?	*Can you smell that strange odor?*

Complete the following sentences choosing a verb among those listed above.

1. Apri le orecchie e _____!

2. Il naso serve per _____ e
   _____.

3. Con gli occhi si _____, si _____ e si _____.

4. Sta' zitto, per favore. Non riesco a _____ cosa dice.

5. Usiamo la lingua per _____ i cibi.

Emotions and the mind

Individualism, first articulated in its modern form by Italian humanists in the Renaissance, is an important aspect of Italian culture. Italians are individualists not only of the mind but of the heart: they express publicly a wide array of emotions, from anger to great sorrow. This public expression of private feelings, often tempered by irony, creates a relaxed and reassuring social environment: in Italy you know where you stand with another person, even if he or she is only a colleague or an acquaintance.

Needless to say, there are drawbacks. Italian individualism makes it hard for people to act as team players, and the expression of one's own self can be stifling for shy or insecure people.

Here follows a list of nouns which we use to describe emotions, besides those already listed in Units 1 and 2.

l(a)'allegria	*cheerfulness*
l(a)'antipatia	*dislike*
il difetto	*shortcoming; defect*
il dolore	*pain; sorrow*
l(a)'emozione; il feeling	*feeling*
la felicità	*happiness*
la gelosia	*jealousy*
la gioia	*joy*
l(a)'infelicità	*unhappiness*
la noia (sing.)	*boredom*
l(o)'odio	*hatred*
la passione	*passion*
la paura	*fear*
il piacere	*pleasure*
la preoccupazione	*worry; concern*
la rabbia; l(a)'ira	*anger*
la sensibilità	*sensibility; sensitivity*
la simpatia	*sympathy*
la speranza	*hope*
lo stress	*stress*
la tristezza	*sadness*

Che noia! Ma parlerà ancora per molto?	*How boring! Will he speak much longer?*
Ho perso l'aereo! Mi è venuta una rabbia!	*I missed the plane. I'm so angry!*

35

Choose the appropriate noun from the ones listed after each sentence.

1. Abbiamo qualche _____ che nostra figlia guarisca.
   a. speranza   b. paura   c. tristezza

2. Che _____! Hanno dovuto vendere la casa dei nonni.
   a. piacere   b. gioia   c. tristezza

3. Hai _____ ad andare a casa da sola? Ti accompagno.
   a. piacere   b. paura   c. speranza

4. Sei molto severa con lei. Non credi che un po' di _____ la aiuterebbe?
   a. preoccupazione   b. simpatia   c. speranza

5. Marco è davvero strano: non prova né grandi _____ né grandi _____.
   a. piaceri; dolori   b. allegria; tristezza   c. amore; odio

Describing emotions

allegro	*cheerful*
arrabbiato; adirato	*angry*
contento	*glad; content*
emotivo; emozionale	*emotional*
noioso	*boring*
odioso	*hateful*
pauroso	*fearful*
piacevole	*pleasant; agreeable*
preoccupato	*concerned; worried*
sensibile	*sensitive*
stressato	*stressed*
triste	*sad*

Sara ha un bambino allegro.	*Sara has a cheerful boy.*
È un ragazzino molto emotivo.	*He's a really emotional boy.*

Find the adjective that describes the emotion characterizing the following situations. Use the masculine singular.

1. A comedy movie which is OK, but not great. _____

2. A dog left alone by his beloved master for two weeks. _____

3. A person who loses his cool easily. _____

4. A person who uses others' faults and mistakes to advance his career. _____

5. Having lunch with friends on a nice summer day. _____

Emotional states

l(a)'ansia; l(a)'agitazione	*anxiety*
la calma	*calm; peace*
la disperazione	*despair*
il dispiacere	*displeasure*
il dolore	*pain*
la gioia	*joy*
la gratitudine	*gratitude*
l(a)'invidia	*envy*
la nostalgia	*nostalgia*
il panico	*panic*

Mi è preso il panico.	*I was seized by panic.*
Mi ha preso un'ansia terribile!	*I was seized by a terrible anxiety!*

ESERCIZIO

4·3

Provide the antonyms for the following nouns.

1. il dispiacere _____

2. l(a)'antipatia _____

3. la gioia _____

4. l(o)'odio _____

5. la felicità _____

6. la tristezza _____

Verbs

addolorare	*to sadden; to pain (emotionally)*
aver(e) paura (di); temere (aux. avere)	*to fear; to be afraid (of)*
aver(e) ragione	*to be right*
aver(e) torto	*to be wrong*
essere disperato	*to despair; to be desperate*
essere stufo	*to be fed up*
far(e) pena (a)	*to feel sorry (for)*
irritare; dare fastidio (a); infastidire	*to annoy*
preoccupare; far preoccupare	*to worry; to make worry*
rattristare	*to sadden*
spaventare	*to scare*
stressare	*to stress*

Sono proprio stufa di questo lavoro.	*I'm really fed up with this job.*
Ha temuto di perdere il bambino.	*She was afraid of losing the baby.*

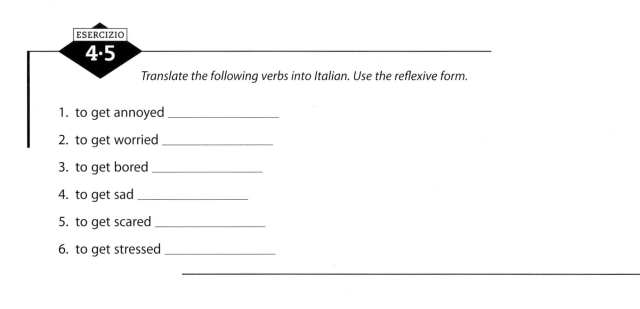

ESERCIZIO
4·4

Complete the following sentences. Choose from the options listed under each of them.

1. I film dell'orrore _____ i bambini.
   a. stressano   b. irritano   c. spaventano

2. La notizia della morte del nonno _____ tutti.
   a. addolora   b. preoccupa   c. irrita

3. Le devo dire che suo marito ha il cancro. _____ molto la sua reazione.
   a. Ammiro   b. Ho paura   c. Temo

We can convey the idea that a person or a thing causes an emotion in ourselves or others. But when we want to emphasize the internal rising of an emotion, in Italian we often use the reflexive form of the verb.

Silvia si spaventa facilmente.	*Silvia gets scared easily.*
Non arrabbiarti, non è una cosa grave.	*Don't get cross, it's not serious.*

ESERCIZIO
4·5

Translate the following verbs into Italian. Use the reflexive form.

1. to get annoyed _____

2. to get worried _____

3. to get bored _____

4. to get sad _____

5. to get scared _____

6. to get stressed _____

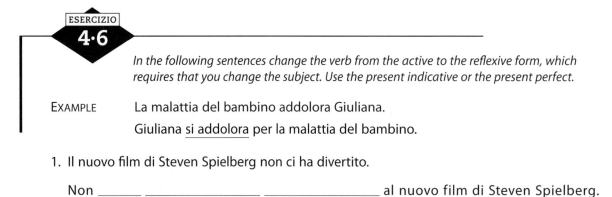

ESERCIZIO
4·6

In the following sentences change the verb from the active to the reflexive form, which requires that you change the subject. Use the present indicative or the present perfect.

EXAMPLE   La malattia del bambino addolora Giuliana.

                 Giuliana <u>si addolora</u> per la malattia del bambino.

1. Il nuovo film di Steven Spielberg non ci ha divertito.

   Non _____ _____ _____ al nuovo film di Steven Spielberg.

2. L'abbaiare del nostro cane irrita i nostri vicini di casa.

   I nostri vicini di casa _____ _____ quando il nostro cane abbaia.

3. Il rumore dell'autostrada lo infastidisce.

   _____ _____ per il rumore dell'autostrada.

4. Il tornado ha terrorizzato i nonni.

   I nonni _____ _____ _____ per il tornado.

5. La notizia della scoperta di una nuova stella ha eccitato il mondo scientifico.

   Il mondo scientifico _____ _____ _____ alla notizia della scoperta di una nuova stella.

One way of conveying that a person or a thing causes an emotion in someone else is to use the construction **fare** + *infinitive of the verb*.

Il clown mi ha fatto ridere tanto!	*The clown made me laugh so much!*

ESERCIZIO
4·7

Complete the following sentences by choosing from the options given after each of them.

1. La massaggiatrice l'ha _____ completamente.
   a. fatta rilassare   b. fatta divertire   c. fatta annoiare

2. Le ultime notizie ci _____ il peggio.
   a. fanno preoccupare   b. fanno temere   c. fanno spaventare

3. Mi _____! Non sapevo che eri in casa.
   a. hai fatto spaventare   b. fatto preoccupare   c. fatto temere

4. Nostra sorella _____ la mamma perché non smette di drogarsi.
   a. fa arrabbiare   b. fa disperare   c. fa temere

5. Se non smetti di _____, niente televisione per una settimana!
   a. farmi spaventare   b. farmi annoiare   c. farmi arrabbiare

Past participles can be used as adjectives. They are formed by replacing the endings of the infinitive of regular verbs with **-ato**, **-uto**, or **-ito**. Consult a grammar book for irregular verbs.

am-are (*to love*) → **am-ato, amata, amati, amate** (*loved*)
tem-ere (*to fear*) → **tem-uto, temuta, temuti, temute** (*feared*)
sent-ire (*to feel*) → **sent-ito, sentita, sentiti, sentite** (*felt*)

Era una cantante amata dal pubblico.	*She was a singer loved by audiences.*
Le mie più sentite condoglianze.	*My most heartfelt condolences.*

Form past participles as adjectives from the following verbs, by replacing the ending of the infinitive with the appropriate ending of the past participle.

1. addolorare _____

2. arrabblare _____

3. annoiare _____

4. imbarazzare _____

5. spaventare _____

6. preoccupare _____

7. stressare _____

When we wish to say that a person or event is causing an emotion in others, we can use the present participle, formed by replacing the ending of the infinitive in **-are** with **-ante**, and verbs in **-ere** and **-ire** with **-ente**. **Commuovere** (*to move emotionally*), **fare** (*to do; to make*), and **sentire** (*to feel*) are irregular.

INFINITIVE	PRESENT PARTICIPLE		PAST PARTICIPLE	
commuovere	**commovente**	*moving*	**commosso**	*moved*
fare	**facente**	*doing, making* (rare)	**fatto**	*done*
sentire	**senziente**	*feeling* (rare)	**sentito**	*felt*

Form the present participle of the following verbs.

1. appassionare _____

2. divertire _____

3. irritare _____

4. preoccupare _____

5. rilassare _____

6. stressare _____

ESERCIZIO 4·10

Add the appropriate adjective to the following sentences, choosing the present or past participle of the verb listed in parentheses.

EXAMPLE   Hanno fatto la pace. È stata una scena _____ (commuovere).

Hanno fatto la pace. È stata una scena <u>commovente</u>.

1. Abbiamo fatto delle vacanze veramente _____ al Club Med. (rilassare)

2. Alla festa è rimasta seduta in un angolo tutta la sera, con un'espressione _____. (annoiare)

3. Beve troppo, ma fa una vita molto _____. (stressare)

4. Ho letto un romanzo poliziesco veramente _____. (appassionare)

5. Mio figlia non è _____, è pigra. (rilassare)

6. Luisa è una donna _____ dalle malattie e dalle preoccupazioni. (stressare)

Adjectives can end in **-oso** (*-ous* or *-ful* in English): **curioso, pauroso.** They are formed by replacing the last vowel of a noun with **-oso: dolor-e** (*pain*) → **dolor-oso** (*painful*); **ansi-a** (*anxiety*) → **ansi-oso.** If the final **i** is accented, **-oso** replaces both the **ì** and the last vowel: **gelos-ia** (*jealousy*) → **gel-oso** (*jealous*).

Mio figlio distrugge i giocattoli perché è curioso.	*My son destroys his toys because he's curious.*
Per Lisa il divorzio è stato molto doloroso.	*For Lisa the divorce was very painful.*

ESERCIZIO 4·11

Reconstruct the nouns from which the following adjectives derive. Add the article.

1. ansioso _____

2. doloroso _____

3. gioioso _____

4. invidioso _____

5. noioso _____

6. odioso _____

We can change an adjective into its opposite by adding the prefixes **in-** (**im-** before **b, m,** and **p**) or **s-**, which correspond to the English *in-, im-, un-,* and *dis-*:

felice	*happy*	**infelice**	*unhappy*
possibile	*possible*	**impossibile**	*impossible*
contento	*content*	**scontento**	*discontent*

Adjectives beginning with **-r** add the prefix **ir-** to ease pronunciation:

razionale   *rational*   **irrazionale**   *irrational*

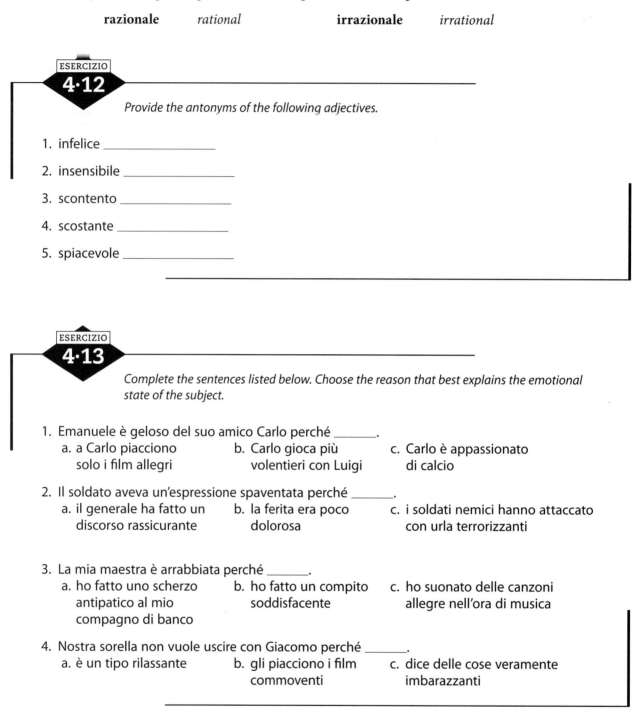

ESERCIZIO
4·12

Provide the antonyms of the following adjectives.

1. infelice _____

2. insensibile _____

3. scontento _____

4. scostante _____

5. spiacevole _____

ESERCIZIO
4·13

Complete the sentences listed below. Choose the reason that best explains the emotional state of the subject.

1. Emanuele è geloso del suo amico Carlo perché _____.
   a. a Carlo piacciono solo i film allegri
   b. Carlo gioca più volentieri con Luigi
   c. Carlo è appassionato di calcio

2. Il soldato aveva un'espressione spaventata perché _____.
   a. il generale ha fatto un discorso rassicurante
   b. la ferita era poco dolorosa
   c. i soldati nemici hanno attaccato con urla terrorizzanti

3. La mia maestra è arrabbiata perché _____.
   a. ho fatto uno scherzo antipatico al mio compagno di banco
   b. ho fatto un compito soddisfacente
   c. ho suonato delle canzoni allegre nell'ora di musica

4. Nostra sorella non vuole uscire con Giacomo perché _____.
   a. è un tipo rilassante
   b. gli piacciono i film commoventi
   c. dice delle cose veramente imbarazzanti

Describing mental and moral traits

attivo   *active*
capace; in grado di   *capable; able*
indipendente   *independent*
intelligente; astuto   *smart*
irrazionale   *irrational*
notevole; grande (a human being) *great*

onesto	*honest*
passivo	*passive*
pigro	*lazy*
razionale	*rational*
responsabile	*responsible*
stupido	*stupid*

Several nouns regarding personality and moral traits can be formed by adding the ending **-ità,** as already seen in Unit 2.

ESERCIZIO
4·14

*Form nouns from the following adjectives by adding the ending **-ità**, add the article, and translate them into English.*

1. capace _____

2. irrazionale _____

3. passivo _____

4. razionale _____

5. stupido _____

ESERCIZIO
4·15

Among the nouns listed after each sentence find the one which is the closest synonym of the word underlined.

1. Mio marito non sopporta l'irrazionalità del leader del partito. _____
   a. la mancanza di   b. l'astuzia   c. la malvagità
      buon senso

2. Non farà mai niente di buono, a causa della sua passività.
   a. paura   b. mancanza di   c. onestà
                     energia

3. Non è sempre possibile agire con razionalità.
   a. con buon senso   b. passione   c. forza
      e freddezza

4. La stupidità è un difetto.
   a. mancanza di   b. poca aggressività   c. poca intelligenza
      sensibilità

Emotions and the mind   **43**

Mental and psychological abilities

l(a)'abitudine	*habit*
l(a)'azione	*action*
la coscienza	*conscience; consciousness*
l(a)'idea	*idea*
l(a)'immaginazione; la fantasia (sing.)	*imagination*
l(a)'intelligenza	*intelligence*
l(o)'istinto	*instinct*
la memoria	*memory*
la mente	*mind*
il pensiero	*thought*
la ragione	*reason*
il ricordo	*recollection*
il riso; la risata	*laughter*
il sogno	*dream*

Sua figlia ha una fantasia vivace.	*Her daughter has a lively imagination.*
Hai idea di dove siamo?	*Do you have any idea of where we are?*

ESERCIZIO
4·16

Provide the words defined in the following sentences. Include the article.

1. A property of <u>mind</u> that includes many <u>mental</u> abilities, such as the capacities to <u>reason</u>, <u>plan</u>, <u>solve problems</u>, think abstractly, <u>comprehend ideas and language</u>, and <u>learn</u>.

   _____

2. An inborn pattern of behavior. _____

3. Any instance of an action performed because we are used to performing it. _____

4. Any instance of what humans can do intentionally to affect the state of the world.

   _____

5. The experience of envisioned images, sounds, or other sensations during <u>sleep</u>.

   _____

Thinking and feeling

agire (aux. avere)	*to act; to do; to behave*
aver[e] bisogno (di)	*to need*
avere; possedere	*to have*
comportarsi	*to behave*
credere (a qualcuno / in Dio) (aux. avere)	*to believe (someone / in God)*
desiderare	*to wish; to want*
diventare	*to become*
dovere (aux. avere/essere)	*to have to / must / shall*
essere abituato (a); avere l(a)'abitudine (di + *infinitive*)	*to be used (to)*

fare	*to do; to make*
lasciare (aux. **avere**); **permettere (a)** (aux. **avere**)	*to let; to allow*
osare (aux. **avere**)	*to dare*
ottenere	*to get*
pensare (a) (aux. **avere**)	*to think (about)*
potere (aux. **avere/essere**); **avere il permesso di**	*to be allowed to; may*
potere (aux. **avere/essere**); **riuscire a**	*to be able to; can*
preferire (aux. **avere**)	*to prefer*
ridere	*to laugh*
stare	*to stay; to be*

Note that **stare** is used both in the expressions **stare bene/male** (*to be well / not well*), **come stai/state?** (*how are you?*), etc., to form the present progressive, and in the expression **stare per +** *infinitive* (*to be about to do something*).

Stanno mangiando?	*Are they eating?*
Sta per partire.	*He's about to leave.*

trattare *to treat*	
usare; avere l(a)'abitudine (di)	*to use (to); to be used to*
volere (aux. **avere/essere**); **aver(e) voglia (di)**	*to want; to will; to feel like*

The Italian verbs **dovere** (*shall, must, to have to*), **lasciare** (*to let*), **desiderare** (*to wish; to want*), **osare** (*dare*), **potere** (*can; may*), **preferire** (*to prefer*), **sapere** (*to know*), and **volere** (*will; to want*) are often used to modify the infinitive that follows, as English does with *can/could, dare, let, may/might, must, shall/should,* and *will/would.*

I bambini devono fare i compiti.	*The children must do their homework.*
Lascia parlare tua sorella!	*Let your sister speak!*
Sapete aprire la cassaforte?	*Do you know how to open the safe?*

ESERCIZIO
4·17

Complete each sentence in the left column by choosing the appropriate phrase from the right column.

1. Che bella giornata! Volete _____   a. aiutarmi a caricarla in macchina?

2. La Sua proposta è interessante, _____   b. andare al mare?

3. La valiga è molto pesante. Puoi _____   c. dire la verità a sua madre.

4. La zia non sta bene. _____   d. Potete passare a trovarla?

5. Luisa non osa _____   e. ma desidero parlarne con il mio socio.

Religion

l(o)'angelo	*angel*
l(a)'anima	*soul*
il bene (sing.)	*good*
la chiesa; la Chiesa	*church; the Church*
il, la credente	*believer*
il cristianesimo	*Christianity*
il diavolo	*devil*
il dio, gli dei; Dio	*god; God*
l(o)'ebraismo	*Judaism*
l(o)'inferno	*hell*
l(o)'Islam	*Islam*
il male (sing.)	*evil*
la moschea	*mosque*
il paradiso	*paradise; heaven*
il peccato	*sin*
la preghiera	*prayer*
il prete; il sacerdote	*priest*
il (tuo) prossimo	*thy neighbor*
la religione	*religion*
la sinagoga	*synagogue*

Ama il prossimo tuo come te stesso.   *Love thy neighbor as thyself.*

ESERCIZIO 4·18

Match each word on the left with its appropriate complement from those listed on the right.

1. la Chiesa _____   a. il bene

2. il diavolo _____   b. il cristianesimo

3. la moschea _____   c. l'ebraismo

4. il paradiso _____   d. l'Islam

5. la sinagoga _____   e. l'inferno

Body care, health, and life ◆·5·

The affluent lifestyle of developed countries is a positive development, but has led us to exercise less and eat junk food, while being more concerned than ever about our appearance. In this respect, Italian and American societies are very similar. People share the same concerns—obesity, diabetes, and anorexia—and they fight the same battles: against sedentary life on the one hand, and obsessive concern for one's body on the other.

i baffi (usually in the pl.)	*moustache*
la barba	*beard*
la fronte	*forehead*
la guancia	*cheek*
il labbro, le labbra	*lip*
il mento	*chin*
il ricciolo	*curl*
la ruga	*wrinkle*
il sudore	*sweat*

Signora, ha la pelle grassa o secca?	*Madam, do you have oily or dry skin?*
Il bimbo ha le guance rotonde.	*The baby has round cheeks.*

ESERCIZIO
5·1

Mark the word that does not belong in each of the following series.

1. a. il sudore   b. le rughe   c. la pelle   d. la barba

2. a. i riccioli   b. le labbra   c. i capelli   d. i baffi

3. a. il sudore   b. la fronte   c. il naso   d. il mento

Complete the following sentences by choosing from the options given after each of them.

1. La barba copre _____.
   a. le labbra   b. le guance   c. la pelle

2. Il sudore bagna _____.
   a. la fronte   b. la pelle   c. il mento

3. I baffi sono sotto _____.
   a. la fronte   b. gli occhi   c. il naso

4. I riccioli coprono _____.
   a. la fronte   b. il mento   c. le rughe

Describing hair

barbuto; con la barba	*bearded*
biondo	*blonde*
calvo; pelato	*bald*
castano	*brown*
con i capelli bianchi; bianco	*white-haired*
liscio	*straight*
lungo	*long*
nero	*black*
riccio, ricci	*curly*
scuro	*dark*

Da bambina avevo i capelli ricci.   *When I was a little girl, I had curly hair.*
È un signore con i capelli bianchi.   *He's a white-haired gentleman.*

Choose the adjectives that can be used to describe the following personal features.

1. Una persona senza capelli è _____.

2. I capelli ricci sono l'opposto dei capelli _____.

3. Le persone anziane hanno i capelli _____.

4. I capelli lunghi sono l'opposto dei capelli _____.

Personal hygiene products

l(o)'asciugacapelli, gli asciugacapelli; il föhn/fon	*hair dryer*
l(o)'asciugamano	*towel*
la carta igienica	*toilet paper*
la crema da barba	*shaving cream*
il dentifricio	*toothpaste*
il deodorante	*deodorant*
il fazzoletto di carta; il kleenex	*(facial) tissue*
il pannolino	*sanitary napkin*
il pettine	*comb*
il rasoio [da barba]	*razor*
la saponetta	*(bar of) soap*
lo shampo(o)	*shampoo*
la spazzola [per i capelli]	*brush*
lo spazzolino [da denti]	*toothbrush*
lo specchio	*mirror*

Mi impresti il fon?	*Can you lend me your hair dryer?*
Non mi piace il rasoio elettrico.	*I don't like electric razors.*

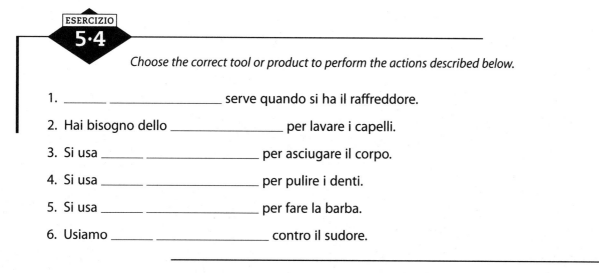

ESERCIZIO
5·4

Choose the correct tool or product to perform the actions described below.

1. _____ _____ serve quando si ha il raffreddore.

2. Hai bisogno dello _____ per lavare i capelli.

3. Si usa _____ _____ per asciugare il corpo.

4. Si usa _____ _____ per pulire i denti.

5. Si usa _____ _____ per fare la barba.

6. Usiamo _____ _____ contro il sudore.

Verbs

In Italian many reflexive verbs can carry a direct object: **bagnarsi i vestiti** (*to get one's clothes wet*); **soffiarsi il naso** (*to blow one's nose*), etc.

asciugare; asciugarsi	*to dry*
bagnare; bagnarsi	*to wet; to get wet*
depilare; depilarsi	*to shave (women); to remove one's hair*
fare il bagno / la doccia	*to take a bath/shower*
farsi la messa in piega	*to do one's hair*
lavarsi (le mani; i capelli / la testa, etc.)	*to wash (one's hands; hair, etc.)*
lavarsi i denti	*to brush one's teeth*
pettinarsi	*to comb one's hair*
radersi; farsi la barba	*to shave (men)*
struccarsi	*to remove one's makeup*

sudare (aux. **avere**)	*to sweat*
tagliarsi i capelli	*to cut one's hair*
truccarsi (gli occhi / il viso, etc.)	*to put on makeup*

When we wish to convey that an action is done to our person or is performed on our behalf, we can use the construction **far fare** (aux. **avere**) or the reflexive form **farsi fare** (aux. **essere**): *to have something done (to/for us); to make someone do something (to/for us).*

Faccio tagliare i capelli.	*I'm having my hair cut.*
Mi sono fatta tagliare i capelli.	*I've had my hair cut.*

ESERCIZIO 5·5

*Change the following sentences to use the constructions **far fare qualcosa** and **farsi fare qualcosa**.*

EXAMPLE   Tingo i capelli.

Faccio tingere i capelli.

Mi faccio tingere i capelli.

1. Depili le gambe?

_____

_____

2. Giovanna lava la testa.

_____

_____

3. Piera e Luciana fanno la messa in piega.

_____

_____

4. Massimo e Giorgio, tagliate la barba?

_____

_____

5. Tagliamo i capelli!

_____

_____

Body care and makeup

l(a)'acconciatura; la messa in piega	*hairstyle; hairdo*
la chirurgia plastica	*plastic surgery*
il cosmetico	*beauty product*

la depilazione	hair removal
la manicure	manicure
il massaggio	massage
la permanente	perm
il rossetto	lipstick
il tatuaggio	tattoo
il trucco	makeup

Silvia porta un trucco molto pesante.	Silvia wears really heavy makeup.
Ti sei fatta fare la messa in piega?	Did you have your hairdo done?

ESERCIZIO
5·6

Complete the following sentences choosing from the words listed above.

1. _____ _____ fa rilassare i muscoli.

2. Quando una parte del tuo corpo non ti piace, puoi fare _____ _____ _____.

3. Quando hai troppi peli, li elimini con _____ _____.

4. Se hai i capelli lisci e vuoi i capelli ricci, ti fai fare _____ _____.

5. Se vuoi delle unghie colorate, ti puoi fare _____ _____.

Professions, establishments, and equipment

il bagno	bathroom; bath
il (negozio di) barbiere (men)	barber's shop
la bilancia	scale
il chirurgo plastico	plastic surgeon
la doccia	shower
l(o, a)'estetista	beautician
il gabinetto	toilet
il parrucchiere / la parrucchiera; la pettinatrice	hairdresser
il peso	weight
la profumeria	cosmetic store
la toeletta; la toilette	washroom; restroom

Dov'è la toeletta, per favore?	Where is the restroom, please?
Hai fatto il bagno?	Did you take a bath?

*Answer yes (**Y**) or no (**N**) to the following questions.*

1. Devi essere un'estetista per fare il chirurgo plastico? _____

2. La vasca da bagno fa sempre parte della doccia? _____

3. Il bagno è un luogo pubblico? _____

4. In profumeria si può comprare il rossetto? _____

5. Vai dal parrucchiere se sei calvo? _____

6. Vai dalla pettinatrice a farti fare la messa in piega? _____

Diet and weight

Life expectancy is very high in Italy: 76.8 years for men and 82.7 for women. Affluence, a good diet, home cooking, and universal health care have all contributed. Cancer and heart disease are the leading causes of death.

l(a)'anoressia	*anorexia*
il benessere (sing.) / **la wellness**	*well-being; wellness*
la bulimia	*bulimia*
il cibo	*food*
la dieta	*diet*
il digiuno	*fast; fasting*
il fast food	*fast food*
i grassi (pl.)	*fat(s)*
il peso	*weight*

Per dimagrire, niente fast food e molto moto.	*To lose weight, no fast food and a lot of exercise.*
Da quando sei a dieta?	*How long have you been on a diet?*

Describing one's diet

anoressico	*anorexic*
bulimico	*bulimic*
grasso	*fat*
magro	*thin*
mediterraneo	*Mediterranean*
nutriente	*nutritious*
obeso	*obese*
robusto	*stout*
slanciato; snello	*slender*
[in] sovrappeso	*overweight*
vegano	*vegan*
vegetariano	*vegetarian*

Nella dieta mediterranea ci sono pochi grassi.	*There are few fats in the Mediterranean diet.*

Choose the appropriate qualifier to complete the sentences listed below.

1. La dieta mediterranea è _____.
   a. grassa   b. vegetariana   c. nutriente

2. Una dieta alimentare senza carne è _____.
   a. mediterranea   b. vegana   c. vegetariana

3. Le persone che mangiano molto fast food sono spesso _____.
   a. in sovrappeso   b. slanciate   c. bulimiche

4. Una persona _____ non riesce a mangiare.
   a. bulimica   b. anoressica   c. obesa

Verbs

digiunare (aux. **avere**)	*to fast*
dimagrire; perdere peso	*to lose weight*
essere a dieta	*to be on a diet*
far bene/male (a qualcuno)	*to be good/bad (for someone)*
ingrassare; mettere su peso	*to put on/gain weight*
mettersi a dieta	*to go on a diet*
pesare; pesarsi	*to weigh*

Troppo alcol fa male.	*Too much alcohol is bad for you.*
Ho messo su tre chili in dieci giorni!	*I gained three kilos in ten days!*

Pair each of the sentences listed on the left with the appropriate conclusion on the right.

1. Da quanto tempo _____   a. aiuta a dimagrire.

2. La dieta vegetariana _____   b. fa ingrassare.

3. Mangiare tanti dolci _____   c. sei preoccupato per il tuo peso.

4. Mia zia ha perso dieci chili _____   d. non mangiare tanti dolci.

5. Se ti pesi tutti i giorni vuol dire che _____   e. perché si è messa a dieta.

6. Se vuoi dimagrire _____   f. sei a dieta?

Illnesses and health issues

l(o)'alcolizzato; l(o, a)'alcolista	*alcoholic*
l(o)'ammalato; il malato	*ill/sick person*
il chirurgo, i chirurg(h)i (m. and f.)	*surgeon*

il, la dentista	dentist
il, la disabile; l(o)'handicappato	disabled
il donatore / la donatrice	donor
l(a)'epidemia	epidemic
il, la farmacista	pharmacist
il, la fisioterapista	physical therapist
l(o)'infermiere / l(a)'infermiera	nurse
l(a)'infezione	infection
il malato di mente	mentally ill person
il medico (m. and f.); il dottore / la dottoressa	physician; doctor
il medico di base / della mutua	primary care physician
la mutua	health care coverage
l(o a)'oculista	eye doctor
il, la paziente	patient
lo, la psichiatra	psychiatrist
lo psicologo	psychologist
la sanità; l(a)'assistenza medica	health care
il, la tossicodipendente; il drogato	drug addict
il vaccino	vaccine

| Mia madre va da un medico privato. | My mother goes to a doctor in private practice. |
| Dal medico della mutua c'è sempre la coda. | At my primary care physician's there's always a long wait. |

To convey physical or metaphorical motion, in Italian you can use the preposition **da** (*from; out of*) followed by *the name of the person or establishment* you are in, at, going to, or coming from.

«Dove sei adesso»? «Sono dal dottore».	"Where are you right now?" "I'm at the doctor's office."
«Dove vai?»? «Vado dal dottore».	"Where are you going?" "I'm going to the doctor's."
«Da dove vieni»? «Torno adesso dal dottore».	"Where are you coming from?" "I've just come back from the doctor."

The person or service in question conveys both the function and the place where the event happens. Compare the following sentences:

| Andiamo a cena da Silvia. | We'll have dinner at Silvia's place. |
| Andiamo a cena con Silvia. | We'll have dinner with Silvia. |

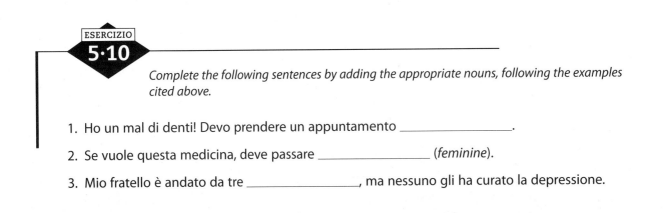

ESERCIZIO
5·10

Complete the following sentences by adding the appropriate nouns, following the examples cited above.

1. Ho un mal di denti! Devo prendere un appuntamento _____.

2. Se vuole questa medicina, deve passare _____ (*feminine*).

3. Mio fratello è andato da tre _____, ma nessuno gli ha curato la depressione.

4. La mia schiena fa male, ma _____ (feminine) vedo delle persone che non riescono più a muoversi.

5. Mia sorella va a farsi fare il lifting _____ che ha operato Madonna.

Ailments

l(a)'allergia	allergy
l(a)'artrite	arthritis
i batteri (usually pl.)	bacteria
la dentiera	dentures
il disturbo; il malanno	ailment
il dolore (a); il male (a)	pain (in)
la febbre	fever
il fumo (sing.)	smoking
l(a)'influenza	flu
l(a)'insonnia	insomnia
il mal(e) di (denti / pancia/stomaco / schiena / testa)	(tooth-/stomach-/back-/head-)ache
il mal(e) di gola	sore throat
la nausea	nausea
il raffreddore	cold
il sintomo	symptom
il tabacco	tobacco
la tosse	cough
il virus	virus

Al nonno dà fastidio la dentiera.	Dentures bother grandpa.
Hai la nausea?	Do you feel nauseous?

ESERCIZIO
5·11

In the following sentences, ailments and the professionals who can take care of them have been mixed up. Reconstruct them so that the right provider will be linked to the proper ailment.

1. Gli infermieri fanno le operazioni.

_____

2. I chirurghi possono curare il raffreddore, la tosse, ecc.

_____

3. L'oculista dice che la nonna deve rifare la dentiera.

_____

4. La dentista mi ha fatto cambiare gli occhiali.

_____

Verbs

aver(e) male (a)	to feel pain (in)
avere mal(e) di/a	to have a(n) -ache
far male (a), farsi male (a)	to hurt, to injure oneself
non sentirsi bene; sentirsi poco bene	to not feel well; to be under the weather
passare (a + *person*)	to get over (an ailment)
prendere; prendersi	to catch
russare (aux. avere)	to snore
sentirsi bene/male	to feel well/unwell
soffrire (di) (aux. avere)	to suffer (from)
starnutire (aux. avere)	to sneeze
tossire (aux. avere)	to cough
vomitare	to throw up

Ti è passata la bronchite?	*Did you get over your bronchitis?*
La mamma non si sente bene.	*Mom is not feeling well.*

ESERCIZIO
5·12

Translate the following sentences.

1. Ho mangiato troppo ieri sera. Ho la nausea.

   _____

2. Mi sono presa il raffreddore.

   _____

3. Mia madre si è fatta male alla schiena.

   _____

4. «Stai male »? «No, ma non mi sento molto bene».

   _____

5. Ti è passata l'influenza?

   _____

Illnesses and addictions

l(a)'AIDS (la sindrome da immuno-deficienza acquisita)	*AIDS (autoimmune deficiency syndrome)*
l(o)'alcolismo	*alcoholism*
l(o)'attacco di cuore; l(o)'infarto	*heart attack*
il cancro	*cancer*
il colpo [apoplettico]; l(o)'ictus	*stroke*
il coma, i coma	*coma*
la depressione	*depression*
il diabete	*diabetes*
la droga; la sostanza stupefacente	*drug*

il fumo	*smoking*
l(a)'infezione	*infection*
la malattia	*disease; illness*
la pazzia	*madness; insanity*
la polmonite	*pneumonia*
lo shock	*shock*
il sintomo da astinenza	*withdrawal symptom*
la tossicodipendenza	*(drug) addiction*
il trauma	*trauma*

Alla nonna è preso un ictus.	*Grandma had a stroke.*
Lo zio è guarito bene dall'infarto.	*Our uncle recovered well from his heart attack.*

ESERCIZIO
5·13

Under each of the headings below, list the appropriate minor ailments, serious illnesses, and addictions.

1. le malattie cardiovascolari

_____

2. le malattie dell'apparato respiratorio

_____

3. le tossicodipendenze

_____

4. i traumi e le loro conseguenze

_____

Describing health conditions

batterico	*bacterial*
cronico	*chronic*
doloroso	*painful*
ereditario	*hereditary*
genetico	*genetic*
grave	*serious*
incurabile; inguaribile	*incurable*
malato	*ill*
medico	*medical*
psicologico	*psychological*
psicosomatico	*psychosomatic*
sano; in salute	*healthy*
sieronegativo	*HIV negative*
sieropositivo	*HIV positive*
virale	*viral*

La mia collega è grave.	*My colleague is seriously ill.*
È una malattia psicosomatica.	*It's a pyschosomatic disease.*

Match each noun in the left column with the appropriate adjective on the right.

1. l'artrite _____   a. batterica

2. il coma _____   b. cardiaco

3. l'infarto _____   c. cronica

4. l'infezione _____   d. incurabile

5. l'infezione _____   e. profondo

6. il malato _____   f. psicosomatici

7. i sintomi _____   g. sieropositivo

8. il test _____   h. virale

Falling ill and recovering

ammalarsi	*to become/fall ill*
curare	*to treat*
disintossicarsi	*to detox*
donare	*to donate*
guarire (aux. **avere/essere**)	*to cure*
guarire (aux. **essere**)	*to recover*
operare	*to perform surgery; to operate*
rianimare	*to revive*
rimarginarsi (a wound)	*to heal*
rompere; rompersi	*to break*
soffrire (aux. **avere**)	*to be in pain*
trapiantare	*to transplant*
visitare	*to visit; to examine (a patient)*

Mio figlio si ammala tutti i momenti.	*My son falls ill very easily.*
Nicola è riuscito a disintossicarsi.	*Nicola was able to detox.*

Replace the words in parentheses in the following sentences with one of the verbs listed above. Use the same mode and tense. Omit the underlined words.

1. (Ha molto male) _____ a causa della gamba rotta.

2. Il medico ha (fatto uscire) _____ il paziente dal coma.

3. La ferita (è guarita) _____ _____ _____ perfettamente.

4. Il chirurgo (sostituisce) _____ il cuore a mio padre.

5. Mia zia (si prende delle malattie) _____ _____ spesso.

Medical practices and instruments

il cerotto [medicato]	*bandage*
la convalescenza; la guarigione	*recovery*
la diagnosi	*diagnosis*
il farmaco; il medicinale / la medicina	*drug; medication*
le gocce (usually pl.)	*drops*
la lente a contatto	*contact lens*
il medicinale senza ricetta	*over-the-counter medication*
gli occhiali (pl.)	*eyeglasses*
la pastiglia; la pillola	*pill*
la ricetta; la prescrizione [medica]	*prescription*
il test; l(o)'esame	*test*
il trapianto	*transplant*
la visita	*visit; (doctor's) examination*

Lucia ha perso una lente a contatto!	*Lucia has lost a contact lens!*
Devi prendere dieci pillole al giorno?	*Do you have to take ten pills a day?*

ESERCIZIO
5·16

You are in Italy on vacation when you suddenly come down with nausea and a temperature. At the emergency room, you explain your symptoms to the doctor on duty. Complete the following conversation.

PAZIENTE: «Mi scusi, Signora, ho bisogno di vedere un medico».

1. Medico: «Sono io il _____ di guardia. Che sintomi ha»?

2. Paziente: «Ho la nausea e _____ di stomaco e la _____ a 39».

3. Medico: «Adesso la misuriamo. Metta il _____ sotto la lingua... Ha trentotto e mezzo. Ha altri _____? _____ di testa»?

4. Paziente: «Sì e ho _____ tutta la notte. Stamattina non sono riuscito a mangiare niente».

5. Medico: «Credo che abbia preso un'_____ gastrointestinale: un virus che ha colpito lo stomaco e il sistema digerente. Deve bere molti liquidi e stare a riposo».

Medical locations and equipment

l(a)'ambulanza	*ambulance*
l(o)'ambulatorio	*walk-in clinic*
la barella	*gurney*
la clinica	*clinic*
il day care	*outpatient care*
l(o)'ospedale	*hospital*
il pronto soccorso, i pronto soccorso	*emergency room*
il reparto	*ward*
la sala operatoria	*operating room*
la sedia a rotelle	*wheelchair*

Chiamate un'ambulanza!   Call an ambulance!
È un intervento da day care.   It's an outpatient surgical operation.

ESERCIZIO
5·17

Complete the following sentences.

1. In un _____ si fanno solo terapie da day care.

2. Non vai al _____ _____ se hai solo un raffreddore.

3. Quando ti portano in sala operatoria, ti mettono su una _____.

4. Se ti rompi una gamba, ti mettono su una _____ _____ _____.

5. Se ti viene un infarto, chiami un'_____.

Life stages and sexual orientation

adolescente	adolescent
adulto	adult; grownup
anziano	elderly
etero(sessuale)	heterosexual; straight
giovane	young
lesbica	lesbian
mortale	mortal
morto	dead
omo(sessuale); gay	homosexual; gay
transessuale	transgender
vecchio	old (person)
vergine	virgin
vivo	alive

Da giovane Dino ha fatto l'astronauta.   As a young man, Dino was an astronaut.
Per piacere, comportati da persona adulta.   Please, behave as a grownup.

ESERCIZIO
5·18

Translate the following sentences into English.

1. Secondo gli antichi greci gli dei intervenirvano nella vita dei mortali.

   _____

2. Il vecchio non riusciva a leggere il cartello.

   _____

3. L'uomo è mortale.

   _____

4. Le funzioni mentali sono meno brillanti nell'adulto che nell'adolescente.

_____

5. Mio fratello era ancora vergine a trent'anni.

_____

Sex and reproduction

l(o)'aborto	*abortion; miscarriage*
l(a)'adozione	*adoption*
la contraccezione	*contraception*
le doglie (pl.)	*labor pains*
l(a)'esistenza	*existence*
il feto	*fetus*
la gravidanza	*pregnancy*
le mestruazioni (pl.)	*menstruation; period*
l(o)'orgasmo	*orgasm*
il parto	*childbirth; delivery*
la pillola [anticoncezionale]	*(birth control) pill*
il sesso	*sex*
la vita	*life*

Bice ha avuto le prime mestruazioni a undici anni.
Bice had her first period at eleven.

Mia sorella ha avuto un parto facilissimo.
My sister had a very easy delivery.

ESERCIZIO
5·19

Complete the following sentences by adding the appropriate noun.

1. Ha avuto un _____ difficile, ma il bambino sta bene.

2. Ha avuto una _____ difficile, ma il parto è stato facile.

3. Le femmine raggiungono lo sviluppo quando hanno le prime _____.

4. Mia sorella prende la _____ perché non vuole avere bambini.

5. Non possono avere figli; stanno pensando all'_____.

Life and death

l(a)'adolescenza	*adolescence*
il cimitero	*cemetery*
l(a)'età	*age*
l(a)'eutanasia assistita	*assisted suicide*
il funerale	*funeral*
la giovinezza	*youth*

l(a)'infanzia	childhood
la menopausa	menopause
la mezza età	middle age
la morte	death
la pubertà	puberty
il suicidio	suicide
la vecchiaia	old age
la vita	life

| L'adolescenza è un'età difficile. | Adolescence is a difficult phase. |
| In Olanda l'eutanasia assistita è legale. | In Holland assisted suicide is legal. |

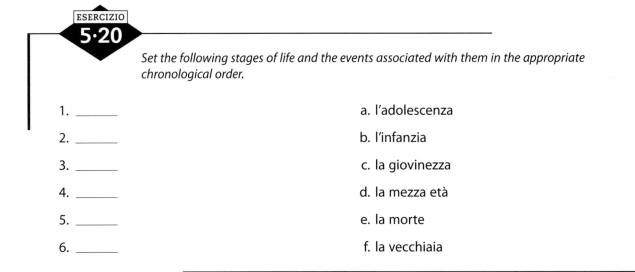

ESERCIZIO
5·20

Set the following stages of life and the events associated with them in the appropriate chronological order.

1. _____
2. _____
3. _____
4. _____
5. _____
6. _____

a. l'adolescenza
b. l'infanzia
c. la giovinezza
d. la mezza età
e. la morte
f. la vecchiaia

Verbs

adottare	to adopt
allevare	to raise
avere un rapporto sessuale (con)	to have sex (with)
crescere	to grow (up)
dare alla luce	to give birth (to)
eccitare	to turn on, to arouse
esistere	to exist
invecchiare	to age; to grow old
morire (di)	to die (from/of)
seppellire	to bury
suicidarsi	to commit suicide
vivere (aux. avere/essere)	to live

| Sua nonna ha allevato dieci figli. | Her grandma raised ten children. |
| Mia cugina ha dato alla luce due gemelli. | My cousin gave birth to twins. |

Complete the following sentences.

1. Giovanna ha _____ _____ _____ tre gemelli.

2. I bambini _____. Le persone anziane _____.

3. In Oregon e in Olanda l'_____ _____ è legale.

4. Le coppie che non possono avere figli spesso _____ un bambino.

5. Quando una persona ha avuto un rapporto sessuale non è più _____.

6. Vivere è l'opposto di _____.

Consumer society

Consumer society has taken hold in Italy in the last fifty years. A refined, long-standing tradition in the visual arts has greatly contributed to making Italy the center of modern design, both in clothing and in household furnishings. Italian luxury products can be found as far away as São Paolo, Shanghai, and Tokyo. Italy makes high-quality items available to the public at large: there is no to-the-trade-only retail sector in Italy.

l(o)'affare (usually sing.)	*bargain; deal*
l(o)'articolo	*article; item*
il, la cliente	*client; customer*
il commercio	*commerce; trade*
il consumatore / la consumatrice	*consumer*
il consumo; i consumi	*consumption*
il lusso	*luxury*
il made-in-Italy (sing.)	*made-in-Italy products*
il magazzino (sing.); lo stock	*stock (inventory)*
la merce	*merchandise*
il prodotto	*product*
la pubblicità; la réclame	*advertisement*
la roba (sing.)	*stuff*
la spesa (alimentare) (sing.); le spese (pl.); l(o)'acquisto	*shopping*

Quanta roba c'è nell'armadio!	*How much stuff there is in that closet!*
Il made-in-Italy si vende bene in Giappone.	*Made-in-Italy products sell well in Japan.*

ESERCIZIO
6·1

*Decide whether the following statements are true (**T**) or false (**F**).*

1. I consumi sono diminuiti negli ultimi trent'anni. _____

2. Il commercio non ha bisogno di consumatori. _____

3. Il made-in-Italy è diventato famoso negli ultimi trent'anni. _____

4. I prodotti di lusso costano poco. _____

5. La pubblicità non serve a vendere i prodotti. _____

Shopping

andare in fallimento; fare fallimento	*to go out of business*
aprire	*to open*
aumentare; alzare	*to raise; to increase*
cambiare	*to change*
chiudere	*to close*
comp(e)rare; acquistare	*to buy; to purchase*
consumare	*to consume*
costare	*to cost*
diminuire	*to lower; to decrease*
(andare a) far(e) la spesa / (le) spese	*to shop; to go shopping (for food)*
(andare a) fare una commissione	*to do / go on an errand*
fare le commissioni	*to do errands*
fare lo/uno sconto	*to give a discount*
pagare	*to pay*
reclamare (aux. **avere**)	*to complain*
rendere; restituire	*to return*
risparmiare	*to save*
spendere	*to spend*
vendere	*to sell*
Vai tu a fare la spesa?	*Will you go shopping?*
Quanto fa?	*How much is it?*

ESERCIZIO

6·2

Complete the sentences below, by choosing from the verbs listed above. Use the infinitive or the present indicative.

1. Sono già le nove! Ma a che ora _____ il supermercato?

2. Mia sorella ha bisogno di un prestito perché _____ troppo.

3. Non abbiamo né latte, né pane. Vai tu a _____ _____ _____?

4. In quel negozio puoi _____ un articolo se non ti piace.

ESERCIZIO

6·3

Complete the following sentences by choosing from the options listed after each of them.

1. È l'ultimo articolo in magazzino. Mi _____?
   a. paga   b. fa uno sconto   c. sconta

2. Ma i prezzi _____ sempre?
   a. costano   b. risparmiano   c. aumentano

3. Non andiamo più in quel negozio perché _____ i prezzi del dieci per cento.
   a. hanno venduto   b. hanno alzato   c. hanno rimborsato

4. Quanto _____ questa lampada?
   a. costa   b. paga   c. rende

Describing shopping

a buon mercato; di bassa qualità; conveniente; che costa poco	*cheap*
aperto	*open*
caro; costoso	*dear; expensive*
chiuso	*closed*
di bassa/cattiva qualità	*low/poor quality*
di buona/alta qualità	*good/high quality*
di moda	*in fashion*
di seconda mano	*secondhand; used*
fatto a mano	*handmade*
fatto su misura	*custom-/tailor-made*
fuori moda	*out of fashion*
gratis; gratuito	*free*
in garanzia	*under warrantee*
in saldo	*on sale*
(fatto) in serie; di serie	*mass-produced*
in vendita	*for sale*
nuovo	*new*

Ho comprato una bella giacca in saldo.	*I bought a nice jacket on sale.*
Queste scarpe sono di bassa qualità.	*These shoes are not good quality.*

ESERCIZIO

6·4

Complete the following sentences, by choosing from the adjectives listed above.

1. Al mercato di quartiere trovi dei prodotti a prezzi _____.

2. «500 euro per un paio di scarpe»?! «Ma sono _____ _____ _____, Signore».

3. I pantaloni larghi in fondo non sono più _____ _____.

4. I prodotti fatti a mano costano molto, ma quelli _____ _____ _____ costano poco.

Paying

l(o, a)'acquirente; il compratore / la compratrice	*buyer*
l(o)'acquisto; le compere (pl.)	*purchase*
l(o)'affare	*bargain; deal*
l(o)'assegno	*check*
la carta di credito	*credit card*
la cartina del bancomat / il bancomat	*ATM/debit card*
la cassa	*cashier's desk*
il cassiere / la cassiera	*cashier*
il contante (often used in the pl.)	*cash*
il prezzo	*price*
la rata	*installment*

il resto (sing.); **gli spiccioli** (pl.)	*change (after a transaction); change (coins)*
la ricevuta; lo scontrino	*receipt*
i soldi (pl.); **il denaro**	*money*
la vendita; il saldo (often used in the pl.)	*sale*
il venditore / la venditrice	*seller*

Signora, dimentica il resto!	*Madam, you're forgetting your change!*
Mio fratello ha perso la cartina del bancomat.	*My brother lost his ATM card.*

ESERCIZIO
6·5

Provide the words described in the following definitions. Add the article.

1. Document issued by vendor acknowledging receipt of an amount of money. _____

2. A written order directing a bank to pay money. _____

3. An advantageous purchase. _____

4. Each installment with which merchandise is paid over a specified period. _____

5. Balance of money received when amount tendered is greater than the amount due.

   _____

ESERCIZIO
6·6

Add the past participle of the appropriate verb to the following sentences.

1. I miei genitori hanno _____ una nuova casa al mare.

2. Il paese ha _____ più di quanto ha prodotto.

3. Ho _____ le commissioni ieri.

4. Avete _____ il conto?

5. «Aspetto il collegamento Internet da due mesi»! «Incredibile! Ma hai _____»?

Stores

The Italian structure of retail and distribution is now made of shopping malls, superstores, and chains, as in the United States. Store hours have become more flexible. Small stores are struggling to survive. Quality has not always been the winner in this change.

la bancarella [del mercato]	*market stand*
la catena	*chain*
il centro commerciale	*shopping mall*
il commesso / la commessa	*salesperson*
il grande magazzino	*department store*

l(a) insegna [del negozio]	[store] sign
il magazzino	warehouse
il mercato	market
il mercato dei contadini	farmers' market
il, la negoziante	shopkeeper; vendor
il negozio di abbigliamento	clothing store
il negozio di casalinghi; i casalinghi	housewares store
il negozio di dischi	music store
il negozio di elettrodomestici	appliance store
il negozio di ferramenta; il ferramenta	hardware store
il negozio di generi vari; il bazaar	drugstore
il negozio di mobili/arredamento	furniture store
l(o)'orario [di apertura]	store hours
il supermercato; il supermarket	supermarket
il venditore / la venditrice ambulante	street vendor

Carrefour è una catena di grandi magazzini.	Carrefour is a supermarket chain.
Che orario fa la panetteria?	What are the store hours of the bakery?
Compro la verdura dalle bancarelle dei contadini.	I buy my vegetables from the farmers' stands.

ESERCIZIO
6·7

In each of the following series, mark the word that does not match the other three.

1. a. il centro commerciale   b. il supermercato   c. il grande magazzino   d. la bancarella

2. a. il mercato   b. il commesso   c. la bancarella   d. il venditore ambulante

3. a. il supermercato   b. il commesso   c. la cassiera   d. la negoziante

4. a. lo stock   b. la merce   c. i prodotti   d. l'insegna

In Italian, names of stores are often formed by adding -**ìa** or -**erìa** to the stem of the noun indicating the merchandise or the vendor.

il farmac-o	drug	il farmacista	pharmacist	la farmacìa	pharmacy
———		il gastronomo	gourmet	la gastronomìa	delicatessen
il libr-o	book	il libr-aio	bookseller	la librerìa	bookstore
il pan-e	bread	il panett-iere	baker	la panetterìa	bakery

ESERCIZIO
6·8

Form the name of the stores where the commercial activities listed below take place. Add the article.

1. il gelato (*ice cream*) _____ _____

2. il gioiello (*jewel*) _____ _____

3. il latte (*milk*) _____ _____

4. il macello (*butcher*) _____ _____

5. il profumo (*perfume*) _____ _____

6. il salame (*salami*) _____ _____

7. il tabacco (*tobacco*) _____ _____

We can use **da** + *article* + *name of the provider* to indicate where we are purchasing something. When we use the name of a store, we use **in** + *noun* which conveys both place where and motion toward; we use **da** to convey motion from.

Sono dal droghiere.	*I'm in/at the greengrocer's.*
Vado in drogheria.	*I'm going to the grocery store.*
Sono tornati i bambini dal gelataio?	*Did the children come back from the ice-cream parlor?*

ESERCIZIO

6·9

In the following sentences, replace the nouns conveying the provider of a service with the nouns indicating the stores.

1. «Che buono questo gelato! Dove l'hai preso»? «Dal gelataio». _____

2. «Dove posso comprare i francobolli»? «Dal tabaccaio». _____

3. Mia figlia ha speso 300 euro dal profumiere! _____

4. Mauro si è dimenticato di passare dal panettiere. _____

5. Vai dal salumaio? Compra due etti di olive, per favore. _____

Italy is famous for its clothes, leather goods, furniture, and modern design in general. Production is still dominated by small- to medium-sized firms which combine flexibility and high quality.

il camerino	*dressing room*
il capo [di vestiario]	*garment; item of clothing*
il manichino	*mannequin*
la misura (shoes, lingerie, and clothes); **la taglia** (clothes only)	*size*
la moda	*fashion*
la ragazza da copertina; **la modella**	*cover girl; model*
la sfilata	*fashion show*
lo, la stilista	*fashion designer*
la vetrina	*window*
il, la vetrinista	*window dresser*

Mi sembra una taglia 52, Signore.	*You look like a size 52 to me, Sir.*
Mia madre ha fatto la modella.	*My mother was a fashion model.*

Consumer society **69**

Complete the following sentences, choosing from the words listed below.

1. _____ sono ben pagate, ma hanno una carriera breve.
   a. I manichini   b. I vetrinisti   c. Le modelle

2. Parigi è ancora il centro mondiale _____.
   a. della moda   b. dell'alta moda   c. dell'abbigliamento

3. Sono andata a Milano a vedere _____ della moda pronta.
   a. le passerelle   b. le sfilate   c. le vetrine

4. _____ vestono i manichini.
   a. Le ragazze da copertina   b. Gli stilisti   c. Le vetriniste

Describing clothing

a righe	*striped*
casual (unchangeable)	*casual*
consumato	*worn out; shabby*
(abbigliamento) da uomo/donna/ bambino	*men's/women's/children's (apparel)*
di buon gusto	*tasteful; in good taste*
fantasia (unchangeable)	*with a pattern*
elegante	*elegant*
scozzese	*plaid*
sportivo	*sporty*
(in) tinta unita	*solid*
volgare; di cattivo gusto	*tacky*

Quel negozio vende abiti da bambino.   *That store sells children's clothes.*
Lei ha molto buon gusto.   *She has very good taste.*

In the sentences below, add the qualifier listed in parentheses, modifying it in gender and number (if possible) when it refers to a noun.

1. Ha tante giacche, ma mette solo quella blu, che è tutta _____. (consumato)

2. Mario si veste sempre _____. (elegante)

3. Mia sorella ha cinquant'anni, ma si veste ancora _____. (casual)

4. Non mi sono mai comprata un abito _____. (fantasia)

5. Stefania porta solo abiti _____. (sportivo)

Clothing items

l(o)'abbigliamento	*apparel*
l(o)'abito lungo / da sera	*evening gown*
la camicia; la camicetta (women)	*shirt*
il cappotto; il giaccone	*(over)coat*
la cerniera lampo; la zip	*zipper*
il golf / la maglia	*sweater*
l(o)'impermeabile	*raincoat*
i (blue) jeans (pl.)	*(blue) jeans*
il panciotto; il gilè / gilet	*vest*
i pantaloni (pl.)	*pants; slacks; trousers*
i pantaloni corti (pl.)	*shorts*
la pelliccia	*fur coat*
il piumone	*down coat*
lo smoking	*tuxedo*
la T-shirt; la maglietta	*T-shirt*
il vestito / l(o)'abito [da uomo/donna]; il tailleur (women)	*suit*
il vestito; l(o)'abito	*dress*
i vestiti (pl.)	*clothes*

Non ho mai avuto un abito da sera.	*I've never had an evening gown.*
Il panciotto è decisamente fuori moda.	*The vest is decidedly out of style.*

ESERCIZIO
6·12

Complete the following sentences with the appropriate garment.

1. Quando piove metti _____.

2. Per la prima alla Scala mio marito metterà _____.

3. Quando fa veramente freddo, serve _____, _____ o _____ da mettere sopra i vestiti.

4. «Quante _____ ti sei messa»? «Ho freddo»!

5. _____ _____ _____ sono adatti quando fa molto caldo.

Clothes and colors

arancione	*orange*
beige (invariable)	*beige*
bianco	*white*
blu (invariable)	*blue*
bordeaux (invariable)	*burgundy*
celeste; azzurro	*sky blue; azure*
giallo	*yellow*
grigio	*gray*
lilla (invariable)	*lilac*
marrone	*brown*
nero	*black*

rosa (invariable)	*pink*
rosso	*red*
verde	*green*
viola (invariable)	*violet*

Paola ha dieci vestiti blu. *Paola has ten blue dresses.*
Ha comprato uno smoking bordeaux. *He bought a burgundy tuxedo.*

ESERCIZIO
6·13

Match adjective and noun. Change the ending of the adjective to match gender and number when possible.

1. arancione   la maglietta _____
2. beige   i pantaloni _____
3. bianco   la T-shirt _____
4. blu   la felpa _____
5. bordeaux   il panciotto _____
6. grigio   la gonna _____
7. lilla   l'abito da sera _____
8. marrone   le pellicce _____
9. nero   gli smoking _____

Dressing and undressing

andar(e) bene (a)	*to fit*
cucire	*to sew*
essere adatto (a); star(e) bene (a)	*to suit; to look good (on)*
intonarsi (con); stare bene insieme	*to match*
mettere/mettersi [addosso]	*to put on*
portare; indossare	*to wear*
provare; misurare	*to try on*
strappare	*to tear*
svestire; svestirsi	*to undress*
tagliare	*to cut*
togliere/togliersi [di dosso]	*to take off*
vestire; vestirsi	*to dress; to get dressed*

Quel vestito è carino, ma non ti va bene. *That dress is nice, but it doesn't fit you.*
Quel vestito è carino, ma non ti sta bene. *That dress is nice, but it doesn't suit you.*

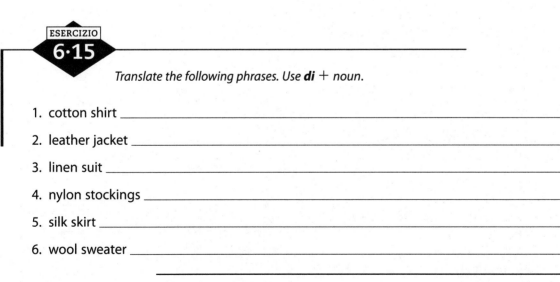

ESERCIZIO
6·14

Replace the verbs in parentheses in the following sentences with the reflexive form.

1. Gianna (ha messo) _____ _____ _____ le scarpe nuove.

2. Noi (abbiamo tolto) _____ _____ _____ prima di fare la doccia.

3. Maria (ha provato) dieci vestiti. _____

4. (Metto) un altro golf. Questo è vecchio. _____

5. Non (tolgono) il cappotto, Signori? Fa caldo qui dentro. _____

Fabrics

il cotone	*cotton*
il cuoio	*leather*
la lana	*wool*
il lino	*linen*
il nylon	*nylon*
il pizzo	*lace*
il poliestere	*polyester*
la seta	*silk*
il velluto	*velvet*
la viscosa	*rayon*

When we wish to convey with what material a garment is made, we can use **di** (more common) or **in** + *noun.*

la camicetta di viscosa	*rayon shirt*
la tenda in velluto	*velvet curtain*

ESERCIZIO
6·15

*Translate the following phrases. Use **di** + noun.*

1. cotton shirt _____

2. leather jacket _____

3. linen suit _____

4. nylon stockings _____

5. silk skirt _____

6. wool sweater _____

Lingerie

la biancheria intima (sing.); **l(o)'intimo** (sing.)	*lingerie; intimates*
il body	*bodysuit, corset*
la calza	*stocking*
il calzino	*sock*
la camicia da notte	*night shirt*
il collant; un paio di collant	*pantyhose; a pair of pantyhose*
le mutande [da uomo]; le mutandine [da donna]; un paio di mutande/ mutandine (pl.)	*briefs; panties; underwear; a pair of underwear*
il paio, le paia (**di** + noun in the plural without the article)	*pair (of)*
la pantofola	*slipper*
il pigiama	*(pair of) pajamas*
il reggiseno	*bra*

Dove sono le calze dei bambini?   *Where are the children's socks?*
Hai un paio di collant da prestarmi?   *Do you have a pair of pantyhose to lend me?*

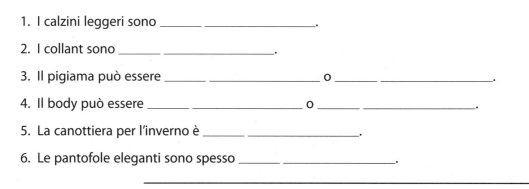

ESERCIZIO
6·16

*In the following sentences, use **di** and add the material/materials with which each piece of lingerie can be made. Choose among the following kinds of fabrics: **lana**, **velluto**, **nylon**, **cotone**.*

1. I calzini leggeri sono _____ _____.

2. I collant sono _____ _____.

3. Il pigiama può essere _____ _____ o _____ _____.

4. Il body può essere _____ _____ o _____ _____.

5. La canottiera per l'inverno è _____ _____.

6. Le pantofole eleganti sono spesso _____ _____.

Accessories

l(o)'accessorio	*accessory*
la borsa	*bag*
la borsetta	*purse; handbag*
il cappello	*hat*
la cintura	*belt*
la cravatta	*tie*
il guanto	*glove*
l(o)'ombrello	*umbrella*
il portafoglio	*wallet*
il sandalo	*sandal*
la scarpa	*shoe*

| **la sciarpa** | scarf |
| **lo stivale** | boot |

La regina Elisabetta adora le borsette. *Queen Elizabeth loves purses.*
Regagliamogli un paio di guanti. *Let's give him a pair of gloves.*

ESERCIZIO
6·17

List the accessories and items of lingerie that usually come in pairs.

Un paio di: _____

_____

Jewelry

l(o)'anello	*ring*
l(o)'argento	*silver*
la bigiotteria	*costume jewelry*
il braccialetto	*bracelet*
la collana	*necklace*
il diamante; il brillante	*diamond*
il gioiello, i gioielli / la gioielleria	*(piece of) jewelry*
l(o)'orecchino	*earring*
l(o)'oro	*gold*
la perla	*pearl*
la pietra preziosa	*precious stone*
la spilla	*pin; brooch*

Le ha regalato un brillante. *He gave her a diamond.*
I gioielli veri sono nella cassaforte. *The real jewelry is in the safe.*

ESERCIZIO
6·18

Complete the following sentences, choosing from the options listed below.

1. Gli orecchini di diamanti stanno bene con _____.
   a. la collana di diamanti b. le perle c. l'anello d(i)'oro

2. Ho perso _____!
   a. la bigiotteria b. un orecchino c. l'orafo

3. La _____ a volte costa quasi come i gioielli veri.
   a. collana b. anelli c. bigiotteria

4. Le ha regalato _____ di fidanzamento con un grosso diamante.
   a. un anello b. una spilla c. un paio di orecchini

Housing

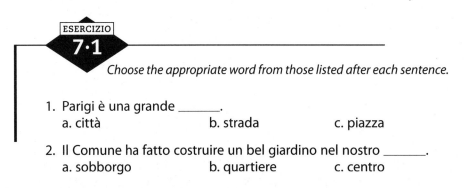

Since Roman times, Italians have lived in multifamily dwellings, in close quarters. Most modern cities have grown around a medieval core of narrow streets, whose renovated buildings now command high prices. Neighborhoods built after World War II are called collectively **la periferia** (*outskirts*), not the same as **i sobborghi** (*suburbs*), because they are contiguous with the geographical and historical city center. They were often built without giving much thought to aesthetics and non-essential services and are usually considered less desirable.

Seventy-two percent of Italians own their own home, usually an apartment. Many of them own a second home, often in the countryside place of origin of their family.

la campagna (sing.)	*countryside*
il centro[città]	*downtown; city center*
la città	*city; town*
la cittadina; il paese	*town*
il corso	*avenue*
il paesino; il villaggio	*village*
la periferia	*outskirts; periphery*
la piazza	*square; plaza*
il quartiere; il vicinato (sing.)	*neighborhood*
il sobborgo	*suburb*
la via; la strada	*street*
il viale (usually lined with trees)	*boulevard*

Abito in periferia, a venti minuti dal centro.	*I live in the outskirts, about twenty minutes away from downtown.*
Vanno a vivere in campagna.	*They're going to live in the country.*

ESERCIZIO 7·1

Choose the appropriate word from those listed after each sentence.

1. Parigi è una grande _____.
   a. città   b. strada   c. piazza

2. Il Comune ha fatto costruire un bel giardino nel nostro _____.
   a. sobborgo   b. quartiere   c. centro

3. I _____ della città sono cresciuti molto negli ultimi dieci anni.
   a. quartiere   b. sobborghi   c. periferie

4. La _____ centrale del paese si riempie di gente verso sera.
   a. periferia   b. viale   c. piazza

5. Non mi piace _____ Garibaldi. È così stretta!
   a. quartiere   b. piazza   c. via

To convey in what kind of place or environment you live, Italian uses different constructions with different words:

> **in** + *noun*: **campagna, centro, città, paese, periferia, piazza**
> **in** + *indefinite article* + *noun*: **paese, paesino, cittadina, ghetto, villaggio**
> **in** + *definite article* + *noun*: **sobborghi**
> **su** + *indefinite article* + *noun*: **viale, corso**
> Note that *out of town* translates to **fuori città**.

ESERCIZIO
7·2

Complete the following sentences by choosing the appropriate construction.

1. Il suo appartamento è _____. (corso)

2. In Italia, la gente preferisce vivere _____ non troppo grande. (cittadina)

3. Non riusciamo a decidere se restare _____, o andare _____. (città; campagna)

4. Siamo andati a vivere _____, ma non siamo molto contenti. (sobborghi)

5. Vive _____ molto piccolo e molto tranquillo. (paesino)

Housing arrangements

l(o)'amministratore (m. and f.)	*condominium manager*
l(o)'appartamento; l(o)'alloggio	*apartment*
l(o)'attico	*penthouse*
la casa	*home; house; place*

Casa and **appartamento** translate as *house* or *apartment*. When either is our primary residence, we call it **casa**, which Americans would call *home*.

Sono a casa / in casa.	*I'm at home.*
Sono riusciti a comprarsi la casa.	*They were able to buy their own home.*

la casa/villetta (unifamigliare)	*single-family house*
la casa di riposo	*nursing home*
la casa per anziani	*retirement community*
le case popolari (pl.)	*projects; subsidized housing*
il condominio	*condominium*
l(o)'edificio; il caseggiato	*building; multi-dwelling building*
il grattacielo	*skyscraper*

il palazzo	*palace; building*
il portinaio	*doorman; concierge*
il senzatetto, i senzatetto	*homeless person*
il villone; il maniero	*mansion*

Ci sono trenta appartamenti nel loro caseggiato.	*There are thirty apartments in their building.*
Dobbiamo pagare la rata del condominio!	*We must pay our condo fees!*

ESERCIZIO
7·3

In each of the following series, mark the word that does not belong.

1. a. il palazzo   b. il caseggiato   c. l'edificio   d. l'attico

2. a. il condominio   b. le case popolari   c. il senzatetto   d. la casa

3. a. il grattacielo   b. l'attico   c. il caseggiato   d. l'edificio

4. a. la villetta   b. la casa   c. il portinaio   d. il condominio

Renting and buying

abitare (aux. **avere**)	*to live; to reside*
affittare; dare in affitto	*to lease; to let*
affittare; prendere in affitto; essere in affitto	*to rent*
fare il mutuo	*to get a mortgage*
fare un(a)'offerta	*to bid*
possedere; essere proprietario (di)	*to own*
sfrattare	*to evict*
stabilirsi	*to settle*
subaffittare	*to sublet*
traslocare (aux. **avere**); **cambiar(e) casa**	*to move*
vivere (aux. **avere/essere**)	*to live*

«Dove abiti»? «Abito in Via Spiga 3».	*"Where do you live?" "I live at 3 Via Spiga."*
Hai fatto un mutuo trentennale?	*Did you get a thirty-year mortgage?*

ESERCIZIO
7·4

*Choosing from the verbs listed above, answer yes (**Y**) or no (**N**) to the following questions. (For basic verbs regarding commercial transactions, review Unit 6.)*

1. Puoi prendere in affitto un intero edificio? _____

2. Quando traslochi vuol dire che cambi casa? _____

3. Puoi vendere l'appartamento che hai affittato? _____

4. Se non paghi l'affitto puoi essere sfrattato? _____

5. Se paghi l'affitto, sei proprietario della casa? _____

Real estate

l(o)'affitto	*rent*
l(o, a)'agente immobiliare	*real estate agent*
la caparra; l(o)'acconto	*deposit; down payment*
la compagnia dei/di traslochi; i traslochi (pl.)	*movers; moving company*
la compravendita	*buying and selling*
il condomino	*condominium (condo) owner*
il contratto (d'affitto)	*lease*
l(o)'inquilino	*tenant*
il mutuo	*mortgage*
il padrone / la padrona di casa	*landlord; owner*
la posizione	*location*
la proprietà	*property*
la proprietà immobiliare; gli immobili (pl.)	*real estate*
il proprietario	*owner*
il subaffitto	*sublet*
il trasloco	*moving*
Sono in subaffitto.	*I'm subletting.*
Sono arrivati quelli dei traslochi.	*The movers have arrived.*

ESERCIZIO 7·5

Complete the beginning of each sentence on the left with the appropriate conclusion taken from those listed on the right.

1. Gli agenti immobiliari _____

2. Il mio inquilino _____

3. Non abbiamo ancora il telefono, _____

4. Potete ottenere un mutuo _____

5. Questo appartamento costa molto _____

6. Sono in affitto _____

a. anche se pagate solo il 10 per cento di acconto!

b. hanno una commissione del 5 per cento.

c. non mi paga l'affitto!

d. perché abbiamo appena fatto il trasloco.

e. perché è in una bellissima posizione.

f. perché non posso comprarmi la casa.

Professionals in the building sector

l(o)'architetto (m. and f.)	*architect*
il decoratore (m. and f.); l(o)'imbianchino	*painter*
l(o)'elettricista (m. and f.)	*electrician*
il falegname (m. and f.)	*carpenter*
l(o)'idraulico (m. and f.)	*plumber*
l(o)'impresario [edile] (m. and f.)	*contractor; developer*
l(o)'ingegnere [civile]	*civil engineer*
il muratore (m. and f.)	*mason; bricklayer*
il, la piastrellista	*tile installer*

Mia figlia studia da architetto.
Papà ha trovato un buon impresario.

My daughter is studying to be an architect.
Dad found a good contractor.

ESERCIZIO
7·6

Provide the male nouns described in the following definitions.

1. Chi costruisce e ripara i sistemi di distribuzione delle acque. _____

2. Chi costruisce muri. _____

3. Chi dipinge i muri di una casa. _____

4. Chi dirige un'impresa di costruzioni. _____

5. Chi disegna e progetta edifici. _____

6. Chi installa le piastrelle. _____

Building and repairing

aggiustare	*to mend; to repair*
avvitare	*to screw*
costruire	*to build*
installare	*to install*
montare	*to assemble*
perdere; avere una perdita	*to leak; to have a leak*
piantare un chiodo	*to drive a nail*
riparare	*to repair; to fix*
ristrutturare	*to remodel*
scavare	*to dig*
segare	*to saw*
svitare	*to unscrew*

L'idraulico ha riparato il rubinetto.
Hai installato tu le piastrelle?! Che brava!

The plumber fixed the faucet.
You installed the tiles yourself?! Bravo!

ESERCIZIO
7·7

Complete the following sentences with the appropriate verb. Use the present indicative or the infinitive.

1. Devo dire all'idraulico di tornare, perché il rubinetto continua a _____.

2. Faccio _____ la vecchia casa dei nonni.

3. I mobili costano poco all'IKEA, ma te li devi _____ da solo.

4. I miei zii hanno deciso di _____ una nuova casa in campagna.

5. L'elettricista viene domani a _____ la televisione.

Tools and materials

l(o)'arnese; l(o)'aggeggio (often useless)	*gadget*
l(o)'attrezzo; l(o)'utensile	*tool*
il cacciavite	*screwdriver*
il chiodo	*nail*
il corto circuito	*short circuit*
l(a)'elettricità; la luce (sing.)	*electricity; power*
il filo/cavo [elettrico]	*(electrical) wire*
il martello	*hammer*
la sega	*saw*
il trapano	*drill*
il tubo / la tubatura	*pipe*
la vite	*screw*
Mio marito si è comprato un altro aggeggio!	*My husband bought another gadget!*
È andata via l'elettricità.	*The electricity went out.*

ESERCIZIO

7·8

Add the tools and materials you need to complete the job in question or to explain what caused the problem you are trying to solve.

1. Hai bisogno del _____ e dei _____ per piantare dei chiodi.

2. Il _____ serve ad avvitare le _____.

3. Mio marito ha il garage pieno di _____ che non servono a niente.

4. Non c'è più corrente perché c'è stato un _____ _____.

5. Signora, per riparare la perdita devo cambiare il _____.

6. La _____ elettrica è comoda, ma bisogna usarla con attenzione.

In Italy, wood has never been builders' material of choice: the Romans built five-story multifamily dwellings made of bricks. Today, a house of any size is built with brick walls (covered with plaster), attached to a structure of reinforced concrete pillars. Marble, tile, and wood are mostly used for flooring.

l(o)'acciaio [inossidabile]	*(stainless) steel*
l(o)'asfalto	*asphalt*
il cantiere [edile]	*construction site*
il cemento; il cemento armato	*cement; (reinforced) concrete*
la colonna	*column*
le fondamenta (pl.)	*foundations*
il ferro	*iron*
la gru, le gru	*crane*
il legno	*wood*
il marmo	*marble*
il materiale	*material*
il mattone	*brick*

il muro (house) / **la parete** (room); **le mura** (city, pl.)	wall(s)
la piastrella [di ceramica]	(ceramic) tile
la pietra	stone
la plastica	plastic
la tappezzeria	wallpaper
la tinta	paint
il vetro	glass

Le case italiane sono di cemento armato.	*Italian houses are built with reinforced concrete.*
Una stanza ha quattro pareti.	*A room has four walls.*

ESERCIZIO

7·9

*As we have seen in Unit 5, in Italian we use the construction **di/in** + noun to say of what material something is made. Translate the following phrases. Use **di** + noun and include the article.*

1. brick wall (of a house) _____

2. plastic objects _____

3. reinforced concrete columns _____

4. stone palaces _____

5. stone walls (of a city) _____

6. wood houses _____

ESERCIZIO

7·10

*Answer yes (**Y**) or no (**N**) to the following questions.*

1. Gli Incas costruivano grandi palazzi di pietra? _____

2. Gli oggetti di plastica sono pesanti e fragili? _____

3. I pavimenti possono essere di alluminio? _____

4. In Italia la maggior parte delle case sono di legno? _____

5. Negli Stati Uniti la maggior parte delle case sono fatte di legno? _____

Building exteriors

il balcone	*balcony*
il cancello	*gate*
il cortile	*courtyard*
la finestra	*window*

il fronte [della casa]	*front*
la persiana	*shutter*
la porta / il portone	*door; front door*
la porta finestra	*French window/door*
la portineria / il portinaio	*doorman; concierge*
la ringhiera	*railing*
la staccionata (di legno); la cancellata (di ferro)	*(wood) fence; (iron) fence*
il tetto	*roof*
la tegola	*roof tile*

I Pizzetto hanno tirato su una cancellata.	*The Pizzettos put up an iron fence.*
Donatella si è affacciata alla finestra.	*Donatella came to the window.*

ESERCIZIO
7·11

Complete the following sentences, choosing from the words listed after each of them.

1. Abbiamo fatto costruire _____ di legno per separarci un po' dai vicini.
   a. una cancellata   b. una staccionata   c. una ringhiera

2. I bambini possono giocare _____ tra le due e le quattro.
   a. sul tetto   b. sul fronte   c. in cortile

3. È caduta _____ dal tetto. Per fortuna non ha colpito nessuno.
   a. una persiana   b. una tegola   c. una porta

4. _____ della casa si vede dalla strada.
   a. La facciata   b. La ringhiera   c. La persiana

Interiors

l(a)'aria condizionata	*air-conditioning*
l(o)'ascensore	*elevator*
la cantina	*(wine) cellar; basement*
la chiave	*key*
il garage	*garage*
l(o)'impianto antifurto; l(o)'allarme	*burglar alarm*
l(o)'interruttore [della luce]	*(light) switch*
il pavimento	*floor*
il piano	*floor; story*
il [sistema di] riscaldamento	*heating (system)*
il rubinetto	*faucet; tap*
la scala	*stair; staircase*
lo scaldabagno, gli scaldabagno; il boiler	*water heater*
il seminterrato	*basement*
il soffitto	*ceiling*

È scattato l'allarme!	*The alarm went off!*
È un edificio a tre piani.	*It's a three-story building.*

ESERCIZIO
7·12

Complete the following sentences choosing from the words listed above.

1. Accendi _____, se no non possiamo fare la doccia.

2. Dai, facciamo le scale invece di prendere _____.

3. Ha voluto una casa con _____ molto grande perché ha tanti vini.

4. _____ c'è posto per tre automobili.

5. _____ di marmo era lucidissimo.

6. La sua casa ha _____ alti quattro metri.

7. Siamo al freddo perché il _____ non funziona.

Verbs

accendere (la luce o qualunque elettrodomestico)	*to switch/turn on (the light or an electric appliance)*
affacciarsi su; dare su; guardare a/verso	*to face*
aprire (il rubinetto / l'acqua / la luce)	*to turn on (the faucet/water/light)*
bussare (alla porta) (aux. **avere**)	*to knock (on/at the door)*
chiudere (il rubinetto / l'acqua / la luce)	*to turn off (the faucet/water/light)*
chiudere a chiave	*to lock*
entrare (in)	*to enter; to come in*
funzionare (aux. **avere**)	*to work (a mechanical/electrical appliance)*
non funzionare; essere guasto	*to be out of order; to be broken*
spegnere (la luce)	*to switch/turn off (the light)*
suonare il campanello	*to ring the bell*
suonare il citofono	*to ring the intercom*
uscire	*to walk out; to leave (exit)*

Non ho acceso il condizionatore.   *I didn't turn on the air conditioner.*
Hai chiuso il rubinetto centrale?   *Did you turn off the main tap?*

ESERCIZIO
7·13

Add the appropriate verb to the following sentences.

1. Fa caldo. Puoi _____ il condizionatore?

2. Hai _____ _____ _____ la porta di casa prima di uscire?

3. Bisogna risparmiare energia elettrica. Per favore, _____ la luce.

4. Il campanello non _____. Bussa quando arrivi.

5. Ragazzi, _____ in casa! Fa freddo qui fuori.

Showing locations

a due arie	*crossed ventilation; double exposure*
acceso	*on*
al pian(o) terreno	*on the ground/first floor*
al primo piano	*on the second floor*
all(o)'ultimo piano	*on the top floor*
dentro (a); all(o)'interno	*in; indoors*
[al piano] di sopra	*upstairs*
[al piano] di sotto	*downstairs*
fuori (di); all(o)'esterno	*out; outdoors*
giù; di sotto	*down; below*
prefabbricato	*prefab(ricated)*
spento	*off*
su; di sopra	*up*
Attenti al cane!	*Beware of the dog!*
Avanti!	*Come in!*

Replace the words in parentheses in each sentence with a synonymous word or phrase.

1. La sua ditta produce case (che si costruiscono in due settimane) _____.

2. Hanno un bellissimo appartamento (che guarda a nord e a sud) _____ _____ _____.

3. Le chiavi sono rimaste (giù) _____ _____.

4. Mia sorella vive al pianterreno. Io abito (un piano sopra il suo) _____ _____ _____.

Domestic life

To furnish their homes Italians favor simple, modern furniture which maximizes the use of space and which can be moved easily from residence to residence when people move. Even kitchens and bathrooms are furnished with modular furniture that can be adapted to any space with minor changes.

la camera da letto	*bedroom*
la camera/sala da pranzo	*dining room*
il corridoio	*hallway*
la cucina	*kitchen*
il giardino; l(o)'orto	*garden; vegetable garden*
l(o)'ingresso / l(a)'entrata	*foyer*
la pergola / il pergolato	*pergola; trellis*
il retro della casa; il giardino	*backyard*
lo sgabuzzino; il ripostiglio; l(o)' armadio a muro	*closet*
il soggiorno; il salotto	*living room (more formal, with or without a dining area)*
lo studio	*study; home office*
la terrazza	*terrace*
il tinello	*living room (informal living and dining room)*
la veranda; il portico	*porch*
Coltivo i pomodori nell'orto.	*I grow my own tomatoes in the garden.*
Non abbiamo abbastanza armadi a muro.	*We don't have enough closets.*

When we want to say where certain activities take place, in Italian we use the following constructions, to indicate both the place where and the motion toward the place.

in + *noun*: (also **a casa**), **terrazza**, **veranda**
in + *noun* (more common) or **in** + *article* + *noun*: **bagno**, **camera** (**da letto/ pranzo**, etc.), **corridoio**, **cucina**, **giardino**, **ingresso**, **soggiorno**, **studio**, **terrazza**, **tinello**
in + *article* + *noun*: **appartamento**, **armadio a muro**, **orto**, **prato**
sotto + *article* + *noun*: **pergola**, **pergolato**
su + *article* + *noun*: **prato**, **terrazza**

Choose the appropriate room where the following activities are performed usually.

1. Dove vai a dormire? _____

2. Dove prepari la cena? _____

3. Dove intrattieni gli ospiti? _____

4. Dove mangia la famiglia la sera? _____

5. Dove mangi quando hai ospiti? _____

6. Dove fai toeletta al mattino? _____

7. Dove si mangia volentieri d'estate? _____

What we do at home

alzarsi	*to get up*
ammobiliare; arredare	*to furnish*
andare a dormire; andare a letto	*to go to bed*
ascoltare	*to listen to*
aver(e) caldo	*to be/feel cold*
aver(e) freddo	*to be/feel warm*
aver(e) sonno	*to be/feel sleepy*
dormire (aux. avere)	*to sleep*
fare del giardinaggio; fare l'orto	*to work in the garden*
guardare (la TV; un DVD, etc.)	*to watch (TV, a DVD, etc.)*
portare fuori / a spasso il cane	*to walk the dog*
salire/scendere le scale; andare su/giù	*to go upstairs/downstairs*
sedersi	*to sit down*
svegliarsi; svegliare	*to wake up; to wake (someone) up*

Puoi chiudere la finestra? Ho freddo.   *Can you close the window? I'm cold.*
Ida ha arredato la casa con mobili antichi.   *Ida furnished her entire house with antiques.*

ESERCIZIO
8·2

Add the verb that describes the activity we perform in each of the rooms or spaces mentioned in the following sentences. Use the present indicative or the infinitive.

1. Accendiamo l'aria condizionata quando _____.

2. Andiamo a dormire quando _____.

3. In camera da letto si va a _____.

4. Andiamo a _____ sul divano.

5. È in giardino a _____.

6. Mi aiuti ad _____ la casa. Sei così brava!

7. Quando abbiamo ospiti, _____ in sala da pranzo.

Furniture

l(a)'armadio / il guardaroba, i guardaroba	*wardrobe*
l(o)'arredamento	*interior decoration; furniture*
l(o)'arredatore / l(a)'arredatrice	*interior decorator*
il camino; il caminetto	*fireplace*
il [mobile] componibile	*modular furniture*
i confort (pl.); le comodità (pl.)	*comforts*
la coperta	*blanket*
il cuscino	*cushion; pillow*
la lampada	*lamp*
il lenzuolo, le lenzuola	*sheet*
il letto	*bed*
il materasso	*mattress*
il mobile, i mobili	*piece of furniture; furniture*
la moquette	*carpet*
la poltrona	*armchair*
il quadro	*picture; painting*
lo scaffale / la libreria	*bookshelf*
la scrivania	*desk*
la sedia	*chair*
il sofà; il divano	*sofa*
il soprammobile	*knickknack*
lo specchio	*mirror*
il tappeto	*rug*
il tavolino	*coffee table*
il tavolo / la tavola	*table*
la tenda	*curtain*

Non abbiamo abbastanza scaffali per i libri.	*We don't have enough bookshelves for our books.*
La loro casa è piena di quadri astratti.	*Their house is full of abstract paintings.*

ESERCIZIO
8·3

Match the sentences listed in the left and right columns.

1. Come passi il fine settimana? _____
   a. Hai letto bene le istruzioni?

2. Che cosa gli piacerebbe fare? _____
   b. In giardino a piantare fiori.

3. Non riesco a montare il mobile. _____
   c. ma a me non piacciono i mobili antichi.

4. Quanto avete pagato l'appartamento?! _____
   d. Un milione di euro, ma ha tutte le comodità.

5. Vendono una bella poltrona Luigi XV, _____
   e. Vorrebbe diventare arredatore.

Complete the following sentences. Choose one of the options listed after each of them.

1. Hai messo _____ sullo scaffale?
   a. i soprammobili   b. i quadri   c. le candele

2. Ho acceso _____ perché faceva freddo.
   a. la lampada   b. la luce   c. il camino

3. Ho messo il tappeto _____.
   a. sullo specchio   b. sotto il tavolo   c. sul quadro

4. Le _____ servono quando è buio.
   a. lampade   b. tende   c. tavolini

Describing interior decoration

(la cucina) abitabile	eat-in (kitchen)
ammobiliato; arredato	furnished
antico; di antiquariato	antique
classico	classic
comodo	comfortable
moderno	contemporary; modern
postmoderno	postmodern
scomodo	uncomfortable
tradizionale	traditional
vuoto	empty

A me non piace lo stile postmoderno.	I don't like the postmodern style.
Quella sedia è bella, ma scomoda.	That chair is beautiful, but uncomfortable.

Replace the phrases and sentences underlined with the appropriate qualifier from those listed on the right.

1. il letto che fa venire il mal di schiena   _____   a. ammobiliato

2. l'appartamento con tutti i mobili   _____   b. antiche

3. la lampada disegnata da Philip Stark   _____   c. comode

4. sei sedie Chippendale   _____   d. moderna

5. le poltrone con dei cuscini morbidissimi   _____   e. scomodo

Household appliances

l(a)'aspirapolvere, gli aspirapolvere / il battitappeto, i battitappeto (for wall-to-wall carpet)	*vacuum cleaner*
il congelatore	*freezer*
la cucina (a gas / elettrica)	*(gas/electric) range; stove*
l(o)'elettrodomestico	*appliance*
l(o)'essicatore	*dryer*
il ferro [da stiro]	*iron*
il forno	*oven*
il forno a microonde	*microwave oven*
il frigo[rifero], i frigo[riferi]	*refrigerator*
il, la lavapiatti, le lavapiatti; il, la lavastoviglie, le lavastoviglie	*dishwasher*
la [macchina] lavatrice; la macchina da lavare	*washing machine*
il lettore di DVD/CD	*DVD/CD player*
la radio, le radio	*radio*
il telecomando	*remote control*
il televisore / la televisione; la TV, le TV	*TV set*
la stufa	*stove*
la sveglia	*alarm clock*

Compriamo una TV con lo schermo piatto?	*Shall we buy a flat-screen TV?*
Hanno un congelatore più grande del frigo.	*They have a freezer bigger than the refrigerator.*

ESERCIZIO 8·6

Complete the following sentences.

1. Accendi la _____ per sentire il giornale radio.

2. Il _____ serve a tenere freschi i cibi.

3. L'energia elettrica fa funzionare tutti gli _____.

4. La lavastoviglie nuova è stata installata in _____.

In Italian we can form compound nouns by joining a verb and a noun, an adverb and a verb, or a prefix and a noun.

aprire + scatole → l(o)'apriscatole	*can opener*
bene + essere → il benessere	*well-being*
mini + gonna → la minigonna	*miniskirt*

Form one word out of the verb + noun pairs listed below. Include the article for the newly formed word. All the words you will form appear in previous units of this book or in the later sections of this unit.

1. asciugare i capelli _____

2. asciugare la mano _____

3. cavare i tappi _____

4. colare la pasta _____

Match the words listed on the left with their complementary parts on the right.

1. fisio_____   a. (a) sciutta

2. pasta_____   b. dipendente

3. tossico_____   c. registratore

4. video_____   d. terapista

Match the prefixes listed on the left with their complementary parts on the right. Omit the letters in parentheses before creating the new word.

1. anti_____   a. aceti

2. extra_____   b. mercato

3. sott(o)_____   c. pasto

4. super_____   d. terrestre

Housework

apparecchiare	*to set the table*
asciugare	*to dry*
fare il bucato; lavare la biancheria	*to do the laundry*
(ri)fare il letto	*to do/make the bed*
fare le pulizie [di casa]	*to do the housecleaning*
lavare	*to wash*
lucidare	*to polish*

mettere in ordine	*to put in order; to straighten up*
passare l(o)'aspirapolvere / il battitappeto	*to vacuum*
pulire	*to clean*
scopare	*to sweep*
sparecchiare	*to clear the table*
sporcare	*to soil*
stirare	*to iron; to press*

Bambini, rifate il letto!	*Children, remake your beds!*
Mio marito fa tutte le pulizie.	*My husband does all the housecleaning.*

ESERCIZIO
8·10

Add the verb indicating what cleaning activity is being performed in each sentence.

1. Il cane ha lasciato i peli sulla moquette. Devo proprio _____.

2. L'essiccatore serve ad _____ il bucato.

3. Mio marito si è comprato un ferro nuovo per _____ le camicie.

4. Nel lavello si _____ i piatti.

5. Pietro, devi _____ _____ _____ la tua stanza, se no niente televisione!

Housecleaning

il bucato	*laundry*
la cameriera; la domestica	*maid; housekeeper*
la casalinga (il casalingo, ironic)	*housewife*
il detersivo; il detergente	*detergent*
il maggiordomo	*butler*
la polvere (sing.)	*dust*
la roba sporca (sing.)	*dirty clothes*
la scopa	*broom*
lo Scottex	*paper towel*
lo spazzettone	*mop*
lo straccio; lo strofinaccio	*rag*

ESERCIZIO
8·11

Mark the word that does not belong in each of the following sequences.

1. a. sporcare   b. pulire   c. lucidare   d. lavare

2. a. la domestica   b. lo spazzettone c. la cameriera   d. il maggiordomo

3. a. la scopa   b. la polvere   c. lo strofinaccio   d. lo spazzettone

4. a. il bucato   b. il detersivo   c. la roba sporca   d. lo Scottex

Food

Italian cuisine is known for the flavor of its ingredients and products, for its regional variations, and for cooking tasty but simple dishes. In the late 1970s the association Slow Food was launched in Piedmont. Its name was chosen in antithesis to fast food; its founders chose a snail as its symbol. Slow Food now has over 80,000 members all over the world. It encourages organic agriculture, supports traditional products and modes of production, and fair trade practices.

l(o)'antipasto	*appetizer*
il buongustaio	*gourmet*
la cena	*dinner*
il cibo	*food*
la [prima] colazione	*breakfast*
il contorno	*side dish*
il cuoco; lo chef (m. and f.)	*cook; chef*
il dolce; il dessert	*dessert*
la gola (sing.)	*gluttony*
l(o)'ingrediente	*ingredient*
l(a)'insalata	*salad*
la minestra; la zuppa	*soup*
il panino; il sandwich	*sandwich*
la pastasciutta	*pasta course*
il pasto	*meal*
il piatto	*dish; course (of a meal)*
il pranzo	*lunch*
la portata	*course*
la porzione	*portion*
la ricetta	*recipe*

Vi piace la minestra di lenticchie?	*Do you like lentil soup?*
A pranzo mangiano solo un panino.	*They only have a sandwich for lunch.*

ESERCIZIO
8·12

Match each noun on the left with its complementary qualifier among those listed on the right.

1. il cuoco conosce _____
2. il panino di _____
3. la minestra di _____
4. la porzione di _____
5. la ricetta del _____

a. mozzarella, basilico e pomodoro
b. pastasciutta
c. verdura
d. i segreti di un grande chef
e. dolce della nonna

Cooking

andare a male; guastarsi	*to spoil; to go bad*
aver(e) fame	*to be hungry*
aver(e) sete	*to be thirsty*

bastare; essercene abbastanza	*to be enough*
bere	*to drink*
(far) bollire	*to boil*
condire	*to dress (food)*
cucinare; preparare; cuocere	*to cook*
(fare) cuocere al forno	*to bake*
far da mangiare	*to prepare a meal; to cook*
fare il caffè / il tè	*to brew/make coffee/tea*
finire; esaurire	*to run out*
(far) friggere	*to fry*
grigliare; cuocere alla griglia	*to grill*
mangiare	*to eat*
(far) [ri]scaldare	*to warm up*
scongelare	*to thaw; to defrost*
servire	*to serve*
tagliare	*to cut*

Il pesce si è guastato.	*The fish has gone bad.*
Abbiamo finito il burro.	*We've run out of butter.*

ESERCIZIO
8·13

In the following sentences the beginning of each sentence has been mixed up with the end of another sentence. Take them apart and put them back together so that each sentence makes sense.

1. Fanno bollire il pesce alla griglia.

_____

2. Ho fatto friggere per venti persone.

_____

3. La mamma ha fatto da mangiare le patate.

_____

4. Mia nipote mi aiuta a pelare le zucchine.

_____

5. Renato ha fatto il latte.

_____

Kitchenware

l(o)'apriscatole, gli apriscatole	*can opener*
il cavatappi, i cavatappi	*corkscrew*
il colapasta, i colapasta; lo scolapasta, gli scolapasta	*colander*
il coperchio	*lid*
l(a)'immondizia	*garbage*

l(a)'insalatiera	bowl
il macinacaffè, i macinacaffè	coffee grinder
il mestolo	ladle
la padella	pan
la pentola	pot
le stoviglie (pl.)	kitchenware (dishes, pots and pans, silverware, glasses, etc.)
il tagliere	cutting board
il tappo [da sughero]	cork
la teglia da forno	baking dish
il vassoio	tray

Ho buttato l'apriscatole nell'immondizia!   *I threw the can opener into the garbage!*
Il suo negozio ha delle stoviglie particolari.   *Her store has special kitchenware.*

ESERCIZIO
8·14

Complete the following sentences with one of the nouns listed below each of them.

1. Non possiamo fare il caffè perché _____ non funziona.
   a. l'apriscatole   b. il macinacaffè   c. l'insalatiera

2. Non puoi aprire la bottiglia di vino senza _____.
   a. il cavatappi   b. l'apriscatole   c. il colapasta

3. Non vuoi _____ per portare tutti quei piatti?
   a. un tagliere   b. un vassoio   c. una padella

4. Per coprire la pentola usi _____.
   a. il mestolo   b. il vassoio   c. il coperchio

Flatware, glassware, and dinnerware

il bicchiere	glass
il boccale	mug
la bottiglia	bottle
il coltello	knife
il cucchiaino	teaspoon
il cucchiaio	spoon
la forchetta	fork
i piatti (pl.)	dishes; dinnerware
il piattino	saucer
il piatto fondo / da minestra	soup bowl
il piatto piano / da pietanza	plate; dish
il servizio (di/da)	set
la tazza	cup
la tovaglia	tablecloth
la tovaglietta [all'americana]	table/place mat
il tovagliolo	napkin

Metti delle forchette da frutta in tavola.   *Put some fruit forks on the table.*
In Italia la pastasciutta si mangia nel   *In Italy we use bowls for pastasciutta.*
    piatto fondo.

In this unit we have encountered several words made of a noun accompanied by a qualifier introduced by the preposition **da**, which conveys the idea of something *used for/with some purpose.*

Usa il piatto **da minestra**.   Use the soup bowl.) Use the bowl meant for serving soup.

ESERCIZIO
8·15

Match the following nouns on the left with their appropriate complements on the right. Then translate the compound words into English. All the words appear in this book, up to and including Unit 12.

1. abito _____   a. da barba

2. bicchiere _____   b. da denti

3. camera _____   c. da letto

4. camicia _____   d. da notte

5. crema _____   e. da sera

6. servizio _____   f. da tè

7. spazzolino _____   g. da vino

Bread and desserts

il biscotto	cookie
la caramella	candy
il cioccolatino	chocolate
la crostata	pie; tart
il gelato	ice cream
il grissino	breadstick
la marmellata	preserve; jam; marmalade
il pane (sing.)	bread
il pane tostato (sing.) / la fetta biscottata	toast
la pasta (sing.) / l(o)'impasto	dough; pasta
la pasta / il pasticcino	pastry
la torta	cake

Mia figlia sta male perché ha mangiato
dieci paste!
Portiamo dei cioccolatini a sua madre.

My daughter is feeling sick because she ate
ten pastries!
Let's bring chocolates for her mother.

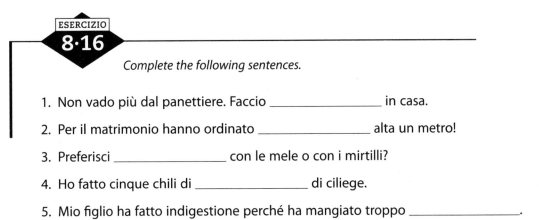

ESERCIZIO
8·16

Complete the following sentences.

1. Non vado più dal panettiere. Faccio _____ in casa.

2. Per il matrimonio hanno ordinato _____ alta un metro!

3. Preferisci _____ con le mele o con i mirtilli?

4. Ho fatto cinque chili di _____ di ciliege.

5. Mio figlio ha fatto indigestione perché ha mangiato troppo _____.

Meat and fish

l(o)'arrosto	roast
la bistecca	steak
la carne	meat
i frutti di mare (usually pl.)	seafood; shellfish
i gamberetti (usually pl.)	shrimp
il maiale	pork
il manzo	beef
il pesce	fish
il pollo	chicken
il salmone	salmon
la salsiccia	sausage
il surgelato	frozen food product
il tacchino	turkey
il tonno	tuna
la trota	trout
il vitello	veal

Faccio il roast beef per cena.
Non mangia i frutti di mare.

I'm doing a roast beef for dinner.
He doesn't eat shellfish.

ESERCIZIO
8·17

Match the left and right parts of the following sentences.

1. Del maiale _____

2. Il pesce puzza _____

3. Il salmone _____

4. La parola *bistecca* _____

a. è buono cotto al vapore.

b. alla griglia.

c. perché è andato a male.

d. si usa molto il tonno.

| 5. Nel sushi _____ | e. si usa proprio tutto. |
| 6. Puoi cuocere la salsiccia _____ | f. viene dall'inglese *beefsteak*. |

Vegetables and legumes

l(o)'aglio	*garlic*
gli asparagi (pl.)	*asparagus*
la carota	*carrot*
il cavolo	*cabbage*
la cipolla	*onion*
i fagiolini (pl.)	*string beans*
il fagiolo	*bean*
il finocchio	*fennel*
il fungo	*mushroom*
l(a)'insalata	*salad; the leafy vegetables used in a salad*
la melanzana	*eggplant*
l(a)'oliva	*olive*
la patata	*potato*
il peperone	*sweet pepper*
il pomodoro	*tomato*
i piselli (pl.)	*peas*
il sedano	*celery*
gli spinaci (pl.)	*spinach*
la verdura (collective sing.)	*vegetables*
lo zucchino	*zucchini*

Gli asparagi sono buoni in primavera.	*Asparagus are good in spring.*
Le cipolle fanno piangere quando le tagli.	*Onions make you cry when you cut them.*

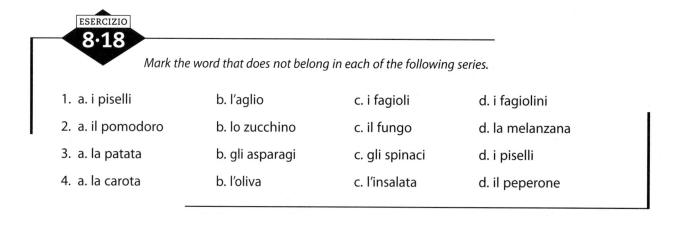

ESERCIZIO
8·18

Mark the word that does not belong in each of the following series.

1. a. i piselli   b. l'aglio   c. i fagioli   d. i fagiolini

2. a. il pomodoro   b. lo zucchino   c. il fungo   d. la melanzana

3. a. la patata   b. gli asparagi   c. gli spinaci   d. i piselli

4. a. la carota   b. l'oliva   c. l'insalata   d. il peperone

Fruit

l(a)'albicocca	*apricot*
l(a)'arancia	*orange*
la banana	*banana*
la ciliegia; le cilieg(i)e	*cherry*
la fragola	*strawberry*
il frutto / la frutta (collective sing.)	*fruit*

il limone	lemon
la mela	apple
il melone	canteloupe
i mirtilli (usually pl.)	blueberries
la pera	pear
la pesca	peach
il pompelmo	grapefruit
l(a)'uva (collective sing.)	grape(s)

L'uva va bene nella macedonia.   Grapes are good in a fruit salad.
Adoro le fragoline di bosco.   I love wild strawberries.

ESERCIZIO
8·19

Complete the following sentences by choosing from the words listed after each sentence.

1. Le _____ sono buone in primavera.
   a. fragole   b. limoni   c. uva

2. Il _____ non è molto dolce.
   a. pesca   b. pompelmo   c. pera

3. La _____ è una frutta che cresce nei paesi caldi.
   a. banana   b. pesca   c. mela

4. L'_____ e il _____ sono degli agrumi.
   a. uva; melone   b. arancia; limone   c. albicocca; mirtilli

Products from the grocery store and the deli

l(o)'aceto	vinegar
il burro	butter
il cibo in scatola	canned food
la farina	flour
il formaggio	cheese
il latte	milk
la maionese	mayonnaise
l(o)'olio	oil
le patatine [fritte] (pl.)	chips
i [pomodori] pelati (pl.)	peeled tomatoes
il pepe	pepper
il prosciutto (crudo o cotto)	(cured or baked) ham
il riso	rice
il sale	salt
la senape	mustard
i sottaceti (pl.)	pickled vegetables
l(o)'uovo, le uova	egg
lo zucchero	sugar

Piero, smetti di ingozzarti di patatine fritte.   Piero, stop binging on chips.
Faccio la panna montata.   I'll make whipped cream.

Match the first half of the sentences listed on the left to the appropriate conclusion among those listed on the right.

1. Il sugo si fa _____   a. crudo o quello cotto?

2. Il cibo in scatola _____   b. è comodo in campeggio.

3. Luciana fa _____   c. la maionese a mano.

4. Metti la senape _____   d. con i pelati.

5. Ti piace il prosciutto _____   e. sugli hot dog.

Beverages

l(a)'acqua minerale	*mineral water*
la bevanda gassata	*soda*
la bibita	*beverage; drink*
la birra	*beer*
il caffè; l'espresso	*coffee*
la cioccolata calda	*hot chocolate*
il liquore / la bevanda alcolica	*spirit/liqueur; alcoholic drink*
la spremuta (di) / il succo (di)	*juice*
il tè / la tisana	*tea*
il vino	*wine*

Vuole acqua minerale naturale o gassata? *Would you like natural or sparkling mineral water?*

Complete the following sentences.

1. Con il pesce si beve il _____ bianco; con l'arrosto va meglio il _____ rosso.

2. Dopo cena perché non servi un _____ invece del caffè o del tè?

3. La coca cola è una _____ gassata.

4. Mia madre fa la _____ di arance fresca ogni mattina.

Describing food

commestibile	*edible*
da asporto	*takeout*
dolce	*sweet*
fresco	*fresh*

integrale	*whole wheat*
macinato	*ground*
mangiabile	*edible; acceptable, but not great*
marcio	*rotten*
maturo	*ripe*
salato	*savory; salty*
secco	*dry*

ESERCIZIO
8·22

Replace the phrases in paretheses in each sentence with the appropriate qualifier.

1. il caffè (pronto per essere messo nella caffettiera) _____

2. l'acqua (dove metti a cuocere la pasta) (che sa troppo di sale) _____

3. la pizza (che compri dal pizzaiolo e mangi a casa) _____ _____

4. il pane (fatto con la farina non raffinata) _____

5. una bistecca (non male, ma niente di speciale) _____

Transportation, traffic, and travel

·9·

Italians can travel by car, bus, taxi, train, and airplane—not to mention walking and biking. Despite all these means of transportation, congestion on urban and suburban roads and on highways is the normal state of affairs. When air pollution reaches dangerously high levels, public authorities in large cities forbid the use of private cars.

Italians are usually good drivers, but they love speeding, even in urban traffic. More and more ecologically minded people bike in heavy traffic, showing determination and courage.

l(o)'autobus, gli autobus; il bus, i bus	bus
l(o, a)'autostoppista	hitchhiker
la bici[cletta]; le bici[clette]	bicycle
il biglietto	ticket
il, la ciclista	biker; cyclist
la fermata [dell'autobus / del tram / della metropolitana]	(bus/streetcar/subway) stop
l(o)'ingorgo	gridlock; traffic jam
il marciapiede	sidewalk
la metropolitana / il, la metro, i metro	subway
il mezzo [di trasporto] pubblico	public means of transportation
la moto[cicletta], le moto[ciclette]	motorcycle
il, la motociclista	motorcyle rider
il motorino; lo scooter	moped; scooter
l(o)'ora di punta	rush hour
il passaggio	ride
il, la passante	passerby
il pedone (m. and f.)	pedestrian
il, la pendolare	commuter
le strisce pedonali; le zebre (pl.)	crosswalk
il taxi, i taxi; il tassì, i tassì	taxi
il traffico	traffic
il tram[way], i tram[way]	streetcar

Mi dai un passaggio, per favore?	Could you give me a ride, please?
Dov'è la fermata del metro?	Where's the subway stop?

Complete the following sentences choosing from the words listed above.

1. Bisogna comprare il _____ del tram prima di salire a bordo.

2. Diamo un passaggio a quell'_____?

3. I marciapiedi sono riservati ai _____.

4. I pedoni hanno il diritto di precedenza sulle _____ _____.

5. Lavora lontano da casa. Fa il _____ da vent'anni.

Italian uses the construction **in** + *noun* (*by* + *noun*) to convey the means of transportation we are using. When we add a qualifier, we use the construction **con** + *article* + *noun* (*with* + *article* + *noun*).

Vado a lavorare in autobus.	*I go to work by bus.*
Arrivo con il treno delle 8.	*I will arrive with the 8 A.M. train.*

But we say: **andare a piedi**, *to go on foot*; **andare a cavallo**, *to go horseback riding*.

Add the appropriate construction conveying the means of transportation to the following sentences. The means used is indicated in parentheses after each sentence.

1. A me piace andare _____ _____ non _____ _____. (macchina; aereo)

2. Andate in giro _____ _____ _____ di suo fratello? (moto)

3. Arrivo domani sera _____ _____ delle 18. (aereo)

4. Mia madre va in centro _____ _____ tutti i pomeriggi. (tram)

5. Vai a scuola _____ _____? (piedi)

6. Vengo da tuo fratello _____ _____. (bici)

In Unit 9 we will encounter several words composed of a noun and an adjective, as are **mezzo pubblico** (*public means of transportation*), **effetti personali** (*personal belongings*), and **stazione ferroviaria** (*railway/train station*). In some compound nouns the adjective precedes the noun; in others it follows it: **il grande magazzino** (*department store*), **il vicolo cieco** (*blind alley*). The word order either can't be inverted or changes the meaning completely when it is inverted: **il magazzino grande** means *large warehouse.*

Match each of the following nouns with its appropriate qualifier listed on the right.

1. l'acqua _____   a. adottivo

2. l'alta _____   b. educazione

3. l'aria _____   c. igienica

4. la buona _____   d. minerale

5. la carta _____   e. moda

6. le cattive _____   f. stradale

7. il figlio _____   g. unita

8. il genere _____   h. soccorso

9. la mezza _____   i. umano

10. il pronto _____   j. mobile

11. la scala _____   k. maniere

12. il segnale _____   l. età

13. la tinta _____   m. condizionata

Getting around

andare in bici[cletta]	*to bike*
andare in moto[cicletta]	*to ride a motorcycle*
camminare (aux. **avere**)	*to walk*
convalidare/obliterare il biglietto	*to validate/stamp one's ticket*
fare il pendolare	*to commute*
fare la coda; essere in coda	*to be in line*
investire; prendere sotto	*to hit; to run over*
noleggiare una macchina; prendere una macchina a noleggio	*to rent a car*
passare (aux. **essere** in this context)	*to go/come/stop by*
prendere; usare	*to ride/take (a means of transportation)*
salire (su)	*to get on*
scendere (da)	*to get off*

L'autobus passa ogni dieci minuti. *The bus comes by every ten minutes.*
Signore, si metta in coda! *Sir, get in line!*

ESERCIZIO
9·4

In the following sentences replace the words in parentheses with one of the verbs listed above.

1. Una lunga fila di persone (aspetta) _____ _____ _____ di comprare il biglietto per la partita di calcio.

2. Luigi (va a piedi) _____.

3. Mio marito ed io (prendiamo) _____ una macchina alla Hertz.

4. Mio fratello (guida un'ora e mezza ogni giorno per andare e venire dal lavoro) _____ ____ _____ _____.

5. Una persona che sale su un mezzo pubblico deve (usare una macchinetta che stampa la data e l'ora sul biglietto) _____ _____ _____.

Describing urban transportation

entrata	entrance; in
fermata prenotata	*stop requested*
giù; discesa	*off*
guasto	*broken; out of order*
in direzione + *name of destination*	*bound/headed for*
metropolitano	*metropolitan*
su; salita	*on*
suburbano	*suburban*
urbano	*urban*
uscita	*exit; out*
valido (fino a)	*valid (until)*

Il biglietto del treno è valido per tre mesi.
Prenda l'autobus in direzione Colosseo.

The train ticket is valid for three months.
Take the bus bound for the Coliseum.

ESERCIZIO
9·5

Choose the word or phrase that best fits the description.

1. Gli autobus suburbani ti portano _____.
   a. fuori città   b. in centro città   c. alla stazione

2. Quando il segnale «fermata prenotata» è acceso vuol dire che _____.
   a. il conducente non si fermerà alla prossima fermata   b. il conducente si fermerà alla prossima fermata   c. l'autobus è guasto

3. Quando vedi la parola «uscita» sulla porta di un autobus vuol dire che puoi _____.
   a. sederti   b. usarla per salire   c. usarla per scendere

4. Se vuoi prendere la metropolitana devi cercare il segnale che dice _____
   a. uscita   b. entrata   c. salita

We can add a qualifier to a noun by adding another noun preceded by the preposition **di**.

la carta dei vini	*wine list*
la cartina del bancomat	*ATM/debit card*
la lista di attesa	*waiting list*
il negozio di casalinghi	*housewares store*

Some of these phrases can be reduced to just one of their components when the context is unambiguous.

la cartina del bancomat → il bancomat, i bancomat	*debit card*
il distributore di benzina → il distributore, i distributori	*gas station*

ESERCIZIO
9·6

*Match the following nouns with the qualifiers introduced by **di** listed on the right. Some words are listed in the remainder of this chapter or in other units in the book.*

1. la carta _____   a. d(i)'arte

2. la cintura _____   b. d(i)'imbarco

3. la città _____   c. di sicurezza

4. il divieto _____   d. di salvataggio

5. il limite _____   e. di sorpasso

6. la lista _____   f. di velocità

7. l'ora _____   g. dei consumi

8. la scialuppa _____   h. di punta

9. la società _____   i. d(i)'attesa

Cars and drivers

l(a)'automobile	*automobile*
l(o, a)'automobilista; il guidatore / la guidatrice	*(car) driver*
la benzina	*gasoline*
il camion	*truck*
il furgone	*van*
la gomma a terra	*flat tire*
la macchina	*car*
il motore	*engine; motor*

l(o)'officina [meccanica]; l(a)'auto officina, le auto officine; il meccanico	*repair garage; mechanic (mechanic's shop)*
la patente [di guida]	*driver's license*
la polizza d(i)'assicurazione	*insurance policy*
la scuola guida, le scuole guida	*driving school*
la targa [della macchina]	*license plate*
il TIR, i TIR; il camion a rimorchio	*eighteen-wheeler; tractor-trailer*
l(a)'utilitaria	*economy car*

Hai portato la macchina dal meccanico?	*Did you take the car to the repair garage?*
Va a scuola guida per prendere la patente.	*She's going to driving school to get her driver's license.*

ESERCIZIO
9·7

Complete the following sentences by choosing from the words listed after each of them.

1. La macchina si è fermata perché siamo rimasti senza _____.
   a. polizza   b. benzina   c. patente
      di assicurazione

2. Non devi guidare se non hai _____.
   a. la macchina   b. la patente   c. la gomma a terra

3. Quando la macchina è rotta, bisogna portarla _____.
   a. dal benzinaio   b. alla scuola guida   c. dal meccanico

4. Vai a scuola guida per _____.
   a. prendere la patente b. comprare una   c. riparare la gomma
                        polizza

Driving

accelerare (aux. avere)	*to accelerate; to speed up*
cambiare [la marcia]	*to shift gear*
fare benzina; fare il pieno (di benzina)	*to get gas; to fill up (the gas tank)*
fare marcia indietro; fare retromarcia	*to reverse*
fermare; fermarsi	*to stop*
frenare (aux. avere)	*to brake*
girare (aux. avere); svoltare (aux. avere)	*to turn*
guidare (aux. avere)	*to drive*
parcheggiare	*to park*
passare da/per (aux. essere in this context)	*to pass/drive through*
rallentare	*to slow down*
sorpassare; passare (aux. avere in this context); superare	*to pass; to overtake*

Può farmi il pieno, per favore?	*Can you fill the tank, please?*
Passerò per Roma.	*I'll drive through Rome.*

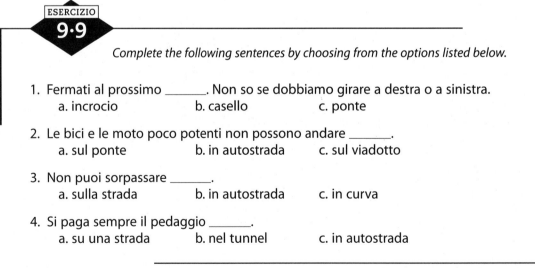

ESERCIZIO
9·8

Match each of the partial sentences on the left with the appropriate conclusion from those listed on the right.

1. Ho solo 5 euro: _____	a. come facciamo a fare benzina?
2. La macchina davanti a noi va piano, _____	b. frena.
3. Per andare a Roma _____	c. non posso fare il pieno.
4. Se tutti i benzinai sono chiusi, _____	d. perché non la sorpassi?
5. Se vuoi fermare la macchina, _____	e. siamo passati da Bologna.

Roads

il casello	*tollbooth*
la curva	*curve*
l(o)'incrocio	*crossing; intersection*
il pedaggio	*toll*
il ponte	*bridge*
la strada	*road*
la superstrada; l(a)'autostrada (a toll road)	*highway*
il tunnel; la galleria	*tunnel*
il viadotto	*viaduct*

Con la ViaCard non devi fermarti al casello.	*With the Easy Pass you don't have to stop at the tollbooth.*
Prendiamo l'autostrada per fare in fretta.	*Let's take the highway to speed things up.*

ESERCIZIO
9·9

Complete the following sentences by choosing from the options listed below.

1. Fermati al prossimo _____. Non so se dobbiamo girare a destra o a sinistra.
   a. incrocio   b. casello   c. ponte

2. Le bici e le moto poco potenti non possono andare _____.
   a. sul ponte   b. in autostrada   c. sul viadotto

3. Non puoi sorpassare _____.
   a. sulla strada   b. in autostrada   c. in curva

4. Si paga sempre il pedaggio _____.
   a. su una strada   b. nel tunnel   c. in autostrada

Road signs

la deviazione	*detour*
la direzione	*direction*
il diritto di precedenza	*right of way*
il divieto di parcheggio	*no parking*
il divieto di sorpasso	*no passing zone*
l(o)'incidente	*accident*
l(a)'indicazione; il segnale stradale	*road sign*
i lavori in corso (pl.)	*roadwork*
il limite di velocità	*speed limit*
la mappa; la cartina	*map*
la multa	*ticket; fine*
il parcheggio	*parking; parking place*
il parchimetro	*parking meter*
il semaforo	*traffic light*
lo stop	*stop (sign)*
la velocità	*speed*
il vigile (m. and f.)	*traffic officer*

Questa strada ha il diritto di precedenza.	*This street has the right of way.*
C'è il divieto di sorpasso in questo tratto.	*There's no passing on this stretch of road.*

ESERCIZIO
9·10

In each of the following series, mark the word that does not belong.

1. a. l'ora di punta b. l'ingorgo c. il traffico d. la multa

2. a. il segnale stradale b. il parchimetro c. il semaforo d. lo stop

3. a. la cartina b. la multa c. il vigile d. il divieto di parcheggio

4. a. la cartina b. l'indicazione c. la direzione d. il parcheggio

Giving directions

a destra; alla tua/sua/vostra destra	*at/on/to the right; at/on/to your right*
a sinistra; alla tua/sua/vostra sinistra	*at/on/to the left; at/on/to your left*
(in) avanti	*forward*
da nessuna parte	*nowhere*
da qualche parte	*somewhere*
da quella parte	*that way*
da questa parte	*this way*
dappertutto	*everywhere*
(strada a) doppio senso	*two-way (street)*
(sempre) dritto	*straight (ahead)*
indietro	*back*
più avanti	*ahead; further ahead*
(strada a) senso unico	*one-way (street)*

| (di) sopra | above; over |
| (di) sotto | under; below; beneath |

Questa strada porterà pure da qualche parte!

This road will go somewhere!

Il camion non passa sotto il ponte.

That truck can't clear the bridge.

ESERCIZIO
9·11

Complete the following sentences by choosing from the qualifiers listed above.

1. In Italia la guida è _____, come negli Stati Uniti, mentre in Gran Bretagna è _____.

2. Se non giri mai il volante la macchina va sempre _____.

3. Una strada che finisce in mezzo a un prato non porta _____ _____ _____.

4. Una strada che puoi prendere in due direzioni è _____ _____ _____.

5. Una strada che puoi prendere solo in una direzione è _____ _____ _____.

Travel

l(a)'agenzia di viaggio	travel agency
l(o)'arrivo	arrival
la biglietteria	ticket counter
la coincidenza	connection
il controllo passaporti	passport control
la dogana	customs
gli effetti personali (pl.)	personal belongings
l(o)'orario	schedule; timetable
la partenza	departure
il passeggero	passenger
il posto; il sedile	seat
la prenotazione	reservation
il rimborso	refund
il ritardo	delay
la stazione	station
la tariffa	fare
l(o)'ufficio oggetti smarriti	lost and found
il viaggiatore / la viaggiatrice	traveler
il viaggio	journey; trip
il visto	visa

Il volo ha tre ore di ritardo.

The flight has a three-hour delay.

Vorrei un posto vicino al finestrino.

I'd like a window seat.

*Answer yes (**Y**) or no (**N**) to the following questions.*

1. Hai bisogno della prenotazione per prendere il tram? _____

2. Il visto serve per entrare in un paese straniero? _____

3. L'arrivo precede la partenza? _____

4. Si comprano i panini alla biglietteria? _____

5. Sei in viaggio se stai andando da Parigi a Helsinki? _____

Verbs

allacciare	*to fasten*
andare	*to go*
annullare; cancellare	*to cancel*
arrivare	*to arrive*
atterrare (aux. **avere**)	*to land*
aver(e) fretta	*to be in a hurry*
confermare	*to confirm*
decollare (aux. **avere/essere**)	*to take off*
disfare le valigie	*to unpack*
fare in fretta; sbrigarsi	*to hurry up; to haste*
fare le valigie	*to pack (one's suitcases)*
imbarcare il bagaglio	*to check luggage*
imbarcarsi	*to board*
partire (per)	*to leave (for)*
passare da/per (aux. **essere** in this context)	*to go/fly/pass through*
perdere	*to miss*
prendere	*to catch; to take*
rimandare	*to postpone; to put off*
rimanere; restare	*to remain*
(ri)tornare; rientrare	*to return; to come back*
venire	*to come*
viaggiare (aux. **avere**); **andare (a/in)**	*to travel; to go (to)*
volare (aux. **avere/essere**)	*to fly*
volerci (aux. **essere**); **metterci** (aux. **avere**)	*to take (time)*

(Note that **volerci** takes as its subject the period of time needed to perform an action, whereas **metterci** is coordinated with the person performing the action.)

Ci sono volute tre ore per arrivare da te.	*It took three hours to get to your place.*
Ci ho messo tre mesi per arrivare a casa.	*It took me three months to get home.*

In the following sentences, substitute the words in parentheses with the appropriate verb from those listed above.

1. Hanno (spostato la data della) _____ partenza.

2. L'aereo (si è alzato in volo) _____ _____.

3. Ho deciso di (far caricare le valigie sull'aereo) _____ _____ _____.

4. (Non sono riuscito a prendere) _____ _____ l'aereo perché sono arrivato all'aeroporto in ritardo.

5. Quante ore di viaggio (sono necessarie) _____ _____ per andare da Parigi ad Amsterdam?

6. Roberto (ha impiegato) _____ _____ _____ due giorni per andare da Milano ad Amburgo.

Air travel

l(o)'aeroplano; l'aereo, gli aerei	*airplane; plane*
l(o)'aeroporto	*airport*
l(o, a)'assistente di volo	*flight attendant*
il bagaglio a mano	*carry-on (luggage)*
il biglietto elettronico	*e-ticket*
la carta d(i)'imbarco	*boarding pass*
la cintura di sicurezza	*seat belt*
la classe turistica	*economy class*
il comandante (m. and f.)	*captain*
il corridoio	*aisle*
il duty free	*duty-free shop*
l(o)'equipaggio	*crew*
la fila	*row*
il finestrino	*window*
il jet lag	*jet lag*
il metal detector	*metal detector*
il pilota (m. and f.)	*pilot*
la porta d'imbarco; l(a)'uscita	*boarding gate*
la procedura d'imbarco / il check-in	*check-in*
il terminal	*terminal*
i trasporti a terra (pl.)	*ground transportation*
il volo	*flight*
la zona; l(a)'area recupero bagagli / il ritiro bagagli	*baggage claim area*

Può portare dieci chili nel bagaglio a mano. *You can carry ten kilos as carry-on luggage.*
Per il volo da Parigi, andate al carosello n. 3. *For the Paris flight, go to carousel no. 3.*

Replace the words in parentheses in each sentence with one of the nouns listed above.

1. Come (valigia da portare sull'aereo) _____ _____ _____ quella borsa è troppo grande.

2. Dove devo andare per prendere (gli autobus o i taxi che portano dall'aeroporto in città) _____ _____ _____?

3. Gentili passeggeri, (l'aereo) _____ che state aspettando ha mezz'ora di ritardo.

4. (La persona che guida questo aereo) _____ ha un messaggio per i passeggeri.

5. Preferisco il sedile vicino al(la parete esterna dell'aereo) _____.

6. Se ha un (documento di viaggio stampato con il computer) _____ _____, può fare il check-in da solo.

7. Su questa linea aerea, (le persone che fanno il servizio a bordo) _____ _____ _____ _____ sono molto competenti.

By rail

In the early 1970s the French railway system introduced **i treni ad alta velocità** (*high-speed trains*). They have made transportation by rail in Europe competitive with air travel, even though low-cost flights are on the offensive. You can now fly from London to Rome for 20 or 30 euros one way.

la banchina	*platform*
la barca	*boat*
il bigliettaio; il capotreno (m. and f.), **i capitreno, i capotreni**	*conductor*
il binario	*track*
la cabina	*cabin*
il faro	*lighthouse*
la ferrovia	*railway; railroad*
il mal di mare	*seasickness*
la nave	*ship*
il porto	*port; harbor*
la scialuppa di salvataggio	*lifeboat*
la stazione [ferroviaria / dei treni]	*railway station*
il treno	*train*
il treno ad alta velocità (la TAV, sing.)	*high-speed train*
il vagone	*railcar*

L'Eurostar per Parigi parte dal binario 3.   *The Eurostar train for Paris will leave from track no. 3.*

Abbiamo solo tre scialuppe di salvataggio.   *We only have three lifeboats.*

Match each noun on the left with the appropriate qualifier on the right.

1 la stazione _____   a. ad alta velocità

2. la stazione _____   b. letto

3. il treno _____   c. merci

4. il treno _____   d. ristorante

5. il vagone _____   e. degli autobus

6. il vagone _____   f. ferroviaria

Describing travel

a bordo	*aboard; onboard*
a terra	*on the ground*
(il biglietto di) andata e ritorno	*round-trip (ticket)*
appena in tempo	*just in time*
dopo	*afterward*
fermo	*still; stopped*
in fretta	*in a hurry; fast*
in orario	*on time*
in tempo	*in time*
lento; lentamente; piano; adagio	*slow; slowly*
presto; in anticipo	*early*
presto; tra poco	*soon*
prima	*before*
(il biglietto di) sola andata	*one-way (ticket)*
tardi; in ritardo	*late*
veloce; velocemente; forte (speed)	*fast*
via	*via*

Vai piano, non si vede niente!   *Slow down, you can't see a thing!*
Ho fatto in fretta, ma ho perso il treno. *I hurried up, but I missed the train.*
Sei arrivata appena in tempo.   *You arrived just in time.*

Find the antonym or the complementary expression for the words listed below.

1. a bordo _____ _____

2. di sola andata _____ _____ _____

3. forte _____

4. in anticipo _____ _____

5. tardi _____

6. veloce _____

Comparatives and superlatives are often used when talking about time, being early, and being late. **Meno di/che** and **più di/che** translate as *more than* and *less than*. In Italian only a few adjectives can take a modified form when we use them as comparatives.

buono	*good*	**migliore, più buono**	*better*
cattivo	*bad*	**peggiore, più cattivo**	*worse*
grande	*big; large; great*	**maggiore, più grande**	*greater; major*
piccolo	*small*	**minore, più piccolo**	*smaller; minor*

Preceded by the article, comparatives convey the top ranking in a series.

Mario è il miglior calciatore della squadra.   *Mario is the best player on the team.*
Nicoletta è la più piccola delle sorelle.   *Nicoletta is the youngest of the sisters.*

Italian does modify qualifiers to form absolute superlatives, or adds other qualifying words such as **molto, assai, parecchio** (*much; a lot*).

buono	*good*	**buonissimo; ottimo; molto buono**	*best; very good*
cattivo	*bad*	**cattivissimo; pessimo; molto cattivo**	*worst; very bad*
grande	*big; large; great*	**grandissimo; massimo; molto grande**	*greatest; very great/huge*
piccolo	*small*	**piccolissimo; minimo; molto piccolo**	*smallest; very small/tiny*
presto	*early; soon*	**prestissimo; molto presto**	*very early*
veloce	*fast*	**velocissimo; molto/assai veloce**	*very fast*

Translate the following sentences.

1. Dario è il figlio più grande.

_____

2. Dario ha due anni più di Gianni.

_____

3. Hanno comprato un'automobile di seconda mano a un prezzo bassissimo.

_____

4. Il sedile vicino al finestrino è meno scomodo del sedile vicino al corridoio.

_____

5. La Cinquecento era un'automobile piccolissimo, ma molto divertente.

_____

6. La Ferrari è più veloce della Mercedes.

_____

7. Sull'autostrada in Germania puoi andare fortissimo.

_____

8. Vincenzo ha fatto un ottimo viaggio in Patagonia.

_____

Tourism

Despite high prices, Italy remains a favorite tourist destination, thanks to its climate, its cuisine, and its artistic heritage, as reflected in our calling Italian cities and towns **città d'arte** (*cities of art*). Some smaller cities, Venice and Florence in particular, are so overwhelmed by visitors that locals now see their presence as a blessing and a curse at the same time. But revenues from tourism are an essential component of the Italian GDP.

le antichità (pl.)	*antiquities*
il castello	*castle*
il cicerone (m. and f.) / **la guida [turistica]** (m. and f.)	*tour guide*
il fine settimana, i fine settimana; il weekend	*weekend*
la guida (turistica dell'Italia / della Francia, etc.)	*guidebook (of Italy/France, etc.)*
l(a)'informazione; le informazioni	*(piece of) information; information*
l(o)'operatore turistico / l(a)'operatrice turistica	*tour operator*
il paesaggio	*landscape*
il panorama, i panorama	*panorama*
il passeggero	*passenger*
il turismo	*tourism*
il, la turista	*tourist*
la vacanza (used more often in the plural, **le vacanze**)	*vacation*
il viaggio organizzato	*package tour*
il villaggio turistico	*all-inclusive vacation resort*
Chiediamo all'ufficio informazioni!	*Let's ask the tourist information office!*

Complete the following sentences by choosing from the options given after each of them.

1. Abbiamo visto un _____ con dieci torri.
   a. panorama   b. castello   c. turismo

2. L'Italia ha dei bellissimi _____.
   a. turisti   b. guide   c. panorami

3. Nei _____ del Club Med si possono fare tante attività divertenti.
   a. villaggi turistici   b. viaggi organizzati   c. fine settimana

4. Siamo andati in Russia con un _____.
   a. villaggio turistico   b. viaggio organizzato   c. paesaggio

The active tourist

Here follow verbs we use frequently when talking about tourism and vacations. Several of them are used in set phrases, with the addition of a direct object or a complement. As you will see, the verbs **fare** and **andare** (+ **a** when followed by a verb in the infinitive) appear frequently.

abbronzarsi; prendere la tintarella	*to get a tan*
andare a cavallo	*to go horseback riding*
andare a fare il bagno; fare il bagno	*to go swimming*
andare in crociera	*to go on a cruise*
andare in gita	*to go on an excursion; to go hiking*
andare in vacanza	*to go on vacation*
arrampicare (aux. **avere**); **fare alpinismo**	*to climb; to go climbing*
campeggiare (aux. **avere**); **andare in campeggio**	*to camp; to go camping*
essere da solo; essere in due/tre, etc.	*to be by oneself; to be a party of two/three, etc.*
fare del turismo	*to go sightseeing*
fare il ponte	*to make a long weekend of it; to take a long weekend*
fare sub	*to go scuba diving*
fare un giro	*to take a tour; to walk around*
fare una passeggiata	*to take a stroll; to go for a walk*
girare; visitare	*to tour*
lasciare la camera	*to check out*
nuotare (aux. **avere**)	*to swim*
pagare/saldare il conto	*to pay the bill*
passare il tempo (aux. **avere**); **passare le vacanze** (aux. **avere**)	*to spend time; to spend one's vacation*
prendere possesso della camera	*to check in*
vedere; visitare	*to see; to visit*

I tuoi fratelli sono andati a nuotare.	*Your brothers went swimming.*
Andiamo in gita domani?	*Shall we go hiking tomorrow?*
Fa alpinismo da quando aveva dieci anni.	*She's been climbing since we was ten.*

Match each verb on the left with the appropriate complementary object and/or qualifier on the right. Translate the combined expression into English.

1. andare _____   a. del turismo

2. andare _____   b. il tempo

3. essere _____   c. in campeggio

4. fare _____   d. in sei

5. fare _____   e. il conto

6. passare _____   f. il ponte

7. prendere _____   g. in crociera

8. saldare _____   h. la tintarella

Accommodations

l(o)'albergo	hotel
l(a)'albergatore / l(a)'albergatrice	hotel manager; hotel owner
il bed & breakfast	bed and breakfast
la camera	room
la cameriera (hotel maid, usually female)	maid
il concierge	receptionist; concierge
il deposito; la caparra	deposit
l(o)'ostello [della gioventù]	youth hostel
la pensione	inn; family-run hotel
la reception	front desk; reception desk
il servizio in camera	room service
la sistemazione	accommodation

Siamo stati in un albergo a cinque stelle.	*We stayed in a five-star hotel.*
Da giovane stavo negli ostelli.	*When I was young, I stayed in youth hostels.*

*Complete the following sentences. Use the prepositions listed in parentheses. When a definite article is required, remember to turn the **preposition** + **article** into one word. Omit the underlined words.*

1. Hai dato la mancia _____ _____ che ci fa la camera? (a)

2. È ora di partire. Hai saldato il conto con _____ dell'albergo? (feminine)

3. La colazione nel nostro _____ _____ _____ era deliziosa e molto abbondante.

4. Possiamo domandare _____ _____ l'indirizzo di un buon ristorante. (a)

5. Hai prenotato l'albergo? A Natale, è difficile trovare una _____ a Parigi.

Eating out

il bar	*bar*
il, la barista, i baristi	*bartender*
il caffè, i caffè	*café*
il cameriere / la cameriera	*waiter/waitress; server*
la carta dei vini	*wine list*
il coperto	*cover charge*
il cuoco (m. and f.); **lo chef** (m. and f.)	*cook; chef*
la mancia	*tip*
il menù	*menu*
la paninoteca	*sandwich place*
il ristorante	*restaurant*
il self-service	*self-service/cafeteria-style restaurant*
la trattoria	*neighborhood restaurant*

Andiamo al bar a prendere un caffè?	*Shall we go get a coffee?*
Lascia un po' di mancia alla cameriera.	*Leave a small tip for the waitress.*

Complete the following sentences.

1. Dalla torre del castello si gode un magnifico _____.

2. Ho prenotato per sei nel _____ in cima alla torre del castello.

3. Lo _____ di quel ristorante ha ricevuto tre stelle dalla guida Michelin.

4. In quell'albergo, le _____ sono splendide, ma il ristorante vale poco.

5. A pranzo mangiamo un panino in una _____, e alla sera andiamo al _____.

Describing your destination

al completo	*no vacancy*
al lago	*at the lake*
al mare	*at the sea*
disponibile	*available; vacancies*
(la camera) doppia/matrimoniale	*double (room)*
esotico	*exotic*
in campagna	*in the country(side)*
in collina	*in the hills; on the hill*
in montagna	*in the mountains*
in spiaggia	*at the beach*
pittoresco	*picturesque*
(la camera) singola	*single (room)*
tipico	*typical*
turistico	*touristic*
tutto incluso	*inclusive (of all expenses/charges)*

Ha bisogno di una singola o una doppia?	*Do you need a single or a double room?*
Andiamo in spiaggia!	*Let's go to the beach!*

ESERCIZIO
10·5

You're speaking to an Italian travel agent about a two-week trip to Tuscany with your wife and two daughters. You need airplane tickets and an accommodation outside Florence. Rely on Units 6 and 9 for words regarding purchases and travel.

Agente: «Qui è l'agenzia Nuovi viaggi. Mi chiamo Carla. Come posso aiutarla»?

Turista: «Le telefono dagli Stati Uniti».

Agente: «Buongiorno, Signore. Come si chiama»?

Turista: «(1) _____ _____ Robert Brown. Vorrei (2) _____ un viaggio di due settimane in Toscana».

Agente: «Ha bisogno del (3) _____ aereo»?

Turista: «Sì per quattro (4) _____. Da Boston a Firenze. A Firenze stiamo con degli amici, ma ho bisogno di una (5) _____ fuori Firenze».

Agente: «Le consiglio una piccola (6) _____ nella campagna tra Firenze e Siena. Non è (7) _____ ed ha un ottimo (8) _____».

Turista: «Benissimo. Grazie e (9) _____ _____».

Agente: «Buon giorno a lei e (10) _____».

Match each of the nouns on the left with the appropriate qualifier on the right.

1. il prezzo _____   a. al completo

2. l'albergo _____   b. a quattro stelle

3. la pensione _____   c. disponibili

4. le camere _____   d. esotici

5. dei paesaggi _____   e. pittoresco

6. un panorama _____   f. tutto incluso

Camping and natural parks

l(a)'antizanzare	*mosquito repellent*
il campeggiatore / la campeggiatrice	*camper*
il campeggio	*campground; camping*
il camper	*camper (van)*
il fuoco	*campfire*
il, la guardaboschi; la guardia forestale (m. and f.)	*forest ranger*
il parco naturale	*natural park*
la pila; la torcia (elettrica)	*flashlight*
la riserva naturale	*natural reserve*
la roulotte	*trailer*
il sacco a pelo	*sleeping bag*
la tenda	*tent*
il termos	*thermos*

Tiriamo su la tenda, che sta per piovere!   *Let's put up the tent, it's about to rain!*
Siete andati in campeggio?   *Did you go camping?*

March the first part of each sentence on the left with the appropriate conclusion from those listed on the right.

1. Gli insetti mi mangeranno viva! _____   a. al guardaboschi.

2. Nel parco ho chiesto indicazioni _____   b. ci sono parecchi campeggi pubblici.

3. Lungo la Route 1 in California _____   c. Mi sono dimenticata l'antizanzare.

4. Nella riserva naturale non ci sono
   alberghi, _____   d. non hai il servizio in camera!

5. Se vai in campeggio, _____   e. sbrighiamoci a tirare su la tenda!

6. Sta per piovere, _____   f. solo campeggi.

At the beach

l(a)'abbronzatura; la tintarella	*tan*
il bagnino (m. and f.)	*lifeguard*
il calcetto, i calcetto; il calciobalilla, i calciobalilla	*foosball*
il costume da bagno	*bathing suit*
la crema antisolare	*sunblock (cream)*
il lungomare, i lungomare	*beachfront*
l(o)'ombrellone (da spiaggia)	*beach umbrella*
l(o)'onda	*wave*
la sabbia (sing.)	*sand*
il salvagente, i salvagente / i salvagenti	*life jacket*
lo sci d(i)'acqua (sing.)	*waterskiing*
la sedia a sdraio	*beach chair; deck chair*
la spiaggia	*beach*
lo stabilimento balneare	*beach resort*
il sub[acqueo] (m. and f.), i sub	*diver*

Il lungomare è lungo sei chilometri.	*The beachfront walkway is 6 km long.*
Ma tu giochi sempre solo a calcetto?	*Do you always only play foosball?*

ESERCIZIO 10·8

Complete the following sentences.

1. «Che bella _____ hai preso»! «Sono stata un mese al mare»!

2. Al bar dello stabilimento possiamo giocare a _____.

3. Che bella _____! Chilometri e chilometri di sabbia e pochissima gente.

4. Dopo cena, andiamo a fare una passeggiata sul _____.

5. Quando sono stato nei Caraibi, sono andato a _____ _____ a guardare i pesci.

In the mountains

l(o, a)'alpinista	*mountain climber*
la borraccia	*canteen*
la cima; la vetta	*summit*
l(o, a)'escursionista; il, la gitante	*hiker*
la gita; l(a)'escursione	*hike; excursion*
la meta; la destinazione	*destination*
la montagna	*mountain*
il pendio, i pendii / la pista [da sci]	*slope; (ski) slope*
la picozza	*ice ax*
il rifugio	*shelter*
il sacco [da montagna]	*rucksack; (back)pack*
il sentiero	*trail*

Gli alpinisti hanno raggiunto la vetta.	*The climbers reached the summit.*
Abbiamo perso il sentiero.	*We lost the trail.*

Complete the following sentences choosing from the nouns listed above.

1. Agli alpinisti piace arrivare in _____.

2. La _____ serve a portare l'acqua in gita.

3. Per portare le provviste ed i vestiti in montagna, usi il _____.

4. Le persone che vanno ad arrampicare sono _____.

5. Si usa la _____ quando si cammina sul ghiaccio.

Countries and people

Adjectives conveying nationality or ethnic origin can be turned into nouns by adding the definite article, the indefinite article, or indefinite qualifiers. Used in the singular they indicate the language in question. They are never capitalized. They mostly end in **-ano**, **-ana**, **-ani**, **-ane**, and **-ese**, **-esi**, except for words such as **britannico**, **britannici** (*British*), **greco**, **greci** (*Greek*), **turco**, **turchi** (*Turk*), **ceco**, **cechi** (*Czech*), etc.

Un americano vuole parlarti.	*An American man wants to talk to you.*
I francesi non erano d'accordo.	*The French didn't agree.*
Parlate [il] cinese?	*Do you speak Chinese?*

africano	*African*
americano	*American*
arabo; l(o)'arabo	*Arab (person); Arabic (language)*
asiatico	*Asian*
australiano	*Australian*
europeo	*European*
francese; il francese	*French; French (language)*
giapponese; il giapponese	*Japanese; Japanese (language)*
inglese; l'inglese	*English; English (language)*
norvegese; il norvegese	*Norwegian; Norwegian (language)*
portoghese; il portoghese	*Portuguese; Portuguese (language)*
russo; il russo	*Russian; Russian (language)*
spagnolo; lo spagnolo	*Spanish; Spanish (language)*
svizzero	*Swiss*
tedesco; il tedesco	*German; German (language)*

Translate the following sentences into English.

1. Conosci un brasiliano?

_____

2. I greci imparano le lingue facilmente.

_____

3. L'interprete sta traducendo dal russo al tedesco.

_____

4. L'Unione Europea ha ventitré lingue ufficiali, incluso il maltese e lo slovacco.

_____

5. Sono italiana, ma i miei figli sono americani.

_____

We increasingly use names of countries and cities in the original language, **Argentina**, **Nicaragua**, **Canada**, **New York**, **Oslo**, **Buenos Aires**, etc. Names of countries and continents do not take the plural, except for **America**, **le Americhe** (*the Americas*), and **India**, **le Indie** (*the Indies*).

Berlino	*Berlin*
il Brasile	*Brazil*
la Cina	*China*
Città del Messico	*Mexico City*
l(o)'Egitto	*Egypt*
Genova	*Genoa*
Gerusalemme	*Jerusalem*
la Gran Bretagna	*Great Britain*
la Grecia	*Greece*
Londra	*London*
il Medio Oriente	*Middle East*
Milano	*Milan*
Mosca	*Moscow*
Napoli	*Naples*
la Nuova Zelanda	*New Zealand*
i Paesi Bassi (pl.); **l(a)'Olanda**	*the Netherlands; Holland*
Parigi	*Paris*
Pechino	*Beijing*
Roma	*Rome*
gli Stati Uniti (d'America); **gli USA/Usa** (pl.)	*the United States (of America); the U.S.(A.)*
Stoccolma	*Stockholm*
la Svezia	*Sweden*
Torino	*Turin*
la Turchia	*Turkey*
l(a)'Ungheria	*Hungary*
l(a)'Unione Europea; **l(a)'UE**	*the European Union; the EU*

Ci sono 27 paesi nell'UE.	*There are 27 countries in the EU.*
Sei mai stato negli USA?	*Have you ever been to the U.S.?*

In Unit 8 we encountered the prepositions **in/a**, which translate as *in/at/to*; **da** meaning *to/at, from*, and *through*; and **per**, *through*. When we mention names of places as our travel destination, we use the following constructions:

◆ **a**; **da/per** + *city name*

Sono a Parigi.	*I'm in Paris.*
Vado a Parigi.	*I'm going to Paris.*
Vengo da Parigi.	*I'm coming from Paris.*
Passo da/per Parigi.	*I'm going (driving/flying/passing) through (via) Paris.*

Note that *I'm from Paris / I'm a Parisian* translates as **sono <u>di</u> Parigi**.

◆ **in** + *country name / definite article + country name in the plural;* **da/per** + *definite article + country name*

Vado in Germania.	*I'm going to Germany.*
Sono stato in Germania.	*I was in Germany.*
Vado negli (in + gli) Stati Uniti.	*I'm going to the United States.*
Vengo dalla Francia.	*I'm coming from France.*
Passo dalla/per la Svezia.	*I'm going (driving/flying/passing) through (via) Sweden.*

Note that **vengono dalla Francia** has a range of meanings as *they come from France: they are traveling from France* or *they are French.*

ESERCIZIO
10·11

Translate the following sentences. Use the present simple or the present perfect.

1. Are you going to Jerusalem?

   _____

2. When Elena goes to Russia, she'll drive through Poland.

   _____

3. His wife is from Stockholm.

   _____

4. Gabriella has been to Japan.

   _____

5. His wife is returning from Stockholm.

   _____

6. My parents will arrive from Finland tomorrow.

   _____

7. She wants to go to China.

   _____

8. They are traveling through the Netherlands.

   _____

Speech, languages, and speakers

la capitale	*capital*
il dialetto	*dialect*
il dizionario; il vocabolario	*dictionary*
l(o, a)'interprete	*interpreter*
il lessico; il vocabolario	*vocabulary*
la lingua dei segni	*sign language*
la madre lingua; la lingua madre	*mother tongue*
la parola	*word; speech*
il popolo	*population*
la traduzione	*translation*
la tribù, le tribù	*tribe*
gli usi (pl.); **i costumi** (pl.)	*customs; mores*

Gli italiani parlano ancora i dialetti.	*Italians still speak dialects.*
Fa la traduttrice simultanea.	*She's a simultanous translator.*

ESERCIZIO
10·12

Translate the following sentences into English.

1. Anche negli Stati Uniti ci sono i dialetti.

_____

2. Che cosa vuol dire *autoctono*? Nel mio vocabolario non c'è.

_____

3. È bilingue. Farà la traduttrice simultanea.

_____

4. Lalla ha imparato la lingua dei segni perché suo figlio è sordomuto.

_____

5. Mia sorella ha imparato il tedesco e il russo da sola.

_____

·11· Education and technology

In Italy most children go to public school, from preschool (which is not mandatory) through university. Private institutions are often affiliated with the Catholic Church or other denominations. English is a requirement starting in elementary school and young people are encouraged to study abroad. Most of them go to another European country, thanks to the Erasmus and Socrates programs sponsored by the European Union.

l(a)'anno scolastico	school year
l(o)'asilo	preschool; kindergarten
l(o)'asilo nido, gli asili nido	nursery school
la classe	class; classroom
l(a)'istruzione (sing.)	education
il liceo	high school
la scuola elementare; le elementari (pl.)	elementary school
la scuola media [inferiore]; le inferiori (pl.)	middle school
la scuola media superiore; le superiori (pl.)	high school
la scuola privata	private school
la scuola pubblica / di stato	public school
la scuola tecnica/professionale	professional/vocational school

A Bruno non piace andare all'asilo.	Bruno doesn't like to go to kindergarten.
Aldo frequenta ancora le medie.	Aldo is still in middle school.

ESERCIZIO
11·1

Complete the following sentences choosing from the nouns listed above.

1. L'_____ _____ dura da settembre a giugno.

2. Se hai otto anni, vai alle _____.

3. Se hai sedici anni, vai alle _____.

4. Se hai dodici anni, vai alle _____.

5. Se tuo figlio ha tre anni, va all'_____.

6. Se tuo figlio ha tre mesi, va all'_____ _____.

128

As indicators of place, **a** and **in** are used without the article when we wish to convey the function a place performs rather than its physical qualities: **scuola** (*school*), **casa** (*home*), **ospedale** (*hospital*), **chiesa** (*church*), **bus** (*bus*), **hotel** (*hotel*), etc.

Vado a scuola.   *I'm going to school.*
Andate in chiesa?   *Are you going to church?*

ESERCIZIO
11·2

Translate the following sentences into English.

1. I bambini sono in chiesa.

_____

2. I miei figli vanno alla chiesa del nostro quartiere.

_____

3. In clinica mi hanno fatto aspettare due ore.

_____

4. Mio marito va in ospedale domani.

_____

5. Nella nostra casa di campagna possiamo ospitare venti persone.

_____

6. Sono nella macchina di tuo fratello.

_____

7. Stai in casa stasera?

_____

8. Vai a teatro sabato?

_____

Instructors and students

l(o)'allievo	*pupil*
il consiglio dei professori	*teacher board*
il diplomato	*high school graduate*
l(o, a)'insegnante	*teacher*
l(o)'istruttore/l(a)'istruttrice	*instructor*
il maestro	*elementary school teacher*
il, la preside	*principal*
il professore (m. and f.) / la professoressa	*professor; high school teacher*
lo studente / la studentessa	*student*
il, la supplente	*substitute teacher*

Sua madre fa la maestra.   *Her mother is an elementary school teacher.*

*Answer yes (**Y**) or no (**N**) to the following questions.*

1. Puoi fare il preside se sei un allievo? _____

2. Puoi fare il professore se hai studiato all'università? _____

3. Se fai il maestro insegni alle superiori? _____

4. Se sei diplomato vai ancora a scuola? _____

Learning

capire	to understand
copiare	to cheat
fare attenzione (a)	to pay attention (to)
frequentare	to attend
imparare	to learn
imparare a memoria	to memorize; to learn by heart
non prendere la sufficienza; prendere l(a)'insufficienza	to fail
passare l(o)'esame	to pass an exam
prendere appunti	to take notes
prendere la sufficienza	to pass
prendere (un corso)	to take (a course)
prendere (un voto)	to get (a grade)
sforzarsi; impegnarsi	to try hard
studiare	to study
tagliare	to play hooky

Ho preso tre insufficienze di fila.   *I failed three tests one after the other.*
Anna ha preso tre corsi di filosofia.   *Anna has taken three philosophy courses.*

Replace the words in parentheses in each sentence with the appropriate verb from the above list. Use the same modes and tenses. Add prepositions and articles if necessary.

1. Invece di andare a scuola, gli studenti hanno (passato la mattinata al cinema) _____.

2. Gli studenti (sono stati molto contenti dei risultati degli) _____ _____ _____ esami.

3. La studentessa (ascolta la professoressa e prende appunti) _____ _____.

4. Le studentesse (vanno a) _____ _____ scuola tutti i giorni.

5. Lo studente (prova a ricordare) _____ la poesia (senza guardare il testo) _____ _____.

Teaching

bocciare	*to hold back one year; to flunk*
correggere	*to correct*
dare	*to assign*
dare il voto / i voti (a)	*to grade; to give/assign grades*
espellere	*to expel*
impegnare; interessare	*to engage*
insegnare (a)	*to teach*
premiare	*to reward*
promuovere	*to promote to the next grade*
punire	*to punish*
spiegare (a)	*to explain (to)*

Mi hanno bocciato in seconda liceo.	*They held me back in my second year of high school.*
Insegno ai bambini di terza.	*I teach third grade children.*

ESERCIZIO
11·5

Complete the following sentences by choosing from the verbs listed above.

1. Il preside _____ _____ gli studenti che hanno tagliato.

2. La maestra _____ _____ _____ all'allieva.

3. La professoressa _____ gli errori nei compiti.

4. Il professore _____ _____ tre traduzioni da fare a casa.

5. Se il professore _____ bene, lo studente capisce e impara.

Describing education

brillante	*brilliant*
confermato; di ruolo	*tenured*
difficile	*difficult*
distratto	*absent-minded*
dotato (in/per + *definite article*)	*gifted/talented (in)*
e/con lode	*with distinction; cum laude*
facile	*easy*
facoltativo	*elective*
giusto	*correct; right*
ignorante	*ignorant*
negato (per)	*hopeless (at)*
obbligatorio	*mandatory*
sbagliato	*incorrect; erroneous*

Lina è negata per la chimica.	*Lina is hopeless at chemistry.*
Ha una bambina molto dotata, Signora.	*You have a very gifted girl, Madam.*

Translate the following sentences.

1. Are you taking three mandatory courses?

   _____

2. He's not a brilliant student.

   _____

3. His answers are correct.

   _____

4. I'm taking two elective courses.

   _____

5. That student is absent-minded.

   _____

6. Your brother is hopeless at chemistry.

   _____

Tools for teaching and learning

l(o)'apprendimento a distanza	*distance learning*
il banco	*desk*
la biro / le biro; la penna a sfera	*ballpoint pen*
la calcolatrice	*calculator*
il compito [a casa]	*homework (assignment)*
il compito in classe	*in-class test*
l(a)'enciclopedia	*encyclopedia*
l(o)'errore	*mistake*
l(o)'esempio	*example*
l(o)'esercizio	*exercise*
l(o)'intervallo	*recess*
il lavoro di gruppo	*teamwork*
il libro di testo	*textbook*
la matita	*pencil*
la penna	*pen*
il problema di matematica	*math quiz/test*
il quaderno	*notebook*
lo studio	*study*
il tema, i tema	*essay; composition*

Il professor Giugni dà molti compiti.   *Professor Giugni assigns a lot of homework.*
Per esempio, 2 più 2 fa 4.   *For example, 2 plus 2 is 4.*

Mark the word that does not belong in each of the following series.

1. a. il tema   b. l'esercizio   c. la matita   d. il compito

2. a. la matita   b. la biro   c. la calcolatrice   d. il banco

3. a. il compito   b. il tema   c. l'intervallo   d. il problema di matematica

Graduating

In Italian education, oral tests, called **interrogazioni** or **esami orali** (*oral interrogations/exams*) are widely used. At the end of high school students go through the rite of passage called **la maturità** (*leaving exam; exam to graduate high school*), when they face a **commissione esterna** (*external examining board*). But nowadays 99 percent of the students taking it receive at least a passing grade.

il diploma di scuola media superiore;	*high school diploma*
il diploma di maturità; la maturità	
l(o)'esame	*exam*
l(o)'esame con scelta su opzioni multiple	*multiple-choice test*
l(o)'esame di ammissione	*admission test*
l(o)'esame di Stato	*board exam*
la pagella	*report card*
il titolo di studio	*degree*
il voto	*grade*

Ha preso il diploma di ragioneria.	*He took a high school accountancy diploma.*
Ho passato l'esame di ammissione a medicina!	*I passed the admission test to medical school!*

Complete the following sentences, choosing from the words suggested under each of them.

1. Giovanna ha preso il massimo dei _____ alla maturità.
   a. problemi   b. voti   c. errori

2. Ho preso l'insufficienza nell'ultimo _____.
   a. lavoro di gruppo   b. studio   c. compito in classe

3. Massimo è stato _____ alla maturità.
   a. bocciato   b. espulso   c. punito

4. Siamo _____ solo in cinque su cento all'esame di ammissione.
   a. passati   b. frequentati   c. premiati

Subjects

Here follow the names of some subjects and disciplines taught from elementary school through postgraduate studies.

il disegno	*drawing*
l(a)'economia	*economics*
l(a)'educazione civica	*civics*
la geografia	*geography*
la giurisprudenza	*law*
la fisica	*phyiscs*
l(a)'informatica	*computer science*
l(a)'ingegneria	*engineering*
il latino	*Latin*
la letteratura; le lettere	*literature*
la matematica	*mathematics*
la materia	*subject*
la medicina	*medicine*
la musica	*music*
le scienze naturali	*natural sciences*
le scienze umane	*humanities*
la storia	*history*

Si laurea in giurisprudenza.	*She's getting a law degree.*
Fa il dottorato in economia.	*She's getting a Ph.D. in economics.*

ESERCIZIO
11·9

Provide the disciplines defined in each sentence. List them with the article.

1. La disciplina che studia i diritti e i doveri dei cittadini. _____

2. La disciplina che studia le relazioni astratte tra i numeri, le figure geometriche, ecc. _____

3. La lingua parlata dagli antichi romani, usata ancora dalla chiesa cattolica. _____

4. La materia che narra le vicende dell'umanità dalla preistoria ad oggi. _____

5. La materia che studia il mondo in cui viviamo dal punto di vista fisico e politico. _____

Higher education

The Italian college and university system was modeled on the German one, but as higher education has become "mass education," some features of the American system have been introduced. All countries belonging to the European Union (and several outside it, such as Norway) have signed the Bologna Convention, pledging to establish a homogenous university-level system to encourage the movement of young citizens and professionals throughout the Union.

l(o)'anno accademico	*academic year*
la biblioteca	*library*
la borsa di studio	*fellowship; scholarship*
il collegio	*boarding school*
il convegno; il congresso	*conference*

i crediti (pl.)	*credits*
il curricolo; il piano di studio	*curriculum*
il dottorato [di ricera]	*Ph.D. program*
il dipartimento	*department*
la domanda di ammissione (a)	*application for admission*
la laurea; il baccalaureato	*college degree*
la lezione; la conferenza	*lecture*
il, la preside	*chairperson*
la ricerca	*research*
il seminario	*seminar*
il sillabo	*syllabus*
le tasse universitarie (pl.)	*tuition fees*
l(a)'università	*college; university*
Hai fatto la domanda di ammissione all'università?	*Did you apply to college?*
Quando prendi la laurea?	*When will you get your college degree?*

ESERCIZIO
11·10

Complete in the following sentences.

1. Ho venti studenti di dottorato iscritti al mio _____.

2. Ho vinto una _____ _____ _____ per andare a studiare a Oxford!

3. Il professore di storia moderna è stato eletto _____ del Dipartimento di Storia.

4. Nelle università statali, le _____ _____ non sono alte.

5. Per diventare _____ all'università devi avere pubblicato molti articoli.

6. In una università europea ci vogliono almeno 60 _____ per prendere il baccalaureato.

7. Professore, sul _____ non ha elencato tutti i libri per il suo corso.

Studying at the university

ammettere (a)	*to admit (to)*
discutere la tesi/dissertazione	*to defend one's dissertation*
fare domanda (a/per)	*to apply (to/for)*
fare lezione	*to lecture*
fare ricerca	*to do research*
fare una conferenza	*to give a lecture*
iscriversi all'università	*to enroll in college/university*
laureare; laurearsi; prendere la laurea (in)	*to graduate (from university)*
presiedere	*to chair*
Discuto la tesi giovedì.	*I'll defend my dissertation on Thursday.*
Presiede la riunione il rettore Bindi.	*Rector Bindi will chair the meeting.*

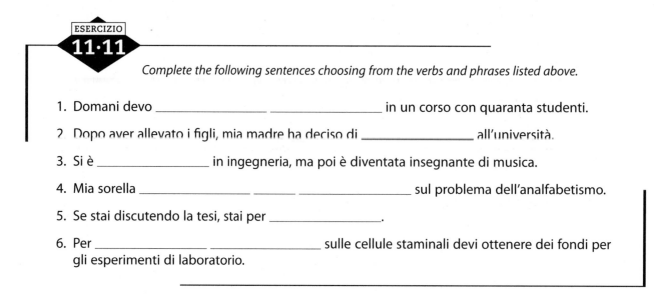

Complete the following sentences choosing from the verbs and phrases listed above.

1. Domani devo _____ _____ in un corso con quaranta studenti.

2. Dopo aver allevato i figli, mia madre ha deciso di _____ all'università.

3. Si è _____ in ingegneria, ma poi è diventata insegnante di musica.

4. Mia sorella _____ _____ _____ sul problema dell'analfabetismo.

5. Se stai discutendo la tesi, stai per _____.

6. Per _____ _____ sulle cellule staminali devi ottenere dei fondi per gli esperimenti di laboratorio.

Computers

English dominates the vocabulary of computers and electronic media in general. Readers can assume that most of the terms listed below are used in English, but the Italian version is given when it is used as much as the original English.

il computer; il PC	*(personal) computer; PC*
il crash	*crash*
il cursore	*cursor*
il dischetto	*diskette*
l(o)'hardware	*hardware*
il lettore ottico di caratteri; lo scanner	*scanner*
la memoria (ROM e RAM)	*memory (ROM and RAM)*
il mouse	*mouse*
la pila	*battery*
la porta / il port	*port*
il portatile; il laptop	*laptop*
lo schermo; il video	*screen*
il sostegno; il supporto	*support*
la stampante	*printer*
il tasto di ritorno	*return key*
la tecnologia	*technology*

Il suo computer ha tre porte USB. — *His computer has three USB ports.*
Il mio PC non ha abbastanza memoria operativa. — *My PC doesn't have enough ROM.*

ESERCIZIO
11·12

Give the names of computing equipment parts described in the following sentences. Include the article.

1. Disco magnetico in materiale plastico, usato per la registrazione di dati. _____

2. Dispositivo per personal computer che permette di spostare il cursore sullo schermo. _____

3. Elaboratore elettronico. _____

4. Sorgente di energia elettrica che fa funzionare un elettrodomestico senza collegamento in rete. _____

5. Strumento per l'elaborazione di dati che si può spostare facilmente. _____

Software

la banca dati	*databank*
la cibernetica; l(a)'intelligenza artificiale	*cybernetics*
il ciberspazio	*cyberspace*
la cifra; il numero	*digit*
la copia	*copy*
il dato, i dati	*datum, data*
l(a)'elettronica	*electronics*
il file	*file*
il programmatore / la programmatrice	*programmer*
il reboot	*reboot*
il software	*software*
la stampa	*print*

Hai fatto un backup dei file? *Did you back up your files?*
La cibernetica ha creato un mondo virtuale. *Cybernetics has created a virtual world.*

ESERCIZIO
11·13

In each series, mark the word that does not belong.

1. a. il cursore b. il mouse c. il tasto di ritorno d. il reboot

2. a. la banca dati b. il file c. il programmatore d. le cifre

3. a. la stampa b. la cibernetica c. l'elettronica d. il software

4. a. il programmatore b. il reboot c. il crash d. i dati

Using a computer

archiviare	to file
avere un crash	to crash
cliccare [su] (aux. avere)	to click (on)
copiare	to copy
duplicare; fare un backup	to back up
eliminare	to delete
inserire	to enter
masterizzare un CD	to burn a CD
premere	to press
riavviare il sistema; fare il reboot	to reboot
salvare	to save
scaricare	to download
stampare	to print

Ho fatto il reboot tre volte.	I rebooted three times.
Ho scaricato tante canzoni da quel sito.	I downloaded many songs from that site.

ESERCIZIO
11·14

Complete the following sentences by choosing from the verbs listed above.

1. Il tasto Enter serve per _____ i dati.

2. Quando il computer ha un crash, provi a fare un _____.

3. Quando usi un CD per salvare dei dati, si dice che lo _____.

4. Se non vuoi perdere i file, devi fare spesso un _____.

5. Usi il mouse per _____.

The World Wide Web

l(o)'allegato	attachment
la casella e-mail	e-mail box
l(a)'homepage	home page
l'indirizzo e-mail	e-mail address
l(a)'internet	Internet
il menù	menu
il messaggio di posta elettronica; l(a)'e-mail	e-mail message
il motore di ricerca	search engine
la pagina web	web page
la parola d'ordine; la password	password
la posta elettronica; l(a)'e-mail	e-mail
il sito (web)	(web)site
l(o)'SMS (esse-emme-esse), gli SMS	SMS (Short Message Service); text message
lo spam; la posta elettronica spazzatura	spam
il videogioco; il videogame	video game
la (world wide) web	the (World Wide) Web

Ti mando un SMS.
Se clicchi qui torni alla homepage.

I'll send you a text message.
If you click here you'll go back to the home page.

ESERCIZIO
11·15

Match the first part of each sentence on the left with the appropriate conclusion among those listed on the right.

1. I nostri affari vanno molto meglio _____

2. Nella mia casella e-mail _____

3. Non scegliere il tuo compleanno _____

4. Se vuoi trovare un'informazione su internet _____

5. Ti ho mandato un documento _____

a. come allegato a un messaggio.

b. come parola d'ordine.

c. da quando abbiamo il nuovo sito web.

d. devi usare un motore di ricerca.

e. ho dieci messaggi spazzatura al giorno.

Describing the Internet

[la] chiocciola	*@; at*
di base	*basic*
facile da usare; user friendly	*user-friendly*
home	*home*
in linea; on line; collegato all'internet	*online*
indietro; back	*back*
interattivo	*interactive*
modulare	*modular*
per default	*by default*
precedente	*previous*
punto	*dot*
scollegato; off line	*off-line*
tecnologico	*technological*

Indirizzo e-mail: alessandra punto bossi chiocciola telenet punto it

E-mail address: alessandra@telnet.it

Ti ho chiamato con skype, ma eri scollegato.

I called you on Skype, but your were off-line.

ESERCIZIO
11·16

Translate the following sentences into Italian, keeping as many English words as possible.

1. Giorgio is online five hours a day (**al giorno**).

_____

2. My e-mail address is valeria.guidi@fastnet.net.

_____

3. She isn't answering her e-mail messages. She must be off-line.

_____

4. The Back option sends you to the previous page.

_____

5. The new software is really (**davvero**) user-friendly.

_____

Verbs

allegare	*to attach*
andare su google	*to google*
chattare (aux. **avere**)	*to chat (online)*
fare il log in; connettersi (a)	*to log in/on*
fare [il] log off; disconnettersi (da)	*to log off*
inoltrare	*to forward*
mandare; inviare	*to send*
navigare (aux. **avere**)	*to navigate; to surf*
personalizzare	*to customize*

Si collega anche quando viaggia.   *He logs on even when he travels.*
Ha navigato su internet tutta la notte.   *He surfed the Internet all night.*

ESERCIZIO
11·17

Complete the short report about your Internet-related activities, using as many words in English as possible.

Gianni si collega a (1) _____ per (2) _____ con degli altri utenti su You Tube. Quando riceve un' (3) _____ divertente, la inoltra ai suoi amici. Il suo (4) _____ web ha una pagina interattiva, dove può giocare a dei (5) _____ con altra gente. Quando si alza la mattina, (6) _____ subito a (7) _____ per controllare la sua casella (8) _____. È bravo a risolvere alcuni malfunzionamenti del (9) _____.

Culture, the arts, and leisure time

Over the centuries Italians have produced great literature. They have also been avid consumers of foreign literary products: the translation business is lively in Italy. And they publish a great number of daily newspapers, which reflect the importance of local cultures, and the wide array of Italian points of view and ideological stands.

And yet, Italians are not great readers. They prefer spending their leisure time with friends, watching TV, going to the movies, and enjoying the outdoors. They are proficient at sports, but, as happens in most countries, the majority of Italians is sedentary and needs to add more physical activities to their lives.

l(o)'alfabeto	*alphabet*
l(o)'autore/l(a)'autrice	*author*
la casa editrice	*publishing house*
la cultura (sing.)	*culture*
l(o)'editore (m. and f.) / l(a)'editrice (rare)	*publisher*
la letteratura	*literature*
il lettore / la lettrice	*reader*
la lettura	*reading*
il libro	*book*
la narrativa; la fiction	*fiction*
la poesia	*poem; poetry*
il poeta, i poeti / la poetessa	*poet*
il romanziere / la romanziera	*novelist*
il romanzo	*novel*
lo scrittore / la scrittrice	*writer*
la scrittura (sing.)	*writing*
la storia	*story*
il titolo	*title*

Legge solo libri gialli.	*He reads only murder mysteries.*
Mondadori è un editore importante.	*Mondadori is an important publisher.*

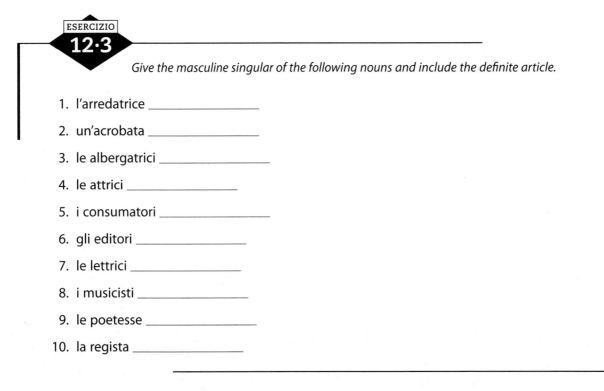

ESERCIZIO
12·1

Mark the word that does not belong in each series.

1. a. l'autore   b. il romanziere   c. il titolo   d. lo scrittore

2. a. il poeta   b. lo scrittore   c. il libro   d. l'autore

3. a. la cultura   b. la scrittrice   c. la romanziera   d. l'autrice

4. a. la poesia   b. l'alfabeto   c. la letteratura   d. la narrativa

ESERCIZIO
12·2

Answer yes (Y) or no (N) to the following questions.

1. In generale i poeti pubblicano dei best seller? _____

2. Il redattore decide che libri pubblicare? _____

3. L'autore scrive il testo? _____

4. La poesia è facile da tradurre? _____

5. Un lavoro di fiction è un lavoro di fantasia? _____

Many names of professionals form the feminine by adding **-essa** to the stem of the noun: **il dottore** (*male physician*) → **la dottoressa** (*female physician*), by changing **-tore** into **-trice**: **lo scrittore** (*male writer*) → **la scrittrice** (*female writer*), or by changing the article: **il cantante** (*male singer*) → **la cantante** (*female singer*).

ESERCIZIO
12·3

Give the masculine singular of the following nouns and include the definite article.

1. l'arredatrice _____

2. un'acrobata _____

3. le albergatrici _____

4. le attrici _____

5. i consumatori _____

6. gli editori _____

7. le lettrici _____

8. i musicisti _____

9. le poetesse _____

10. la regista _____

Writing and publishing

abbonarsi (a)	*to subscribe (to)*
(in)cominciare	*to begin*
dire lettera per lettera	*to spell*
finire	*to end*
intervistare	*to interview*
intitolare	*to title*
leggere	*to read*
pubblicare	*to publish*
raccontare; narrare	*to tell; to recount; to narrate*
scrivere	*to write*
stampare	*to press; to print*

Il romanzo finisce male.	*The novel ends badly.*
Può dirmi il suo nome lettera per lettera?	*Can you spell your name for me?*

ESERCIZIO
12·4

Complete the following sentences by choosing from the verbs listed above. Use the present simple and the present perfect of the indicative or the present infinitive.

1. «Signore, quanti libri _____ di media all'anno»? «Diciotto, venti».

2. «Quanti libri ha _____ quella scrittrice»? «Ha _____ otto romanzi».

3. Ha _____ il suo primo romanzo *La campagna*. Uscirà a marzo.

4. I libri vengono _____ su carta.

5. La mamma _____ una storia al bambino.

6. Il lavoro di una casa editrice è _____ libri.

Newspapers

l(o)'abbonamento (a)	*subscription (to)*
l(o)'articolo	*article*
l(a)'attualità; la cronaca (sing.)	*current affairs*
il direttore [del giornale]	*newspaper editor; publisher*
l(a)'edizione web	*web edition*
il giornale; il quotidiano	*newspaper*
il giornalismo	*journalism*
il, la giornalista	*journalist*
la notizia, le notizie	*news*
la prima pagina	*front page*
la rivista; il rotocalco	*magazine*
la stampa	*press*
il titolo	*headline*

Vorrei un abbonamento semestrale.	*I'd like a six-month subscription.*
Il direttore ha licenziato la giornalista.	*The publisher fired the journalist.*

ESERCIZIO

12·5

Complete the following sentences by choosing from the options listed after each of them.

1. È uscita una nuova _____ settimanale che si indirizza ai lettori giovani.
      a. giornalista   b. quotidiano   c. rivista

2. Il _____ della nostra città ha 150 anni.
      a. stampa   b. giornale   c. notizia

3. Hanno pubblicato il suo articolo in _____.
      a. prima pagina   b. notizia   c. stampa

4. Sul _____ di oggi non c'è la notizia delle dimissioni del primo ministro!
      a. rivista   b. titolo   c. giornale

Radio and TV

l(o)'ascoltatore/l(a)'ascoltatrice	*listener*
il canale [televisivo]	*TV channel*
il conduttore / la conduttrice	*host; anchor*
il giornale radio, i giornali radio	*radio news*
i [mass] media	*(mass) media*
la [antenna] parabolica	*satellite dish*
il programma	*program*
la radio, le radio	*radio*
il, la radiocronista; il, la telecronista	*newscaster*
la rete	*network*
lo spettacolo; lo show	*show*
lo spettatore / la spettatrice	*spectator*
il telegiornale; il TG, i TG	*TV news*

Mia madre guarda solo il TG.	*My mother watches only the TV news.*
Hanno installato la parabolica.	*They installed a satellite dish.*

ESERCIZIO

12·6

Complete the following sentences by choosing from the words listed above.

1. Hanno dato la notizia del rapimento al _____ _____, ma non al telegiornale.

2. Il suo programma ha tre milioni di _____.

3. La _____ è stata inventata prima della televisione.

4. Nostro nonno era _____ sportivo ai Campionati Mondiali di calcio del 1934.

5. Rupert Murdoch possiede molte _____ televisive.

Describing the media

a cura di	*edited by*
dal vivo; in diretta	*live*
di fantasia	*fictional*
esaurito	*out of print*
famoso	*famous*
giornalistico	*journalistic*
in onda	*on the air*
in stampa	*in print*
registrato	*recorded*
sensazionale	*sensational*
televisivo	*TV-related; television*
(TV) via cavo	*cable (TV)*

È una raccolta di saggi a cura di Bocci.   *It's a collection of essays edited by Bocci.*
Il suo romanzo è esaurito.   *His novel is out of print.*

ESERCIZIO 12·7

Complete the following sentences by choosing from the qualifiers listed above.

1. Grazie alla TV _____ _____ si possono vedere centinaia di canali.

2. Il suo nuovo libro ha avuto tanto successo che è già _____.

3. L'intervista con il primo ministro è stata trasmessa _____ _____.

4. Silenzio! Siamo _____ _____!

5. Quel programma non è in diretta, è _____.

Cinema, theater, and photography

l(o)'applauso	*applause*
l(o)'attore/l(a)'attrice	*actor*
il cinema (sing.)	*cinema*
il cinema[tografo], i cinema[tografi]	*(movie) theater*
il film	*film; movie*
la foto[grafia], le foto[grafie]	*photograph; photography*
il fotografo	*photographer*
l(a)'immagine	*image*
la macchina fotografica; la cinepresa	*camera*
la multisala	*multiplex*
il palcoscenico	*stage*
la [sera della] prima	*opening night*
il pubblico	*audience*
il, la regista	*director*
il sipario	*curtain*
i sottotitoli (pl.)	*subtitles*

la star, le star (f. and m.); la stella   *star*
    (f. and m.); il divo / la diva
il teatro   *theatre/theater*

Calò il sipario.   *The curtain came down*
Al cinema danno il *Titanic*.   Titanic *is showing in movie theaters.*

ESERCIZIO 12·8

Complete the following sentences by choosing from the nouns listed above.

1. Cartier Bresson è stato un grande _____.

2. Ingmar Bergman è stato un _____ importante.

3. Danno venti film alla _____.

4. Lo zoom, il grandangolo e il teleobiettivo sono delle lenti per
   la _____ _____.

5. I film stranieri hanno tutti i _____.

Acting and film

applaudire   *to applaude*
dirigire (un film)   *to direct*
doppiare   *to dub*
filmare   *to film*
fischiare   *to boo*
girare (un film)   *to shoot (a film)*
prendere; fare una foto[grafia]   *to take a photo(graph)*
provare; fare le prove   *to rehearse*
recitare (in + *article*)   *to act; to play in*

Chi ha diretto *Ben Hur*?   *Who directed* Ben Hur?
Ha recitato nell'*Amleto*.   *He played in* Hamlet.

ESERCIZIO 12·9

Match the first part of each sentence on the left with the appropriate conclusion among those listed on the right.

1. Ha doppiato _____

2. Hanno finito le prove. _____

3. Il regista che ha vinto l'Oscar _____

4. Un film è un serie _____

a. di immagini fotografiche in movimento.

b. Dopodomani c'è la prima.

c. ha diretto cinquanta film.

d. John Wayne per trent'anni.

Music and dance

Since the Renaissance, Italy has played a major role in the development of Western music, opera especially. But Italy has imported much of the twentieth century's popular music from Great Britain, the United States, and Central and South America.

la ballerina	*ballerina*
il ballerino	*dancer*
il balletto (sing.)	*ballet*
il bis, i bis	*encore*
il, la cantante	*singer*
la canzone	*song*
il compositore (m. and f.)	*composer*
il concerto	*concert*
il coro	*choir; chorus*
la danza; il ballo	*dance*
il direttore / la direttrice [d'orchestra]	*conductor*
la discoteca	*disco*
il dj; il disc jockey (m. and f.)	*DJ; disc jockey*
l(a)'esecuzione; la performance	*performance*
il gruppo; la banda	*band*
la musica (sing.)	*music*
il, la musicista	*musician*
l(o)'opera	*opera*
l(a)'orchestra	*orchestra*
il ritmo	*rhythm*
lo strumento [musicale]	*musical instrument*
il suonatore, la suonatrice	*player*
la voce	*voice*

Canto da soprano nel coro della chiesa.	*I sing soprano in the church choir.*
Segue molto bene il ritmo.	*He follows the rhythm very well.*

ESERCIZIO
12·10

Complete the following sentences by choosing from the nouns listed above.

1. Balla benissimo, perché ha un gran senso del _____.

2. Beethoven fu un grandissimo _____.

3. I Beatles sono stati il _____ rock più famoso del XX secolo.

4. Il soprano ha cantato benissimo. Il pubblico ha chiesto a gran voce il _____.

5. Mia sorella è la prima donna _____ d'orchestra alla Scala.

6. Pavarotti è stato un grande _____ d'opera.

Singing and dancing

andare a ballare	to go dancing
cantare	to sing
comporre	to compose
condurre; guidare	to lead
danzare; ballare	to dance
registrare	to record
seguire	to follow
suonare (a musical instrument)	to play

Il ballerino guida la ballerina.	The gentleman leads the lady.
Suoni la tromba?	Do you play the trumpet?

ESERCIZIO 12·11

Answer the following questions.

1. Chi dirige gli attori, la regista o la romanziera? _____

2. Chi compone musica, il compositore o il direttore d'orchestra? _____

3. Chi scrive la colonna sonora di un film, il musicista o la regista? _____

4. Chi dirige l'orchestra, il direttore o il cantante? _____

5. Se guardi delle immagini in movimento, guardi delle fotografie o un film? _____

The fine arts

In no cultural endeavor has the contribution of Italy been greater than in the **belle arti**, the *fine arts*, which have filled the museums of so many countries. Here follows a list of nouns regarding painting, sculpture, architecture, and design.

l(o)'architetto/l(a)'architetta	architect
l(a)'arte	art
l(o, a)'artista	artist
la ceramica	pottery
il design	design
il designer (m. and f.)	designer
la galleria	gallery
il modello	model
il monumento	monument
la mostra	exhibit; show
il museo	museum
il pittore / la pittrice	painter
il quadro; il dipinto / la pittura (sing.)	painting
il restauro	restoration
il ritratto	portrait
lo scultore / la scultrice	sculptor
la scultura	sculpture
la statua	statue

| lo stile | style |
| il vaso | vase |

| Vivono in una casa stile liberty. | *They live in an arts nouveaux–style building.* |
| Fa la modella per uno scultore. | *She's a model for a sculptor.* |

Mark the word that does not belong in each of the following series.

1. a. la galleria   b. il monumento   c. la statua   d. lo scultore

2. a. il museo   b. il vaso   c. la galleria   d. la mostra

3. a. lo scultore   b. la statua   c. il marmo   d. il ritratto

4. a. lo stile   b. la pittrice   c. l'artista   d. il designer

Complete the following sentences by adding the profession of the artist.

1. L'_____ americano più famoso è Frank Lloyd Wright.

2. La lampada Arco venne disegnata da Achille Castiglioni, un grande _____.

3. La moglie del pittore gli fa anche da _____.

4. Michelangelo è uno dei più grandi _____, _____ e _____ di tutti i tempi.

5. Picasso è stato un _____ importantissimo.

Producing art

cuocere (al forno)	*to bake; to fire*
dipingere	*to paint*
disegnare	*to draw*
essiccare; far asciugare	*to dry*
intagliare	*to carve*
mostrare (a); far vedere (a)	*to show (to)*
posare	*to pose*
progettare; disegnare; fare il design (di)	*to design*
scolpire	*to sculpt*

| Michelangelo ha scolpito il *David*. | *Michelangelo sculpted the* David. |
| Posso farti vedere le mie foto? | *Can I show you my photos?* |

In the following sentences, artists and verbs have been mixed up. Match the artist with the verb describing his/her artistic endeavor.

1. L'architetto posa per il pittore.

_____

2. La grafica dipinge l'affresco.

_____

3. La modella scolpisce la statua.

_____

4. La pittrice progetta lo stadio.

_____

5. Lo scultore disegna il logo della ditta.

_____

Italian can form compound nouns that specify the function of an object by adding **da** + *noun*. When the context is clear, the qualifier can be dropped.

le carte [da gioco]	*playing cards*
il guantone [da baseball]	*baseball mitt*

Match the nouns on the left with the appropriate complement among those listed on the right. Translate the compound words into English.

1. il costume _____   a. da bagno

_____

2. la macchina _____   b. da ginnastica

_____

3. la pallina _____   c. da montagna

_____

4. il pallone _____   d. da scrivere

_____

5. la racchetta _____   e. da calcio

_____

6. il sacco _____   f. da golf

_____

7. le scarpe _____   g. da tennis

_____

8. gli scarponi _____   h. da sci

_____

Having fun

barare (a) (aux. **avere**)	*to cheat*
dare scacco matto (a)	*to checkmate*
divertire	*to amuse*
divertirsi	*to enjoy oneself; to have fun*
giocare (a) (aux. **avere**)	*to play*
giocare d'azzardo (aux. **avere**)	*to gamble*
intrattenere	*to entertain*
scommettere	*to bet*
tagliare il mazzo	*to cut the deck*

Carlo ha barato a poker.   *Carlo cheated at poker.*
Vi siete divertiti allo zoo?   *Did you have fun at the zoo?*

ESERCIZIO
12·16

Add the appropriate verb to the following sentences.

1. I clown fanno _____ i bambini.

2. I giocatori di carte _____ a poker.

3. Paolo _____ moltissimo allo zoo.

4. Il gran maestro ha _____ al computer.

5. Nei film western, spesso il giocatore d'azzardo _____ e viene ucciso.

Keeping in shape

l(a)'aerobica (sing.)	*aerobics*
l(o)'allenatore/l(o)'allenatrice personale	*personal trainer*
l(a)'attrezzatura	*exercise gear*
la cyclette	*stationary bike*
l'esercizio fisico (sing.); **la ginnastica**	*exercise*
la fitness	*fitness*
la palestra	*gym*
i pesi (pl.)	*weights*

la piscina	*swimming pool*
le scarpe da ginnastica; le sneaker(s)	*sneakers*
la tuta da ginnastica	*gym clothes; tracksuit*

Vado in palestra tre volte la settimana.	*I go to the gym three times a week.*
Lalla fa ginnastica tutti i giorni.	*Lalla exercises every day.*

ESERCIZIO
12·17

Complete the following sentences by choosing from the words listed above.

1. Lavoro in palestra con un'_____ _____.

2. Non faccio più l'_____. Mi facevano male le ginocchia.

3. Se vuoi dimagrire devi fare molta _____.

4. Signora, non può stare in palestra scalza. Deve mettersi le _____.

Sports

l(o)'allenamento	*training*
l(o, a)'atleta	*athlete*
l(a)'atletica [leggera] (sing.)	*athletics*
la barca a vela	*sailboat*
il campione / la campionessa	*champion*
la classifica	*placement*
la corsa	*running*
la gara	*race*
il giocatore / la giocatrice (di baseball / football americano / calcio/football, etc.)	*(baseball/football/soccer, etc.) player*
il golf	*golf*
la medaglia	*medal*
la parità / il pareggio	*tie*
il perdente (m. and f.); lo sconfitto	*loser*
la pista [da atletica]	*track*
il pugilato / la box	*boxing*
la racchetta	*racquet*
il record	*record*
lo sci (sing.)	*skiing*
lo sport	*sport*
il tennis	*tennis*
la vela	*sail; sailing*
la vittoria	*victory*
il vincitore / la vincitrice	*winner*

Max ha una barca a vela di dodici metri.	*Max has a 12-meter sailing boat.*
Mio figlio vuole fare il giocatore di calcio.	*My son wants to become a soccer player.*

Complete the following sentences choosing from the options given below each of them.

1. Alle Olimpiadi hanno battuto _____ dei 200 metri piani.
   a. la classifica   b. il record   c. la corsa

2. L'Italia è quarta in _____ ai giochi olimpici.
   a. pareggio   b. vittoria   c. classifica

3. Suo marito è in gran forma perché ha fatto _____ tutta la vita.
   a. il perdente   b. sport   c. il vincitore

4. Mia figlia ha vinto _____ di bronzo ai mondiali di atletica!
   a. la medaglia   b. il record   c. la gara

The preposition **da** can be followed by a verb in the present infinitive to convey the idea that something *can be done, must be done, needs to be done,* or *is worth doing.*

Hai dei libri da leggere?	*Do you have any books to read?*
Vi assegno tre libri da leggere.	*I'm assigning you three books to read.*
La mia automobile è da lavare.	*My car needs washing.*
È un posto da vedere.	*It's a place worth seeing.*

Match each noun on the left with the appropriate complementary phrase among those listed on the right.

1. i diritti d'autore _____

2. il nuovo film di Scorsese _____

3. il sacco da montagna _____

4. l'articolo di giornale _____

5. l'atleta _____

6. la commedia _____

7. un motivo musicale _____

8. una poesia carina _____

a. da allenare per la gara

b. da cantare in coro

c. da pagare allo scrittore

d. da preparare per la gita

e. da recitare nel teatro comunale

f. da recitare alla festa di compleanno del nonno

g. da scrivere per l'ultima edizione

h. da vedere assolutamente

The preposition **a** can be used before a noun to indicate the main characteristic of a thing or an activity. **Barca a vela** (*sailboat*): a boat that uses sails; **barca a motore** (*motorboat*): a boat propelled by a motor; etc.

Match the nouns on the left with the appropriate complements on the right. Translate the compound words into English.

1. l'apprendimento _____	a. a contatto
2. il bagaglio _____	b. a distanza
3. la carne _____	c. a mano
4. le lenti _____	d. a sfera
5. la penna _____	e. ad alta velocità
6. il quadro _____	f. a olio
7. il treno _____	g. alla griglia

Team sports

l(o)'allenatore/l(a)'allenatrice	*coach*
l(o)'arbitro (m. and f.)	*referee; umpire*
il baseball	*baseball*
il calcio; il football	*soccer*
il fan (m. and f.); il tifoso	*fan*
il football americano	*football*
il gol; i gol	*goal (point scored)*
il guantone (da baseball / box, etc.)	*(baseball/boxing) glove*
la pallacanestro / il basketball	*basketball*
la pallavolo	*volleyball*
il pallone / la boccia; la palla; la pallina	*ball*
la partita	*game; match*
la porta; la rete (in soccer)	*goal (structure)*
lo stadio	*stadium*

Ho perso cinque palline da golf domenica.	*I lost five golf balls on Sunday.*
Stefanie Graf ha vinto la partita in due set.	*Stefanie Graf won the game in two sets.*

ESERCIZIO
12·21

On the basis of the clues given below, decide what sport is being played.

Se usi questi attrezzi:

1. un pallone, un campo in erba e due porte con le reti _____

2. una palla, un canestro e un campo all'aperto o al chiuso _____

3. una pallina, un campo a forma di diamante, una guantone e una mazza _____

4. un pallone ovale e un campo all'aperto _____

Playing sports

allenare	*to train*
correre (aux. **avere**)	*to run*
fare ginnastica	*to work out; to exercise*
fare pari	*to tie*
fare vela; **andare in vela**	*to sail*
giocare a (calcio/football/baseball/ football americano/tennis, etc.) (aux. **avere**)	*to play (soccer/baseball/football/tennis, etc.)*
perdere	*to lose*
sciare (aux. **avere**)	*to ski*
segnare	*to score*
tuffarsi	*to dive*
vincere	*to win*

Giocano a calcio ogni sabato.	*They play soccer every Saturday.*
Vanno in vela sei mesi all'anno.	*They go sailing six months a year.*

ESERCIZIO
12·22

In each sentence, replace the words in parentheses with the appropriate verb from those listed above.

1. Hanno (preso una barca a vela e sono andati) _____ _____ in giro per il Mediterraneo.

2. I bambini (danno calci a un pallone e cercano di mandarlo verso una delle due porte alle estremità del campo) _____ _____ _____.

3. Il personal trainer (lavora con) _____ l'atleta per prepararlo per le Olimpiadi.

4. Le due squadre di calcio hanno fatto (lo stesso numero di gol) _____.

5. Vittorio (è salito su un trampolino e si è buttato) _____ _____ _____ in acqua.

Work and business

The Italian economy, dominated by agriculture until the 1950s, is now a service economy, even though the manufacturing sector still represents a larger share of the GDP in Italy than in the United States. Italy is a nation where small- and mid-sized firms survive in all sectors thanks to high quality production and their skills in taking advantage of niche markets. Because of a lack of investment in research and development the technology sector is underdeveloped, even though Italy remains the seventh richest country in the world.

l(o)'annuncio di lavoro	*job advertisement*
il biglietto da visita	*business card*
la carriera	*career*
il colloquio [di lavoro] / l(a)'intervista	*job interview*
il concorso	*competition*
il curricolo; il curriculum vitae	*résumé; CV*
i dati personali (pl.)	*personal data/information*
la disoccupazione	*unemployment*
la formazione (sing.)	*training*
l(o)'impiego	*employment; job*
il lavoro	*work*
il mestiere; il (proprio) lavoro	*(one's) job/work*
il pensionamento / la pensione (sing.)	*retirement*
il posto [di lavoro]	*position*
la professione	*profession*
la raccomandazione	*recommendation*
la referenza	*reference*
l'ufficio del personale	*personnel department; human resources*

Il posto fisso è una cosa del passato.	*Job security is a thing of the past.*
È uno con molte raccomandazioni.	*He's well connected.*
Il mio ex datore di lavoro mi ha scritto un'ottima lettera di raccomandazione.	*My former employer wrote an excellent letter of recommendation for me.*

*Answer yes (**Y**) or no (**N**) to the following questions.*

1. Trovi i dati personali sul curriculum vitae? _____

2. L'ufficio del personale si occupa delle risposte agli annunci di lavoro? _____

3. Se lavori ancora a settant'anni sei in pensione? _____

4. Se non hai avuto una promozione in dieci anni, stai facendo una buona carriera? _____

5. Se sei disoccupato hai un posto fisso? _____

Professional roles

l(o)'addetto	*delegate; person in charge of a particular task*
l(o)'artigiano	*craftsman*
l(o, a)'assistente sociale	*social worker*
il boss (m. and f.); il [mio] principale (m. and f.); il [mio] capo (m. and f.) / la [mia] capa	*boss*
la capacità	*skill*
il, la consulente	*consultant*
il datore / la datrice di lavoro	*employer*
il, la dirigente; il manager (m. and f.)	*manager*
l(o, a)'esperto di computer	*computer expert*
l(o)'impiegato; il, la dipendente	*employee*
l(o)'ingegnere (m. and f.)	*engineer*
il lavoratore / la lavoratrice; l'operaio	*worker*
il libero professionista	*self-employed professional*
il personale (collective sing.)	*staff*
la segretaria (il segretario, rare)	*secretary*
il tecnico	*technician*

Chi è l'addetto alla manutenzione?	*Who's the person in charge of maintenance?*
Mia moglie fa la libera professionista.	*My wife is self-employed.*

Find the worker described in each of the following definitions.

1. I giornalisti, gli avvocati, i medici sono spesso dei _____ _____.

2. Il responsabile del progetto per costruire il ponte è un _____.

3. La fabbrica in cui aumenta la produzione di lavatrici assume degli _____.

4. La persona che controlla il tuo lavoro è il tuo _____.

5. La persona che ha funzioni dirigenti in un'azienda è un _____.

Describing work

a tempo parziale; part time	*part-time*
a tempo pieno; full time	*full-time*
disoccupato	*unemployed*
freelance	*freelance*
impiegato; che ha un lavoro	*employed*
in prova	*on probation*
specializzato	*skilled*
stagionale	*seasonal*

Gianni è un operaio specializzato. Gianni is a skilled worker.

ESERCIZIO
13·3

Replace the phrases in parentheses in each sentence with the appropriate qualifier from those listed above.

1. Ho un lavoro (da maggio a ottobre) _____ in un hotel.

2. Il mio fidanzato fa il fotografo (per vari giornali e riviste) _____.

3. Lavori (dalle 9 alle 5) _____ _____ _____.

4. Mia sorella lavora (venti ore la settimana) _____ _____ _____.

5. Sono (senza lavoro) _____.

6. Una persona (con un lavoro) _____.

Working conditions

l(a)'amministrazione / il management / l(a)'azienda (sing.)	*management*
l(o)'aumento	*increase*
la busta paga, le buste paga	*paycheck*
il, la collega	*colleague; coworker*
il contratto [di lavoro]	*contract*
le dimissioni (pl.)	*resignation*
le ferie (pl.)	*vacation time*
il lavoratore extracomunitario	*immigrant worker*
l(o)'orario di lavoro	*working hours*
la pensione	*pension*
la promozione	*promotion*
il salario	*wage*
lo sciopero	*strike*
il sindacato	*trade union*
lo stipendio	*salary*
il sussidio di disoccupazione	*unemployment benefits*
le tasse (pl.)	*taxes*
il turno	*shift*

I sindacati e l'azienda hanno interrotto i negoziati.		The trade unions and the firm broke the negotiations.	
Hanno espulso dieci lavoratori extracomunitari.		They expelled ten immigrant workers.	

ESERCIZIO
13·4

Match the first part of each sentence on the left with the appropriate conclusion among those listed on the right.

1. Fa l'operaio specializzato da trent'anni, _____   a. al direttore di dare le dimissioni.

2. I sindacati e l'azienda _____   b. conosce bene il suo mestiere.

3. Il consiglio di amministrazione ha chiesto _____   c. ha un secondo lavoro.

4. Mi sono licenziato perché _____   d. hanno firmato il contratto.

5. Sara ha un buon posto di lavoro, _____   e. ma fa un orario impossibile.

6. Suo marito guadagna poco; per quello _____   f. mi hanno offerto un lavoro migliore.

Work—from beginning to end

andare in pensione	*to retire*
assumere	*to hire*
impiegare; dare lavoro (a)	*to employ*
lavorare (aux. **avere**)	*to work*
licenziare	*to fire*
licenziarsi; lasciare il lavoro	*to quit (one's job)*
prendere le ferie; mettersi in ferie	*to go on vacation*
scioperare (aux. **avere**)	*to strike*
sfruttare	*to exploit*

Papà va in pensione tra due anni.	*Dad will retire in two years.*
Prendiamo le ferie a luglio?	*Shall we go on vacation in July?*

ESERCIZIO
13·5

Complete the following sentences by choosing from the verbs listed above.

1. Gli extracomunitari costretti a lavorare dodici ore al giorno sono _____.

2. I lavoratori hanno deciso di _____ perché la ditta non ha accettato le proposte del sindacato.

3. La mia azienda è in crisi. Temo che verrò _____.

4. Quando una persona prende dei giorni di vacanza pagati, _____ _____ _____.

5. Quando smetti di lavorare dopo trent'anni di lavoro, _____ _____ _____.

Technology at work

Nowadays most people work at their desks, rather than on the factory floor. Telephones and computers dominate the office environment. Italians start work between 8 and 9 in the morning, take their lunch hour in a nearby **bar** or **caffè**, and crawl home fighting traffic jams between 6 and 7 P.M.

l(a)'agenda	*daily planner; notebook*
la casella vocale; il voice mail	*voice mail*
il cellulare; il telefonino	*cell(ular) phone*
il centralino	*switchboard*
il fax	*fax machine*
l(o)'interno	*extension*
il messaggio	*message*
il numero di telefono; il numero telefonico	*telephone number*
il numero verde	*toll-free number*
l(o)'operatore/l(a)'operatrice	*operator*
la scrivania	*desk*
la segreteria telefonica	*answering machine*
il senzafili, i senzafili; il cordless	*cordless*

Le ho lasciato dieci messagi sul voice mail.	*I left ten messages on her voice mail.*
Se chiami un numero verde non paghi la telefonata.	*If you call an 800 number, you don't pay for the phone call.*

ESERCIZIO 13·6

Complete the following sentences by choosing among the nouns listed above.

1. Ho quindici _____ sulla mia segreteria telefonica!

2. Il mio numero di telefono in ufficio è 02.388.54.000, _____ 312.

3. Può mandare quel documento all'avvocato con il _____, Signora.

4. Si prega di lasciare un messaggio dopo il _____ _____.

5. Avete raggiunto gli uffici delle Società Telefonica Vodafone. Risponde l(a)'_____ numero 54.

The mail

la busta	*envelope*
la cassetta delle lettere	*mailbox*
la consegna	*delivery*
il corriere (m. and f.)	*courier*
il destinatario	*recipient*
il francobollo / la marca da bollo / il timbro	*stamp*
la lettera	*letter*
il mittente	*sender*

il pacco	package; packet
il, la portalettere; i portalettere	mail carrier
la posta	mail
[la] posta aerea	air mail
l(o)'ufficio postale	post office

Ci vuole un francobollo da €1,50.
Ho messo la lettera nella cassetta delle lettere.

You need a €1.50 stamp.
I put the letter in the mailbox.

ESERCIZIO 13·7

Complete the following sentences by choosing from the words listed above. Some sentences require the use of a **preposizione articolata**. The preposition required is suggested in parentheses.

1. Il corriere garantisce _____ del pacco entro le 12 di domani.

2. Il francobollo si incolla _____ _____. (**su**)

3. Sul francobollo mancava _____ dell'ufficio postale.

4. La cartolina viene imbucata _____ _____ _____ _____. (**in**)

5. Le lettere vengono consegnate _____ _____. (**da**)

Communicating

comporre/fare il numero	to dial
firmare	to sign
mandare	to send
mandare un fax	to fax
restare in linea; attendere [in linea]	to hold
riattaccare	to hang up
ricevere	to receive
richiamare	to call again
spedire	to mail; to ship
squillare	to ring

Il telefono ha squillato per mezz'ora.
Devi aver fatto il numero sbagliato.

The telephone rang for half an hour.
You must've dialed the wrong number.

ESERCIZIO 13·8

In the following sentences, replace the words in parentheses with the appropriate verb from those listed above.

1. Devi (mettere il tuo nome) _____ nello spazio indicato.

2. Hai (chiamato) _____ a tua figlia?

3. Il telefono (suona) _____ da dieci minuti.

4. Hai detto a Laura di (telefonare un'altra volta) _____?

5. Non (mettere giù la cornetta del telefono) _____! Non ti ho detto tutto!

6. Può (aspettare al telefono) _____ _____ _____, Signore?

Describing communications and time at work

al lavoro	*at work*
al telefono	*on the phone*
è caduta la linea	*be cut off*
fragile	*fragile*
in attesa	*on hold*
in ferie; in vacanza	*on vacation*
in linea	*online*
in mutua	*on sick leave*
in permesso	*(to take) time off*
in stanza	*at one's desk*
in ufficio	*at the office*
per posta	*by mail*
per telefono	*by phone*
urgente	*urgent*

Non è in stanza. Vuole lasciare un messaggio?	*She's not at her desk. Do you want to leave a message?*
Marina si è messa in mutua.	*Marina called in sick.*

ESERCIZIO
13·9

Complete the following sentences with a synonym that conveys the same idea expressed in each of the situations described below.

1. Sul pacco c'è scritto di fare attenzione. → Il contenuto è _____.

2. Il tuo collega non viene in ufficio perché ha l'influenza. → È _____ _____.

3. Il tuo direttore vuole che tu lo richiami non appena possibile. → È un messaggio _____.

4. La tua collega vuole andare a riposarsi al mare. → Vuole andare _____ _____.

5. La maestra di tuo figlio ti ha cercato nella ditta dove lavori. → Sei _____ _____.

6. Chiami una ditta per ordinare dei prodotti per l'ufficio. → Li ordini _____ _____.

Banking

Modern banking was invented in Italy in the late Middle Ages, as witnessed by many words, starting with *bank* which is related to the Italian word **banco** (*bench*). In the last twenty years average citizens have begun to abandon traditional saving practices in favor of investing in the stock market. As a consequence, in Italian newspapers and websites you will find English words such as *derivatives, futures, stock options,* and *insider trading.*

Several terms relevant to financial and banking operations (*to buy, to sell, cost, price,* etc.) have already been listed in Unit 6.

gli affari (pl.); **il business** (sing.) / **l(a)'attività**	*business*
l(o, a)'agente di borsa	*trader*
l(o, a)'analista [finanziario]	*(financial) analyst*
l(a)'azione	*share*
l(o, a)'azionista	*shareholder; stockholder*
il capitale	*capital*
il crollo; il crac	*crash; crack*
la dichiarazione dei redditi	*tax return*
il dividendo	*dividend*
la finanza (sing.)	*finance*
il guadagno; i profitti (pl.); **le entrate** (pl.)	*earnings*
l(o)'imbroglio	*rip-off*
l(o)'insider trading	*insider trading*
l(o)'investimento	*investment*
l(o)'investitore (m. and f.)	*investor*
il listino di borsa / la borsa (valori)	*stock exchange (list)*
l'obbligazione; il titolo	*bond*
le perdita	*loss*
la prestazione; la performance	*performance*
il profitto; il rendimento	*profit; return*
il rischio	*risk*
la speculazione	*speculation*
il tasso di interesse	*interest rate*

La nostra azienda è quotata in borsa.	*Our firm is listed on the stock exchange.*
Gli azionisti non approvarono il bilancio.	*The shareholders didn't approve the budget.*
Il nonno investe solo in titoli di stato.	*Grandpa invests only in state bonds.*

ESERCIZIO
13·10

In the following series, mark the word that does not belong.

1. a. i profitti   b. i dividendi   c. gli investimenti   d. l'imbroglio

2. a. l'analista   b. il crac   c. le perdite   d. il rischio

3. a. il business   b. la finanza   c. la prestazione   d. la dichiarazione dei redditi

4. a. il rischio   b. il capitale   c. l'agente di borsa   d. il rendimento

Investing

finanziare	*to finance*
giocare in borsa (aux. **avere**)	*to play the stock market*
guadagnare	*to earn; to gain*
investire	*to invest*
perdere	*to lose*
rendere	*to return; to yield*
rischiare	*to risk*
scommettere	*to bet*
speculare (aux. **avere**)	*to speculate*

Lucia ha investito bene i suoi risparmi.   *Lucia invested her savings well.*
Quanto ha reso quel fondo?   *How much did that investment fund yield?*

Answer the following questions with full sentences.

EXAMPLE   I tuoi titoli di stato hanno reso il 3 per cento. Hanno reso molto o poco?

   <u>Hanno reso poco.</u>

1. Delle azioni che hanno reso il 5 per cento hanno reso molto o poco?

   _____

2. Fornisci il capitale di rischio per un nuovo business. Lo stai finanziando o stai speculando?

   _____

3. Hai preso in prestito 20.000 euro per giocare in borsa. Stai rischiando?

   _____

4. Quando il prezzo del petrolio sale del 30 per cento in due giorni, qualcuno sta speculando?

   _____

5. Se hai investito 50.000 euro e dopo sei mesi nei hai 55.000, hai avuto un profitto o una perdita?

   _____

Banking transactions

l(o)'accredito; il credito	*credit*
la banca	*bank*
il banchiere (m. and f.)	*banker*
il bilancio; il budget	*budget*
il cambio	*exchange*
il conto	*account*
il debito	*debt*

il deposito	deposit
il dollaro	dollar
l(o)'estratto conto	statement
l(o)'euro	euro
l(o)'impiegato di banca	bank employee; bank clerk
la percentuale	percentage
il prelievo	withdrawal
il prestito	loan
i risparmi (pl.)	savings
il saldo; la bilancia	balance
la valuta	currency

Vorrei cambiare 100 euro in dollari.	*I'd like to change 100 euro to dollars.*
Le spese sul conto sono del 2 per cento.	*Account charges are 2 percent.*

ESERCIZIO
13·12

Match the first part of each sentence on the left with the appropriate complementary part among those listed on the right.

1. Ho fatto un prelievo ieri _____

2. Il mio conto in banca rende _____

3. La banca ha concesso un prestito _____

4. Puoi passare al bancomat _____

5. Signora, come vuole investire _____

6. Vuole il deposito automatico dello stipendio _____

a. alla ditta.

b. a prelevare dei soldi?

c. dal nostro conto.

d. i suoi risparmi?

e. il 2 per cento!

f. sul suo conto?

Verbs

accreditare; versare	*to credit*
addebitare; prelevare	*to withdraw*
andare in / fare bancarotta; fallire	*to go bankrupt*
cambiare (i soldi)	*to (ex)change (money)*
depositare; versare	*to deposit*
girare	*to endorse*
imprestare; dare in prestito	*to loan*
prendere a/in prestito	*to borrow; to take out a loan*
risparmiare; fare economia	*to save*

La rata del mutuo viene addebitata sul mio conto.	*The mortgage payment is withdrawn from my checking account.*
Maria ha preso in prestito 3.000 euro.	*Maria took out a 3,000 euro loan.*

In the following sentences replace the words in parentheses with the appropriate verb from those listed above. Use the present indicative or the present perfect.

1. Abbiamo (ottenuto) _____ _____ _____ dei soldi dalla banca per comprare la casa.

2. (Diamo) _____ 10.000 euro al nostro amico che ce li restituisce fra un anno.

3. I miei zii hanno (dovuto chiudere la ditta) _____ _____ perché avevano troppi debiti.

4. La mamma è andata in banca a (vendere dei dollari e comprare degli euro) _____ _____ _____.

5. Ogni mese la mia amica Marta (guadagna 2.000 euro, ma ne spende solo 1.500) _____!

6. Marina va in banca a (prendere) _____ 500 euro dal conto.

The economy

l(a)'azienda; la società; la ditta	company; firm
il benessere	affluence
il capitalismo	capitalism
la catena di montaggio	assembly line
il commercio	commerce; trade
la concorrenza	competition
la crisi	crisis
la domanda (sing.)	demand
l(a)'economia (sing.)	economy; economics
la fabbrica	factory
l(a)'industria (sing.) / il settore industriale	industry; industrial sector
il monopolio	monopoly
la multinazionale	multinational company
il padrone / la padrona	owner; boss
l(a)'offerta (sing.)	supply
la povertà	poverty
la produttività	productivity
la ricchezza	wealth
la società per azioni (S.p.A.); la corporation	corporation
il socio (in affari)	business partner
il sottosviluppo	underdevelopment
lo sviluppo	development
l'uomo d'affari / la donna d'affari	businessman/businesswoman

La sua azienda ha fatto fallimento.	His firm went bankrupt.
Adesso alla catena di montaggio ci sono i robot.	Nowadays there are robots on the assembly line.

Complete the following sentences by choosing from the words listed above.

1. Gli operai lavorano in _____.

2. Ho una ditta con tre altri _____.

3. I _____ portano alla crescita dei prezzi.

4. Mia madre è padrona di una ditta: è una _____ _____.

5. Quando la _____ sale i salari e gli stipendi crescono.

6. Si usano i _____ alla catena di montaggio.

7. Una _____ ha fabbriche e uffici in vari paesi.

Describing the economy

arretrato	*backward; underdeveloped*
benestante	*well-off*
economico	*economic; economical*
efficiente	*efficient*
in via di sviluppo	*developing*
inefficiente	*inefficient*
inutile	*useless*
no-profit; nonprofit	*nonprofit; not for profit*
povero	*poor*
privato	*private*
pubblico; statale	*public; government-related*
ricco	*rich; wealthy*
utile	*useful*

*Decide if the following statements are true (**T**) or false (**F**).*

1. L'Italia è un paese arretrato. _____

2. Haiti è un paese arretrato. _____

3. È meglio essere poveri che benestanti. _____

4. È meglio essere efficienti che inefficienti. _____

5. Gli Stati Uniti non hanno un settore nonprofit. _____

6. Il Vietnam è un paese in via di sviluppo. _____

Trade

esportare	*to export*
fabbricare; fare	*to make*
fornire	*to supply*
gestire; dirigere	*to manage*
importare	*to import*
privatizzare	*to privatize*
produrre	*to produce*
scambiare; commerciare	*to trade*
usare; utilizzare	*to use*

Il dottor Pini dirige bene la ditta.	*Dr. Pini manages the company well.*
Il paese importa più di quanto esporta.	*The country imports more than it exports.*

ESERCIZIO
13·16

Answer the following questions by choosing from the options given below each of them.

1. Che paese esporta petrolio?
   a. l'Italia　　　　　b. la Francia　　　　　c. l'Arabia Saudita

2. Che paese esporta scarpe, abiti e mobili?
   a. la Grecia　　　　b. l'Italia　　　　　c. l'Iran

3. Chi fabbrica delle ottime automobili?
   a. il Giappone　　　b. la Russia　　　　c. l'India

4. Chi ha il compito di ridistribuire le risorse di un paese?
   a. l'ONU　　　　　b. lo stato　　　　　c. il Fondo Monetario Internazionale

Government, politics, and society

Italy has been a Republic since 1946, after the fall of Mussolini's fascist regime and the end of World War II. Its government, like the American one, is based on the separation of the legislative, executive, and judicial powers. But its political system and culture are very different: Italy is a country of many parties which give voice to the many souls of the Italian people. Political participation is intense, which makes governing harder.

l(o, a)'abitante	*inhabitant*
la bandiera	*flag*
la carta d'identità, le carte di identità	*identity card*
la cittadinanza	*citizenship*
il cittadino	*citizen*
la frontiera	*frontier*
l(o, a)'immigrante	*immigrant*
il patriottismo	*patriotism*
il permesso di soggiorno	*residence permit*
la popolazione	*population*
il popolo / la nazione	*people*
lo stato	*state*
lo stato nazionale	*nation-state*
lo straniero	*foreigner*

La bandiera italiana è verde, bianca e rossa.	*The Italian flag is green, white, and red.*
Sei di cittadinanza italiana?	*Do you have Italian citizenship?*

ESERCIZIO
14·1

Complete the following sentences by choosing from the words listed above.

1. La _____ americana è a stelle e strisce.

2. Per abitare legalmente in Italia, bisogna avere
   il _____ _____ _____.

3. Se sei nato in Canada, hai la _____ canadese.

4. Quando si va in un altro stato si passa la _____.

5. Se vieni a lavorare in Italia dal Congo sei un _____.

6. Una persona che viene da un altro paese è uno _____.

Government institutions

la burocrazia	*bureaucracy*
il consiglio dei ministri	*council of ministers; cabinet*
il comune	*city; town; municipality*
la camera dei deputati	*chamber of deputies; house of representatives*
la costituzione	*constitution*
la democrazia	*democracy*
la dittatura	*dictatorship*
il governo	*government*
l(a)'istituzione	*institution*
il ministero	*ministry*
la monarchia	*monarchy*
il parlamento	*parliament*
la provincia	*province*
la regione	*region*
la repubblica	*republic*
il senato	*senate*
lo stato assistenziale; il welfare	*welfare state*

L'Italia è divisa in 21 regioni.	*Italy is divided into 21 regions.*
La Costituzione è la legge fondamentale dello stato.	*The Constitution is the fundamental law of the state.*

ESERCIZIO 14·2

In the following series, mark the word that does not belong.

1. a. la monarchia   b. la repubblica   c. la dittatura   d. la provincia

2. a. lo stato assistenziale   b. il parlamento   c. la camera dei deputati   d. il senato

3. a. il comune   b. la provincia   c. il ministero   d. la regione

4. a. il governo   b. il comune   c. il parlamento   d. il consiglio dei ministri

Government officials

l(a)'autorità	*authority*
il deputato; il, la parlamentare; il, la rappresentante	*representative (in Congress); member of Parliament*
il funzionario (m. and f.) / la funzionaria (dello stato)	*civil servant*
il governatore	*governor*
il, la leader; i, le leader(s)	*leader*
il ministro / la ministra	*minister; secretary*
il presidente	*president*
il primo ministro (m. and f.); il, la premier	*prime minister*
il principe / la principessa	*prince/princess*
il re / la regina	*king/queen*

| il senatore / la senatrice | senator |
| il sindaco (m. and f.) | mayor |

Alla sfilata sono intervenute le autorità.
È una funzionaria della regione
  delle Marche.

The authorities came to the parade.
She is a civil servant for the Marche region.

ESERCIZIO
14·3

Complete the following sentences by choosing from the words listed above.

1. I membri del Parlamento sono i _____ e i _____.

2. In Italia, il capo del governo è il _____ _____.

3. In una monarchia, il _____ o la _____ è il capo dello stato.

4. In una repubblica, il capo dello stato è il _____.

5. La maggiore autorità in un comune è il _____.

ESERCIZIO
14·4

Answer yes (Y) or no (N) to the following questions.

1. I deputati costituiscono il senato? _____

2. I funzionari dello stato lavorano nella burocrazia? _____

3. Il primo ministro è il capo del governo? _____

4. La Gran Bretagna è una repubblica? _____

5. Se non sei nato negli Stati Uniti, puoi diventare presidente? _____

6. Una regina è una funzionaria della burocrazia? _____

Governing

il consenso	consensus; consent
la corruzione	corruption
il dissenso	dissent
la leadership	leadership
la legittimità	legitimacy
la maggioranza	majority
la minoranza	minority
l(a)'opposizione	opposition
la politica (sing.)	politics
il provvedimento / i provvedimenti;	policy
le politiche	

la questione / il problema, i problemi	*issue*
la riforma	*reform*
lo scandalo	*scandal*

Non si governa senza maggioranza.	*You can't govern without the majority.*
Le nuove politiche fiscali sono impopolari.	*The new fiscal policies are unpopular.*

ESERCIZIO
14·5

Match the first part of each sentence on the left with the appropriate complementary part on the right.

1. Il consenso dei cittadini è essenziale _____   a. la riforma delle pensioni.

2. Il Ministro della Difesa ha dato _____   b. ha fatto una conferenza stampa.

3. Il nuovo governo ha promesso di fare _____   c. contro la legge sull'immigrazione.

4. L'opposizione ha votato _____   d. le dimissioni a causa di uno scandalo.

5. La portavoce del Primo Ministro _____   e. per governare in democrazia.

Verbs

approvare	*to approve*
dimostrare (contro) (aux. **avere**)	*to demonstrate against*
eleggere	*to elect*
governare	*to govern; to rule*
impadronirsi di	*to take over*
partecipare (a) (aux. **avere**)	*to participate (in)*
passare una legge	*to pass a bill*
presentarsi candidato (a)	*to run (for)*
protestare (contro) (aux. **avere**)	*to protest (against)*
votare (per/contro) (aux. **avere**)	*to vote (for/against)*

Mia sorella si presenta candidata al Senato.	*My sister will run for a seat in the Senate.*
Milioni di persone hanno dimostrato contro la guerra.	*Millions of people demonstrated against the war.*

ESERCIZIO
14·6

Provide the verb that conveys the ideas expressed in the following sentences. Use the infinitive.

1. Cercare di farsi eleggere a una carica pubblica. _____

2. Dare il proprio consenso a una politica, una legge o un provvedimento. _____

3. Esprimere con forza la propria opinione contro una legge o un provvedimento. _____

4. Essere un cittadino attivo che vota alle elezioni, esprime le proprie opinioni, ecc. _____

5. Scegliere una persona per una carica attraverso una votazione. _____

Describing government

a favore (di)	*in favor (of)*
carismatico	*charismatic*
civile	*civil*
contrario (a)	*opposed (to)*
dittatoriale	*dictatorial*
domestico; interno	*domestic*
favorevole (a)	*favorable (to)*
internazionale; estero	*foreign*
politico; di parte	*political*
pubblico	*public*
statale	*government-related; state-related*

I deputati hanno espresso voto contrario.	*The members of the Chamber of Deputies voted against.*
È una in gamba, ma non è carismatica.	*She's capable, but she isn't charismatic.*

ESERCIZIO
14·7

Replace the words in parentheses in the following sentences with the appropriate qualifier from those listed above.

1. I deputati hanno votato (per) _____ la legge che stabilisce il salario minimo.

2. Il governo del generale Pinochet è stato per molti anni un governo (che non permetteva libere elezioni o la libertà di stampa, di parola, di assemblea, ecc.) _____.

3. Il governo inglese (non) è (a favore dell') _____ _____euro.

4. In Italia, l'assistenza medica è un servizio (gestito dallo stato) _____.

5. La decisione di intervenire in Iraq è una questione (che va al di là dei confini del paese) _____.

Elections

la campagna	*campaign*
il candidato	*candidate*
il dibattito	*debate*
l(o)'elettore/l(a)'elettrice	*voter*
l(a)'elezione	*election*
le primarie (pl.)	*primaries*
il referendum	*referendum*
la scheda; la votazione	*ballot*
il seggio [elettorale]	*polling station*
il seggio [in parlamento]	*seat*
il sondaggio post-elettorale; l(o)'exit poll	*exit poll*
il voto / la votazione	*vote*

Chi ha vinto le elezioni?	*Who won the elections?*
Il mio seggio è alla scuola media.	*My polling station is at the middle school.*

Complete the following passage with the appropriate words.

Con la nomina a speaker della Camera dei (1) _____, Nancy Pelosi diventa una delle (2) _____ di origine (3) _____ che si sono affermate in (4) _____. La sua recente (5) _____ nel distretto no. 8 della California con l'80 per cento dei (6) _____ dimostra la sua popolarità. Come speaker, Nancy Pelosi può definire l'agenda dei dibattiti e assegnare le proposte di (7) _____ alle commissioni della Camera. Questo significa che potrà bloccare una (8) _____, oppure facilitarne l'approvazione assegnandola ad una commissione favorevole. Nancy Pelosi è attiva da anni in campo democratico in tutti i settori, ma la sua battaglia principale è legata ai (9) _____ civili.

Political ideologies

la base [del partito]	*(political) base; rank and file*
il centro (sing.)	*center*
la destra	*right*
l(a)'eguaglianza (sing.); **l'uguaglianza** (sing.)	*equality*
la giustizia; l(a)'equità	*fairness*
l(a)'ideologia	*ideology*
la libertà	*freedom; liberty*
l(a)'opinione pubblica	*public opinion*
il partito	*(political) party*
la sinistra	*left*
l(a)'unione	*union*

Il centro ha sempre dominato la politica italiana.	*The center has always dominated Italian politics.*
La base del partito ha scelto un nuovo segretario.	*The rank and file chose a new party secretary.*

In both Italian and English most words referring to ideologies end in **-ismo** (*-ism*): **populismo** (*populism*), **liberalismo** (*liberalism*), etc. We can also form nouns and adjectives by modifying a noun with **-ismo**: **il populismo** → **il, la popul-ista** (*popul-ist*).

From **democrazia** (*democracy*), though, comes the adjective and noun **[il] democratico** (*democratic; democrat*). *Nazi* translates to **nazista**, and *nazism* to **nazismo**.

*Add **-ismo** then **-ista** to the following words. Translate them into English.*

1. centr-o _____

2. comun-e _____

3. estrem-o _____

4. fasci-o _____

5. femmin-ile _____

6. fondamental-e _____

7. progress-o _____

8. social-e _____

ESERCIZIO
14·10

*Add **-ismo** to the following words and translate them into English.*

1. anarch-ia _____

2. conservator-e _____

3. liberal-e _____

4. local-e _____

5. moderat-o _____

6. radical-e _____

Civil rights

Italians are vocal participants in the movements and debates that characterize civil society: in favor of and against abortion, gay marriage, stem cell research, the environment, and so forth. They work in volunteer organizations in great numbers. One issue seems to find them overwhelmingly in agreement: their opposition to the death penalty.

la classe media	*middle class*
la classe operaia	*working class*
la comunità	*community*
la dimostrazione	*demonstration*
la discriminazione	*discrimination*
la diversità (sing.)	*diversity*
l(a)'intolleranza	*intolerance*
le masse (pl.)	*masses*
la minoranza etnica	*ethnic minority*
il movimento antiglobalizzazione/ antiglobal	*antiglobal(ization) movement*
la privacy	*privacy*
il razzismo	*racism*
il, la senzatetto, i senzatetto (m. and f.)	*homeless person*
la società civile	*civil society*
la solidarietà	*solidarity*
la tolleranza	*tolerance*
la tradizione	*tradition*

| il valore | value |
| il volontario | volunteer |

| Hanno aperto un rifugio per i senzatetto. | *They opened a shelter for the homeless.* |
| La tolleranza è un valore nelle democrazie. | *Tolerance is a value in democracies.* |

Throughout this book we have encountered adjectives ending in **-ale** (*-al* in English), which convey the meaning *pertaining to*, or *typical of*. These adjectives are formed by adding that suffix to certain nouns:

la costituzione (*constitution*) → **costituzionale** (*constitutional*)
il sesso (*sex*) → **sessuale, transessuale, asessuale**, etc. (*sexual, transsexual, asexual*)
la nazione (*nation*) → **nazionale** (*national*)

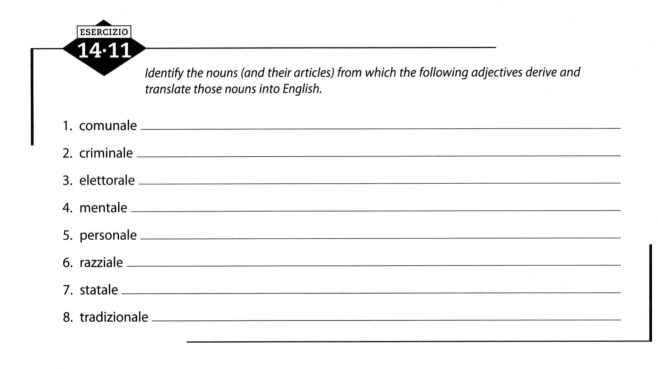

ESERCIZIO
14·11

Identify the nouns (and their articles) from which the following adjectives derive and translate those nouns into English.

1. comunale _____

2. criminale _____

3. elettorale _____

4. mentale _____

5. personale _____

6. razziale _____

7. statale _____

8. tradizionale _____

Crime

In Italy, the most serious offenses are committed by organized crime: the **camorra**, active in Naples and its surroundings, and the **mafia**, more active in Sicily. Apart from a wave of kidnappings for ransom between the 1970s and the 1990s, Italy was otherwise a country of petty crimes, rarely carried out by people with weapons. More recently, criminal activities (trafficking of women and children as slave labor, forced prostitution, robberies, thefts, and so forth) have been growing together with the increase in immigrant population. But crimes of passion committed by family members are also on the rise.

l(o)'abuso	*abuse*
il crimine organizzato	*organized crime*
il delitto	*crime*
il furto d'identità	*identity theft*
il ladro	*thief*
il mafioso	*mafioso*
la molestia	*harassment*
l(o, a)'omicida, gli omicidi; l(o)'assassino	*murderer*

l(o)'omicidio	*murder*
la pornografia	*pornography*
il rapinatore, la rapinatrice	*robber*
il riciclaggio di denaro sporco	*money laundering*
il riscatto	*ransom*
lo stupratore (m.)	*rapist*
lo stupro	*rape*
il traffico	*traffic; trafficking*
la vittima	*victim*

Ho inoltrato un reclamo contro il mio capo per molestie sessuali.	*I filed a complaint against my boss for sexual harassment.*
Hanno identificato l'assassino grazie all'esame del DNA.	*They identified the murderer thanks to a DNA test.*

ESERCIZIO
14·12

Complete the following sentences by choosing from the words listed below each item.

1. Il _____ è entrato in casa dalla finestra.
   a. ladro   b. mafioso   c. stupratore

2. L'Internet ha reso molto più facile il _____.
   a. traffico di bambini   b. furto d'identità   c. delitto

3. Spesso lo _____ è una membro della famiglia della vittima.
   a. mafioso   b. rapinatore   c. stupratore

4. Non si può giustificare la _____ che usa i bambini.
   a. pornografia   b. molestia   c. abuso

5. Quel famoso businessman è diventato ricco grazie al _____.
   a. riscatto   b. riciclaggio di   c. furto di identità
                             denaro sporco

Committing crimes

commettere un omicidio	*to murder*
corrompere	*to bribe*
danneggiare; fare del male (a)	*to harm*
denunciare	*to turn in*
evadere	*to escape*
molestare	*to harass*
rapinare; derubare (qualcuno)	*to rob (a person)*
rapire; sequestrare	*to kidnap*
rubare (qualcosa a qualcuno)	*to steal (something from someone)*
sospettare	*to suspect*
stuprare	*to rape*

Fermatelo! Mi ha derubato!	*Stop him! He robbed me!*
Fermatelo! Mi ha rubato il portafoglio!	*Stop him! He stole my wallet!*

Provide the verb that defines the actions described in the first part of each of the following sentences.

1. Se qualcuno preleva dei soldi dal conto di un altro senza il suo consenso, lo _____.

2. Se sai che qualcuno ha commesso un reato e vai alla polizia, lo _____.

3. Se si causa la morte di un'altra persona volontariamente, si _____.

4. Se il direttore cerca di obbligare la segretaria ad avere una relazione con lui, la _____.

5. Se un gruppo tiene prigioniera una persona per ottenere dei soldi, l'ha _____.

The criminal justice system

The Italian legal and judicial system, based on codified law derived from Roman law, is very different from the American one. Criminal investigations are led by a magistrate overseeing the **Polizia Giudiziaria** (*police*), with help from the **Carabinieri**, a military police corps, and the **Guardia di Finanza** (*Customs and Border Police*).

l(a)'accusa (sing.)	*prosecution*
l(o)'avvocato (m. and f.)	*lawyer*
il carcere	*jail*
il commissario (m.and f.); l(o)'ispettore/ l(a)'ispettrice (di polizia)	*(police) detective; inspector*
il, la complice	*accomplice*
il, la criminale; il, la delinquente	*criminal*
la difesa (sing.)	*defense*
il diritto	*right*
il dovere	*duty; obligation*
l(o)'ergastolo; la condanna a vita	*life sentence*
l(a)'evidenza, la prova	*evidence; proof*
il giudice (m.and f.)	*judge*
la giuria	*jury*
la giustizia	*justice*
l(a)'inchiesta; l(a)'investigazione	*investigation*
l(a)'ingiustizia	*unjust/unfair deed*
la legge	*law*
la pena di morte	*death penalty*
il poliziotto (m. and f.) / la poliziotta (rare)	*police officer*
il processo	*trial*
il sospettato	*suspect*
il sospetto	*suspicion*
il, la testimone	*witness*
il tribunale / la corte	*court*

L'Italia non ha la pena di morte.	*Italy doesn't have the death penalty.*
La giuria l'ha dichiarato innocente.	*The jury acquitted him.*
La testimone ha mentito in tribunale.	*The witness lied in court.*

The components of the following sentences have been assembled incorrectly. Find the right sequence.

1. I poliziotti non hanno convinto la giuria.

_____

2. In Italia la testimone è protetta dalla polizia.

_____

3. Le prove presentate dall'accusa hanno arrestato il sospettato.

_____

4. Non ha un soldo: non esiste la pena di morte.

_____

5. Per paura della mafia, non può prendersi un avvocato.

_____

Prosecuting criminals

accusare	to charge
arrestare	to arrest
assolvere	to acquit
confessare	to confess
difendere	to defend
essere colpa di qualcuno	to be someone's fault
fare causa (a)	to sue
permettere	to permit; to allow
processare	to try
proibire	to forbid
rilasciare	to release

Non è colpa mia se i ladri sono entrati nel magazzino!	It's not my fault if the robbers broke into the warehouse!
Il giudice lo ha condannato a trent'anni.	The judge sentenced him to thirty years.

Provide the verbs defined in the sentences listed below. Use the infinitive.

1. Ammettere con il giudice di aver commesso un reato. _____

2. Consentire a qualcuno di fare qualcosa. _____

3. Decidere che una persona è innocente. _____

4. Liberare una persona dopo averla sospettata ingiustamente. _____

5. Mettere qualcuno in carcere. _____

International relations and war

gli affari internazionali/esteri (pl.)	*foreign affairs*
l(o)'ambasciatore (m. and f.) /	
l(a)'ambasciatrice	*ambassador*
la battaglia	*battle*
il colonialismo	*colonialism*
il colpo di stato; il golpe	*coup d'état*
il console (m. and f.)	*consul*
la diplomazia	*diplomacy*
il disarmo	*disarmament*
la forza	*force*
il genocidio	*genocide*
la guerra	*war*
la guerriglia	*guerrilla war*
l(o)'imperialismo	*imperialism*
le informazioni (pl.); l(a)'intelligence	*intelligence*
il nemico	*enemy; foe*
l(o)'olocausto	*holocaust*
la pace	*peace*
il pericolo	*danger; hazard*
il potere / la potenza	*power*
la pulizia etnica	*ethnic cleansing*
la sconfitta	*defeat*
la sicurezza (sing. in this context)	*security*
la spia	*spy*
la strategia	*strategy*
la tattica	*tactic*
il, la terrorista	*terrorist*
la violenza	*violence*
la vittoria	*victory*

Il terrorismo è una forma di guerra non convenzionale.	*Terrorism is a nonconventional kind of war.*
Che differenza c'è tra genocidio e pulizia etnica?	*What's the difference between genocide and ethnic cleansing?*

ESERCIZIO
14·16

In the following series, mark the word that does not belong.

1. a. il battaglia   b. la guerra   c. la forza   d. le informazioni

2. a. il terrorista   b. il nemico   c. la tattica   d. la spia

3. a. la vittoria   b. l'olocausto   c. il genocidio   d. la pulizia etnica

4. a. il golpe   b. il colonialismo   c. l'imperialismo   d. la pace

5. a. la violenza   b. la battaglia   c. la strategia   d. la guerriglia

Waging war

arrendersi (a)	*to surrender (to)*
catturare	*to capture*
combattere	*to fight; to combat*
dirottare	*to hijack*
fare la guerra	*to wage war*
fare la pace	*to make peace*
ferire	*to wound*
obbedire (a) (aux. avere)	*to obey*
prendere/tenere in ostaggio	*to hold hostage*
proteggere	*to protect*
sconfiggere	*to defeat*
soffrire la fame	*to starve*
sopravvivere	*to survive*
torturare	*to torture*
tradire	*to betray*
uccidere	*to kill*

Il nemico si è arreso.	*The enemy surrendered.*
Hanno dirottato un aereo.	*They hijacked an airplane.*

ESERCIZIO
14·17

Complete the following sentences choosing among the verbs listed above.

1. Fare la guerra è l'opposto di _____ .

2. I soldati devono _____ agli ordini.

3. Quando il nemico riesce a farti del male, ma non a ucciderti, ti ha _____.

4. Quando prendi dei nemici prigionieri li _____.

5. Quando riveli al nemico dei segreti di stato _____ il paese.

6. Quando vieni sconfitto ti _____.

Weapons and combatants

l(a)'arma, le armi	*weapon*
l(a)'arma di distruzione di massa	*weapon of mass destruction*
la bomba	*bomb*
l(o)'esercito	*army*
la flotta	*fleet*
le forze armate (pl.)	*military*
il fucile	*rifle*
il generale (m. and f.)	*general*
il missile	*missile*
la mitragliatrice	*machine gun*
la pistola	*pistol; gun*

il soldato / la soldatessa	soldier
la testata nucleare	nuclear warhead
la trafficante d(i)'armi	arms dealer
l(o)'ufficiale (m. and f.)	officer; official

| Le armi chimiche sono armi di distruzione di massa. | Chemical weapons are weapons of mass destruction. |
| Hanno arrestato il trafficante d'armi. | They arrested the arms dealer. |

ESERCIZIO
14·18

Match each noun on the left with the most plausible complementary noun among those listed on the right.

1. il missile _____   a. i soldati

2. l'ufficiale _____   b. il generale

3. la flotta _____   c. la nave

4. le forze armate _____   d. le mitragliatrici

5. le pistole _____   e. le testate nucleari

Human rights and international aid

l(o)'aiuto	aid
l(o)'asilo (politico)	(political) asylum
la carestia	famine
i diritti umani (pl.)	human rights
l(a)'emergenza	emergency
l(a)'evacuazione	evacuation
il pacifismo	pacifism
il rifugiato; lo sfollato	refugee
la schiavitù	slavery
il soccorso	relief
la tortura	torture
la violazione	violation

| I rifugiati hanno ottenuto asilo politico. | The refugees were granted political asylum. |
| Sto scrivendo un libro sui diritti umani. | I'm writing a book on human rights. |

Complete each sentence with the word from the above list that best completes it.

1. L'ideologia contraria a tutte le guerre si chiama _____.

2. Le Convenzioni di Ginevra vietano la _____.

3. La guerra civile ha creato un milione di _____.

4. Le Nazioni Unite hanno il compito di difendere i _____.

5. Le persone perseguitate nel loro paese chiedono _____.

Nature and the environment

The ancients understood the difference between stars and planets, and they gave us the names of the planets of the solar system, which they believed had a motionless Earth at its center. Italian astronomers and scientists, Galileo in particular, played a key role in revolutionizing that interpretation and giving us the image of the universe which we now take for granted.

l(a)'astronomia	astronomy
il cannocchiale; il telescopio	telescope
la cometa	comet
la galassia	galaxy
Giove	Jupiter
la luna; la Luna	moon; Moon
Marte	Mars
la massa	mass
la materia	matter
Mercurio	Mercury
il meteorite	meteorite
Nettuno	Neptune
il pianeta, i pianeti	planet
Plutone (pianeta mamo)	Pluto (dwarf planet)
Saturno	Saturn
il sistema solare	solar system
il sole; il Sole	sun; Sun
lo spazio	space
la terra; la Terra	earth; Earth
l'universo	universe
Urano	Uranus
Venere	Venus
il vuoto	vacuum

Un meteorite causò l'estinzione dei dinosauri.	A meteorite led to the extinction of the dinosaurs.
C'è luna piena stanotte.	There will be a full moon, tonight.

Write the names of the planets according to their distance from the Sun, beginning with the closest.

1. _____

2. _____

3. _____

4. _____

5. _____

6. _____

7. _____

8. _____

Complete the following passage about the solar system with the appropriate words from the above list.

Il (1) _____ è al centro del sistema solare, che si trova nella (2) _____ chiamata Via Lattea. Il (3) _____ _____ ha otto (4) _____ (gli scienziati hanno deciso nel 2006 che Plutone non è più un (5) _____). Alcuni pianeti hanno dei (6) _____: la Terra ha la (7) _____, Giove ha sessantatré (8) _____. Quattro di loro sono chiamati le (9) _____ di (10) _____. Furono scoperte da Galileo grazie ad un nuovo strumento, il (11) _____. (12) _____ è famoso per i suoi anelli.

The earth

l(a)'aria	*air*
l(a)'atmosfera	*atmosphere*
la calotta polare	*polar ice cap*
il cielo	*sky*
l(o)'equatore	*equator*
il globo	*globe*
la latitudine	*latitude*
la longitudine	*longitude*
il meridiano	*meridian*
il parallelo	*parallel*
il polo	*pole*
il tropico	*tropic*

La calotta polare si sta sciogliendo.
L'equatore divide la Terra in due emisferi.

The polar ice cap is melting.
The equator divides the Earth into two hemispheres.

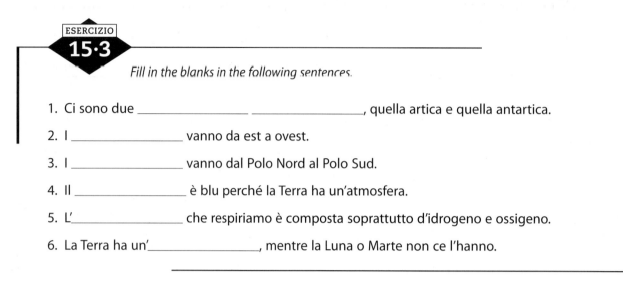

ESERCIZIO
15·3

Fill in the blanks in the following sentences.

1. Ci sono due _____ _____, quella artica e quella antartica.

2. I _____ vanno da est a ovest.

3. I _____ vanno dal Polo Nord al Polo Sud.

4. Il _____ è blu perché la Terra ha un'atmosfera.

5. L'_____ che respiriamo è composta soprattutto d'idrogeno e ossigeno.

6. La Terra ha un'_____, mentre la Luna o Marte non ce l'hanno.

Land and water

l(a)'acqua dolce; l(a)'acqua salata / di mare	*fresh water; salt/sea water*
il canale	*canal; channel*
la cascata	*waterfall*
la collina	*hill*
il continente	*continent*
la costa	*coastline; shoreline*
il fiume	*river*
il ghiacciaio	*glacier*
il golfo	*gulf*
l(o)'iceberg	*iceberg*
l(a)'isola	*island*
il lago	*lake*
il mare	*sea*
la montagna	*mountain*
l(o)'oceano	*ocean*
il passo; il colle	*pass*
la penisola	*peninsula*
la pianura	*plain*
la riva	*bank*
le terra; la terraferma; le terre emerse (pl.)	*land*
la valle	*valley*

Le trote vivono in acqua dolce.
L'Italia ha 7.500 km di costa.

Trout live in fresh water.
Italy has 7,500 km of coastline.

ESERCIZIO
15·4

Answer yes (Y) or no (N) to the following questions.

1. Beviamo l'acqua salata? _____

2. Un iceberg causò l'affondamento del *Titanic*? _____

3. I ghiacciai si stanno sciogliendo? _____

4. Il fiume scorre dal mare verso la montagna? _____

5. Le isole sono collegate alla terraferma? _____

6. Le penisole sono collegate alla terraferma? _____

Climate and weather

l(o)'autunno	*fall; autumn*
il clima	*climate*
l(a)'estate	*summer*
la frana	*landslide*
l(o)'incendio	*wildfire*
l(a)'inondazione	*flood*
l(o)'inverno	*winter*
il maremoto; lo tsunami	*tsunami*
la primavera	*spring*
la siccità	*drought*
la slavina; la valanga	*avalanche*
il solstizio	*solstice*
la stagione	*season*
il tempo	*weather*
il terremoto	*earthquake*
il tifone	*typhoon*
la tromba d'aria; il tornado	*tornado*
l(o)'uragano	*hurricane*
il vulcano	*volcano*

La siccità dura da cinque anni. — *The drought has been going on for five years.*
Era un terremoto di grado 7 sulla scala Richter. — *The earthquake was a magnitude 7 on the Richter scale.*

ESERCIZIO
15·5

Match the first part of the sentences on the left with the appropriate conclusion on the right.

1. D'estate _____   a. capitano in montagna.

2. D'inverno _____   b. è il 20 o il 21 giugno.

3. Il maremoto ha inondato _____   c. è il 22 o il 23 settembre.

4. Il solstizio d'estate _____   d. fa caldo.

5. L'equinozio d'autunno _____   e. fa freddo.

6. L'incendio ha distrutto _____   f. il paese di fango.

7. La frana ha coperto _____   g. mezza foresta.

8. Le valanghe _____   h. tre chilometri di costa.

Verbs

aprirsi; rasserenarsi	*to clear (up)*
cadere	*to fall*
eruttare (aux. avere)	*to erupt*
gelare (aux. avere/essere)	*to freeze*
grandinare (aux. avere/essere)	*to hail*
inondare	*to flood*
nevicare (aux. avere/essere)	*to snow*
piovere (aux. avere/essere)	*to rain*
ripararsi; cercare rifugio	*to take shelter*
salire e scendere	*to ebb and flow*
sciogliere; sciogliersi	*to melt; to thaw*
scorrere; sfociare	*to flow*
sorgere	*to rise*
tramontare	*to set (the sun)*

Il Po sfocia nell'Adriatico.	*The Po River flows into the Adriatic Sea.*
Cade la neve.	*Snow is falling.*

Italian uses several verbs impersonally, including those conveying weather conditions: **piovere** (*to rain*), **nevicare** (*to snow*), **fare caldo/freddo**, etc. (*to be hot/warm/cold*), **importare (a)** (*to matter [to]*), **bisognare** (*to be necessary*), **convenire** (*to be worth[while], to be advantageous/better/easier*). Impersonal verbs are used in the third person singular without any subject. Beware that some verbs can be used personally and impersonally.

accadere (a); succedere (a); capitare (a)	*to happen (to)*
bisognare; occorrere	*to be necessary; to be advisable*
convenire (a)	*to be advantageous*
incominciare	*to begin*
sembrare; parere	*to seem*

Bisogna riparare il telescopio.	*We need to have the telescope repaired.*
È/Ha nevicato.	*It snowed.*
Siamo capitati in un albergo orribile.	*We ended up staying at a horrible hotel.*

ESERCIZIO
15·6

Translate the following sentences into English.

1. Non mi sembra vero.

_____

2. Conviene prendere il treno delle sette.

_____

3. È piovuto per tre notti.

_____

4. Sembra che divorzino.

_____

5. Nevicherà domani.

_____

6. Bisogna parlargli.

_____

7. «È stata punita perché ha detto la verità». «Accade alle persone oneste».

_____

8. Che cosa è successo?

_____

Describing the weather

afoso; umindo	*sultry; hot and humid*
al sole	*in the sun*
all(a)'ombra	*in the shade*
alto	*high; tall*
bagnato	*wet*
basso; poco profondo	*low; shallow*
caldo	*warm*
coperto; nuvoloso	*overcast; cloudy*
est; a est	*east; to the east*
freddo	*cold*
molto caldo; caldissimo	*hot*
nord; a nord	*north; to the north*
ovest; a ovest	*west; to the west*
profondo	*deep*
secco; asciutto	*dry*
sud; a sud	*south; to the south*
temperato	*temperate; mild*
tropicale	*tropical*

Ai gatti piace stare al sole.	*Cats enjoy lying in the sun.*
Il sole tramonta a ovest.	*The sun sets in the west.*

Complete the following sentences.

1. Il cielo è _____. Pioverà.

2. Il clima del deserto è _____.

3. Il clima dell'India meridionale è _____.

4. La Fossa delle Marianne è il punto più _____ dell'oceano.

5. La maggior parte dell'Europa occidentale ha un clima _____.

6. Nel deserto fa _____.

7. Nella foresta tropicale il cima è molto _____.

8. Quando fa molto caldo si sta bene _____.

Forecasting the weather

l(a)'afa; l(a)' umidità	*sultriness; heat and humidity*
l(o)'arcobaleno	*rainbow*
il fulmine	*lightning*
il ghiaccio	*ice*
il grado	*degree*
la grandine	*hail*
la massima	*maximum*
la media	*average*
il meteorologo	*meteorologist*
la minima	*minimum*
la nebbia	*fog*
la neve	*snow*
la nuvola	*cloud*
l(o)'ombra	*shade; shadow*
la pioggia	*rain*
la pressione	*pressure*
la previsione	*forecast*
la temperatura	*temperature*
il temporale; la tempesta	*storm*
il tuono	*thunder*
il vento	*wind*

Le previsioni del tempo dicono che farà nuvolo.	*The weather forecast says it will be cloudy.*
La grandine ha distrutto l'uva.	*The hail storm destroyed the grapes.*

Mark the word that does not belong in each of the following series.

1. a. il ghiaccio   b. la media   c. la minima   d. la massima

2. a. il temporale   b. la grandine   c. il ghiaccio   d. l'arcobaleno

3. a. il fulmine   b. il grado   c. la tempesta   d. il tuono

4. a. il meteorologo   b. l'ombra   c. la previsione   d. la temperatura

5. a. la neve   b. il sole   c. l'ombra   d. l'afa

The environment

The industrial revolution has given us material progress, a longer life span, and pollution. Northern Italy, which is heavily industrialized and shielded from northerly winds by the Alps, is especially affected. But changes in the climate do not bode well for other regions either: desertification is growing in the south, and sea levels may become a greater and greater danger to low-lying lands, and to Venice in particular.

l(o, a)'ambientalista	*environmentalist*
l(o)'ambiente	*environment*
il blackout	*blackout*
il carbone	*coal*
il carburante	*fuel*
la centrale; l'impianto	*plant*
la conservazione	*conservation*
l(a)'ecologia	*ecology*
l(o, a)'ecologista	*ecologist*
l(o)'effetto serra	*greenhouse effect*
l(a)'energia	*energy*
la fonte	*source*
l(o)'inquinamento	*pollution*
il mulino a vento	*windmill*
la natura	*nature*
il pannello solare	*solar panel*
il pesticida, i pesticidi	*pesticide*
il petrolio	*oil*
il riciclaggio	*recycling*
il riscaldamento globale / il surriscaldamento del pianeta	*global warming*
il rumore	*noise*
lo smog	*smog*
lo spreco	*waste*

L'effetto serra causa il surriscaldamento del pianeta.	*The greenhouse effect is causing global warming.*
L'inquinamento da rumore è un problema serio.	*Noise pollution is a serious problem.*

From the words listed above, give those that fit each of the categories below. Turn the noun into the plural when appropriate.

1. le fonti dell'inquinamento:

_____

2. le conseguenze dell'inquinamento:

_____

3. gli strumenti per combattere l'inquinamento:

_____

Describing the environment

acido	*acid*
acustico	*acoustic*
alternativo	*alternative*
ambientale	*environmental*
convenzionale	*conventional*
elettrico	*electric; electrical*
solare	*solar*
sostenibile	*sustainable*

Adjectives ending in *-(a)ble* in English end in **-abile/-ibile** in Italian. They are formed by adding **-abile** to verbs ending in **-are**, and **-ibile** to verbs ending in **-ere** or **-ire**.

affonda-re (*to sink*) → **affond-abile** (*sinkable*)
descrive-re (*to describe*) → **descriv-ibile** (*describable*)
percepi-re (*to perceive*) → **percep-ibile** (*perceivable; perceptible*)

In some cases, the verb is modified: **comprendere** (*to understand*) → **comprensibile** (*understandable*); **bere** (*to drink*) → **bevibile** (*drinkable*); **piegare** (*to fold*) → **pieghevole** (*foldable*), etc. In others, the adjective comes from the past participle: **fatto** → **fattibile** (*doable*), **visto** → **visibile** (*visible*).

Many adjectives in **-abile/-ibile** are used in the negative, which is formed by adding the prefix **in-** (*in-/un-/dis-*), **im-** before **b, m,** and **p** (*im-*), or **ir-** before **r** (*un-*): **raggiungibile** (*reachable*) → **irraggiungibile** (*unreachable*); **correggibile** (*correctable*) → **incorreggibile** (*incorrigible*); **probabile** (*probable*) → **improbabile** (*improbable*).

*Form adjectives ending in **-bile** from the following verbs, and translate them into English.*

1. accettare _____ _____

2. curare _____ _____

3. lavare _____ _____

4. leggere _____ _____

5. montare _____ _____

6. navigare _____ _____

7. portare _____ _____

8. sopportare _____ _____

ESERCIZIO

15·11

Turn each of the following adjectives into its opposite. Then translate them into English.

1. curabile _____ _____

2. descrivibile _____ _____

3. leggibile _____ _____

4. mangiabile _____ _____

5. presentabile _____ _____

6. raggiungibile _____ _____

7. respirabile _____ _____

8. sopportabile _____ _____

9. visibile _____ _____

Agriculture

l'agricoltore (m. and f.)	*farmer*
l(a)'agricoltura	*agriculture*
l'allevatore/l'allevatrice (di bestiame)	*rancher*
il campo	*field*
il contadino	*peasant*
la fattoria; l'azienda agricola	*farm*
il fienile	*barn; hay loft*
il grano	*wheat*
il gran[o]turco; il mais	*corn*
il letame; il concime	*manure*
gli organismi geneticamente modificati (OGM) (pl.)	*genetically modified organisms (GMOs)*
il raccolto; la mietitura; la vendemmia	*harvest*
il seme	*seed*
la stalla	*stable*
il trattore	*tractor*
il veterinario (m. and f.)	*veterinarian*

| la vigna; il vigneto | vineyard |
| il viticoltore / la viticultrice | wine producer |

| A ottobre si fa la vendemmia. | We harvest grapes in October. |
| Sono cresciuta su una fattoria. | I grew up on a farm. |

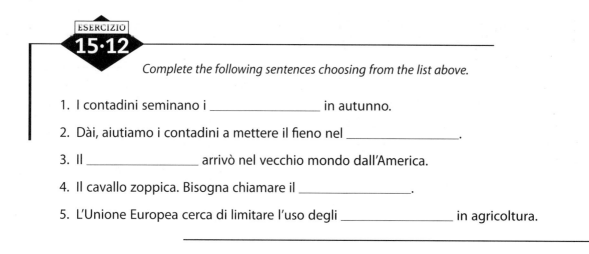

ESERCIZIO
15·12

Complete the following sentences choosing from the list above.

1. I contadini seminano i _____ in autunno.

2. Dài, aiutiamo i contadini a mettere il fieno nel _____.

3. Il _____ arrivò nel vecchio mondo dall'America.

4. Il cavallo zoppica. Bisogna chiamare il _____.

5. L'Unione Europea cerca di limitare l'uso degli _____ in agricoltura.

Farming

addomesticare	to domesticate
allevare	to breed; to rear
arare	to plough
bagnare (i fiori/campi, etc.); annaffiare; innaffiare	to water (the flowers/fields)
coltivare	to cultivate
domare	to tame
mietere; vendemmiare	to harvest
nutrire	to feed
praticare l(a)'agricoltura; coltivare la terra	to farm
segare	to saw

| Non puoi addomesticare un leone, solo domarlo. | You can't domesticate a lion, only tame him. |
| Dobbiamo bagnare le piante nell'orto. | We must water the plants in the vegetable garden. |

ESERCIZIO
15·13

Add the appropriate verb or noun to the following sentences.

1. Gli esseri umani hanno incominciato ad _____ il cane circa 15.000 anni fa.

2. I leoni possono essere _____ non _____.

3. Per coltivare il grano, bisogna _____ in autunno.

4. Quando c'è la siccità, i contadini _____ i campi.

5. Quando il terreno è povero, si aggiungono i _____.

6. Si _____ in autunno per fare il vino.

7. Una volta si _____ i campi con l'aratro tirato da animali.

The natural sciences

l(o)'adattamento	*adaptation*
l(o)'atomo	*atom*
la cellula	*cell*
il clone	*clone*
l(a)'ereditarietà	*heredity*
l(a)'evoluzione	*evolution*
il fatto	*fact*
il gene	*gene*
la genetica	*genetics*
il microscopio	*microscope*
l(o)'organismo	*organism*
la relatività	*relativity*
la selezione naturale	*natural selection; survival of the fittest*

Il primo clone era una pecora.	*The first clone was a sheep.*

ESERCIZIO
15·14

Complete the following sentences choosing from the above list.

1. Darwin ha elaborato il principio della _____ _____.

2. Dolly è stato il primo _____.

3. Einstein è diventato famoso per la teoria della _____.

4. L'_____ spiega perché alcuni organismi riescono a sopravvivere.

5. Per ingrandire un'immagine usi il _____.

Plants

l(o)'abete	*fir*
l(o)'acero	*maple*
l(o)'albero	*tree*
la betulla	*birch*
il bosco	*wood; woods*
il cactus	*cactus*
il castagno	*chestnut*
il cespuglio	*shrub*
l(a)'edera	*ivy*
l(a)'erba	*grass*
il faggio	*beech*

il fiore	*flower*
la foresta	*forest*
il giglio	*lily*
la legna (for the fire); **il legno** (material)	*wood*
la margherita	*daisy*
la palma	*palm*
il pino	*pine*
il pioppo	*poplar*
la quercia	*oak*
la radice	*root*
la rosa	*rose*
il tulipano	*tulip*
la viola del pensiero	*pansy*

L'edera cresce sui muri.	*Ivy grows on walls.*
Cappuccetto Rosso incontrò un lupo nel bosco.	*Red Riding Hood met a wolf in the woods.*

ESERCIZIO 15·15

You are making a bouquet. Which items among the ones listed below would you include?

cinque rose	due gigli
dell'edera	due pioppi
dell'erba	otto tulipani
della legna	una palma
delle radici	un pino
dieci margherite	

Animals

l(o)'animale	*animal*
l(o)'animaletto di casa; il cucciolo	*pet*
l(a)'ape	*bee*
la balena	*whale*
il cammello	*camel*
il cane	*dog*
la capra	*goat*
il cervo	*deer*
il coniglio	*rabbit*
la farfalla	*butterfly*
la formica	*ant*
la gallina	*hen*
il gallo	*rooster*
il gatto	*cat*
l(o)'insetto	*insect*
il leone / la leonessa	*lion/lioness*

il lupo	*wolf*
il maiale	*pig*
il mammifero	*mammal*
la mosca	*fly*
la mucca	*cow*
l(o)'oca	*goose*
l(o)'orso	*bear*
la pecora	*sheep*
il pesce	*fish*
il pinguino	*penguin*
il ragno	*spider*
lo scarafaggio	*cockroach*
la scimmia	*monkey*
lo scoiattolo	*squirrel*
il serpente	*snake*
la tigre	*tiger*
il topo	*mouse*
il toro	*bull*
l(o)'uccello	*bird*
la zanzara	*mosquito*

Il gatto miagola.	*The cat meows.*
Il cane abbaia.	*The dogs barks.*
Gli uccelli cantano.	*Birds sing.*
I serpenti strisciano.	*Snakes slither.*
Il leone ruggisce.	*The lion roars.*

ESERCIZIO

15·16

*Decide whether the following statements are true (**T**) or false (**F**).*

1. Con il latte di capra si fanno degli ottimi formaggi. _____

2. I galli covano le uova. _____

3. Il coniglio è un animale mite. _____

4. Il cane deriva dal lupo. _____

5. Il toro è un animale mite. _____

6. La scimmia è un animale intelligente. _____

7. Il leone è un animale domestico. _____

Measurements, time, and dates

Numbers came to us from India and the Arab world, even though the foundations of modern mathematics, geometry in particular, date to the ancient Greeks. In Italian, cardinal numbers don't take the article when they convey quantity, but they do when they refer to the position they occupy in the numerical sequence. Italian inserts a period every fourth digit, but a comma between integers and decimals. Consult a grammar book to check the Italian words conveying numbers in letters.

Lo zero è un numero affascinante.	*Zero is a fascinating number.*
L'uno viene prima del due.	*One comes before two.*
1.458.751.000,00	*1,458,751,000.00*
25,2	*25.2*

Ordinal numbers are declined like any other adjective: **il terzo, i terzi, la terza, le terze**. They usually carry the article, unless they are added to a proper name or used as adverbs.

Abbiamo perso la terza partita.	*We lost the third game.*
Giovanni Paolo II era molto popolare.	*John Paul II was very popular.*

Mathematics

l(a)'addizione	*addition*
l(o)'angolo	*angle; corner*
il cerchio	*circle*
la cifra / il numero	*figure; digit*
la divisione	*division*
l(o)'esempio	*example*
la frazione	*fraction*
la metà	*half*
la moltiplicazione	*multiplication*
il numero	*number*
il rettangolo	*rectangle*
la sfera	*sphere*
il solido	*solid*
la sottrazione	*subtraction*
il totale	*total*
il triangolo	*triangle*

Il quadrato ha quattro lati eguali.	*A square has four equal sides.*
Il triangolo ha tre angoli.	*A triangle has three angles.*

Fill in the blanks in the following sentences.

1. Se sommi 2 + 2 fai un'_____.

2. Se vuoi sapere quanto fa 72 ÷ 8 devi fare una _____.

3. Se vuoi sapere quanto fa 150 − 18 devi fare una _____.

4. Se vuoi sapere quanto fa 15 × 291 devi fare una _____.

5. Un triangolo è una figura geometrica con tre _____ e tre _____.

Calculating and measuring

calcolare	*to calculate*
contare	*to count*
dividere	*to divide*
durare	*to last*
fare	*to be/equal (arithmetical operation)*
fare il totale	*to total; to add up*
misurare	*to measure*
moltiplicare	*to multiply*
pesare	*to weigh*
sommare; addizionare	*to add*
sottrarre	*to subtract*

Moltiplicate 3 per 8.	*Multiply 3 by 8.*
15 diviso 5 fa 3.	*15 divided by 5 is 3.*
Hai misurato quanto è alto il soffitto?	*Did you measure how high the ceiling is?*

Identify the arithmetical operation you are performing, or replace the words underlined in each sentence below with the appropriate verb.

1. 12 + 5 + 58 + 32 = 107 _____

2. 45 ÷ 9 _____

3. 88 - 13 _____

4. Dire ad alta voce 1, 2, 3, 4, 5, ecc. _____

5. Il film è andato avanti per due ore. Il film è _____ due ore.

6. Mettere sulla bilancia delle arance _____

7. Prendere un metro e calcolare le dimensioni di una stanza _____

Describing numbers

decimale	decimal
d(i)ritto	straight
dispari	odd
due volte	twice
eguale (a)	equal (to)
falso	false
intero	integer
massimo	maximum
meno (di); di meno	less (than)
minimo	minimum
negativo	negative
pari	even
più (di/che); di più	more (than)
positivo	positive
tre volte	three times
una volta	once
unico	unique
vero	true

8 è più di 7.   8 is more than 7.
3 per 3 fa 9.   3 times 3 is 9.

ESERCIZIO
16·3

Find the qualifier described by the following definitions.

1. A number that is greater than 0. _____

2. A number that is less than 0. _____

3. A system of counting using ten digits, 0 through 9 (base 10). _____

4. Not divisible by 2. _____

5. Not in accordance with the fact or reality or actuality. _____

6. Radically distinctive and without equal. _____

Measurements

l(a)'altezza	height
il chilogrammo	kilogram
il chilometro	kilometer
il gallone	gallon
la larghezza	width
il litro	liter
la lunghezza	length
il metro	meter; measuring tape
il miglio, le miglia	mile
la misura	measure; measurement
il peso	weight

il piede	foot
il pollice	inch
la profondità	depth
la qualità	quality
la quantità	quantity
il volume	volume

Quanto pesa la valigia in chilogrammi? — How much does the suitcase weigh in kilograms?
Ci sono circa 3 piedi in 1 metro. — There are about 3 feet in 1 meter.

ESERCIZIO
16·4

Match the first part of each sentence with the appropriate conclusion from those listed on the right.

1. Ci sono circa quattro litri _____

2. Ci sono circa tre piedi _____

3. Il peso di un corpo _____

4. La massa di un corpo _____

5. Un miglio equivale _____

a. a 1.650 metri.

b. cambia secondo la gravità.

c. in un gallone.

d. in un metro.

e. non cambia.

Time

l(o)'anno; l(a)'annata	year
il calendario	calendar
[il] Capodanno	New Year's Eve; New Year's Day
la data	date
il fine settimana; il weekend	weekend
il futuro	future
il giorno; la giornata	day
il giorno feriale	weekday
il giorno festivo; la festa; la festività	holiday
il mattino; la mattina; la mattinata	morning
il mese	month
la mezzanotte	midnight
il mezzogiorno	noon
il millennio	millennium
il minuto	minute
[il] Natale	Christmas
la notte; la nottata	night
l(a)'ora	hour
l(o)'orologio (da polso; a muro)	watch; clock
[la] Pasqua	Easter
il passato	past
il pomeriggio	afternoon
il presente	present
il secolo	century
il secondo	second

| la sera; la serata | evening |
| il tempo | time |

| Ci sono sessanta secondi in un minuto. | *There are sixty seconds in one minute.* |
| Avete passato una bella serata? | *Did you have a nice evening?* |

ESERCIZIO
16·5

Mark the word that does not belong in each of the following series.

1. a. la notte   b. il giorno feriale   c. la mattina   d. il pomeriggio

2. a. il secondo   b. il passato   c. il presente   d. il futuro

3. a. il minuto   b. il presente   c. il secondo   d. l'ora

4. a. il millennio   b. Natale   c. Pasqua   d. Capodanno

The prepositions **di, a, da, in, su, con, per, tra/fra** can be used to convey aspects of time. **Di** (without any article) and **in** are used to convey the idea of a chunk of time within which something happened. **A** conveys a specific point in time. It usually corresponds to the English *at*. **Da** (*from, since*) conveys origin. **Per** conveys duration. And **tra/fra** convey an interval. We often omit prepositions when indicating time.

Andiamo in vacanza d'estate.	*We go on vacation in summer.*
È nata nel 1975.	*She was born in 1975.*
Vedrò la mia famiglia a Natale.	*I'll see my family at Christmas.*
Partiamo alle sette.	*We'll leave at seven A.M.*
Non lo vedo da tre mesi.	*I haven't seen him for three months.*
Non lo vedo dal 2002.	*I haven't seen him since 2002.*
Vado in vacanza per due settimane.	*I'm taking a two-week vacation.*
Passo da te tra le sette e le otto.	*I'll stop by at your place between seven and eight.*
Consegno l'articolo tra due mesi.	*I'll deliver the article in two months.*

ESERCIZIO
16·6

*Complete the following sentences by choosing from the following prepositions: **a, in, da, tra**. At times, you will need no preposition at all.*

1. _____ Capodanno facciamo una grande festa.

2. Capodanno è _____ Natale e Pasqua.

3. È andato a scuola d'inglese _____ anni.

4. Il treno parte _____ 10 (di mattina).

5. Non lo vediamo _____ 1997.

6. Sono stata in vacanza _____ due mesi!

7. Vado dai nonni _____ Pasqua.

Days of the week

lunedì	*Monday*
martedì	*Tuesday*
mercoledì	*Wednesday*
giovedì	*Thursday*
venerdì	*Friday*
sabato	*Saturday*
domenica	*Sunday*

Months of the year

gennaio	*January*
febbraio	*February*
marzo	*March*
aprile	*April*
maggio	*May*
giugno	*June*
luglio	*July*
agosto	*August*
settembre	*September*
ottobre	*October*
novembre	*November*
dicembre	*December*

ESERCIZIO
16·7

Fill in the blanks with the words that best complete the sentences.

1. _____, _____, _____ e _____ hanno trenta giorni.

2. _____, _____, _____, _____, _____, _____ e _____ hanno trentun giorni.

3. _____ ha 28 giorni, 29 in un anno bisestile.

4. Il _____ e la _____ formano il fine settimana.

5. Il mio compleanno è a _____.

6. Il Natale cade sempre il 25 _____.

7. Il solstizio d'estate è a _____.

8. L'equinozio di primavera è a _____.

Describing time

adesso; ora	*now*
l(o)'altro ieri	*the day before yesterday*
ancora	*still; yet*
circa; verso	*about; around*

corre; va avanti	fast (watch; clock)
domani	tomorrow
dopodomani	the day after tomorrow
e mezza; e trenta	half; 30 (minutes)
e tre quarti; e quarantacinque; un quarto all(a)'/alle (+ the following hour)	three quarters; 45 (minutes); a quarter (to)
e un quarto; e quindici	quarter; 15 (minutes)
fa	ago
ieri	yesterday
in anticipo	early
la mezza	12:30 P.M.; noon
il millenovecentosessantotto; il sessantotto (but not il diciannove sessantotto)	1968
[il] prossimo	next
qualche volta	sometimes
ritarda; va indietro	slow (watch; clock)
sempre	always
solo; soltanto	only
spesso	often
subito	at once
l(o)'ultimo; scorso	last; latest; past
una volta	once; one time

C'era una volta una principessa... — *Once upon a time there was a princess . . .*
L'ho letto nell'ultimo numero della rivista. — *I read it in the latest issue of the journal.*

ESERCIZIO
16·8

Replace the words underlined in each sentence with one of the qualifiers listed above.

1. È l'una e 30 minuti. È l'una _____

2. Essere in un posto dieci minuti prima dell'ora prevista. Essere _____ _____.

3. Hai visto il numero della rivista che è appena uscito? Hai visto _____ numero della rivista?

4. Il mio orologio segna le dieci ma sono le dieci e mezza. Il mio orologio _____.

5. L'ho visto il giorno precedente a oggi. L'ho visto _____.

6. Sono le dieci e 15 minuti. Sono le dieci _____.

7. Sono le 12 (A.M.). _____ _____.

8. Sono le 12 (P.M.). _____ _____.

9. Ti vedo il giorno successivo a oggi. Ti vedo _____.

10. Vincenzo vede esclusivamente le persone che gli servono per il lavoro. Vincenzo vede _____ le persone che gli servono per il lavoro.

Answer key

1 Family

1-1 1. la cognata   2. la sorella   3. la nuora   4. la mamma   5. la suocera   6. il cugino
7. il figlio   8. il nipote   9. la zia

1-2 1. c   2. b   3. a   4. b

1-3 1. l(o)'amante   2. il cognato   3. il fidanzato   4. il padre   5. il marito   6. il nipote
7. il genero   8. il parente   9. lo sposo   10. lo zio

1-4 1. gli zii   2. gli sposi   3. i cognati   4. i cugini   5. i fidanzati   6. i nipoti / i nipotini
7. i suoceri   8. i nipoti

1-5 1. some affection   2. the engagement ring   3. an anniversary   4. some lies
5. little trust/faith   6. the honeymoon   7. a marriage / wedding   8. a love affair

1-6 1. vostri   2. mio   3. loro   4. suo   5. mia   6. tua   7. nostre

1-7 1. c   2. c   3. b   4. a   5. a

1-8 1. abbracciarsi   2. aiutarsi   3. amarsi   4. perdonarsi   5. sposarsi   6. tradirsi
7. promettersi   8. volersi bene

1-9 1. mi vizio   2. sposarti   3. si fidanzano   4. si vogliono bene   5. vi amate
6. ci siamo promessi

1-10 1. Si deve parlare ai figli della droga.   2. Si aiutano i propri parenti.
3. Si dice che Elena e Giorgio divorzieranno.   4. Si va al ristorante stasera.

1-11 1. fidanzato   2. intimo   3. divorziato   4. sposato   5. innamorato   6. vedovo

1-12 1. Loro   2. Essi   3. Esso   4. Lei   5. Noi   6. Lui   7. Tu   8. Voi

1-13 1. Li   2. Ti   3. Le   4. Li   5. Ci   6. Vi   7. La   8. La

1-14 1. Mi   2. Vi   3. Gli   4. Gli   5. Le   6. Ci   7. Gli   8. Ti

2 People

2-1 1. c   2. d   3. a   4. f   5. b   6. e

2-2 1. b   2. c   3. a   4. a

2-3 1. l(a)'aggressività, *aggressiveness*   2. la normalità, *normality*   3. la profondità,
profundity/depth   4. la severità, *severity*   5. la superficialità, *superficiality*
6. la vivacità, *vivacity/liveliness*

2-4 1. la curiosità   2. la superficialità   3. la normalità   4. l(a)'aggressività   5. lo severità

2-5 1. affettuosamente   2. intimamente   3. pazientemente   4. saggiamente
5. severamente   6. timidamente   7. vivacemente

2-6 1. a   2. e   3. b   4. d   5. c

2-7 1. e   2. c   3. d   4. a   5. b

2-8 1. d   2. a   3. f   4. e   5. b   6. c

2-9 1. scusarsi   2. aspettare   3. chiedere/domandare   4. chiamare/telefonare   5. passare

2-10	1. pazienza 2. superficiale 3. affetto 4. orgoglio 5. famigliare 6. timidezza
2-11	1. b 2. a 3. d 4. c 5. e 6. f
2-12	1. Pronto 2. aiuti; persone 3. inviti 4. invitare 5. tipo 6. comportamento; maniere 7. festa
2-13	1. d 2. c 3. e 4. b 5. a
2-14	1. volentieri / con piacere 2. malvolentieri 3. da solo / solo 4. in pochi 5. occupato
2-15	1. Chi 2. Quanti 3. Dove 4. Perché 5. Come 6. Quando

3 The body and the senses

3-1	1. b 2. b 3. a 4. c 5. c
3-2	1. un 2. alla 3. a un 4. al 5. un 6. la 7. a un
3-3	1. cardiaci 2. muscoloso 3. facciale 4. nervoso
3-4	1. T 2. F 3. T 4. T 5. F
3-5	1. il braccio 2. il ginocchio 3. la lingua 4. il muscolo
3-6	1. la bocca 2. il braccio 3. il dente 4. il dito
3-7	1. il dente 2. il dito 3. la mano 4. il naso
3-8	1. c 2. a 3. a 4. b
3-9	1. a 2. c 3. b 4. a 5. c
3-10	1. gli occhi; testa/faccia 2. le orecchie; viso 3. le papille gustative; bocca 4. la pelle; corpo 5. il naso; bocca
3-11	1. c 2. a 3. a 4. b 5. a
3-12	1. la bellezza, *beauty* 2. l'amarezza, *bitterness* 3. la freddezza, *coldness* 4. la morbidezza, *softness* 5. la dolcezza, *sweetness*
3-13	1. la bruttezza 2. l'amarezza 3. la bellezza 4. la freddezza
3-14	1. ascolta 2. annusare; sentire (gli odori) 3. guarda; vede; osserva 4. sentire 5. assaggiare

4 Emotions and the mind

4-1	1. a 2. c 3. b 4. b 5. a
4-2	1. piacevole 2. triste/preoccupato 3. emotivo 4. odioso 5. allegro/piacevole
4-3	1. il piacere 2. la simpatia 3. il dolore / la tristezza 4. l(o)'amore 5. l(a)'infelicità 6. l(a)'allegria / la gioia
4-4	1. c 2. a 3. c
4-5	1. irritarsi 2. preoccuparsi 3. annoiarsi 4. rattristarsi 5. spaventarsi 6. stressarsi
4-6	1. ci siamo divertiti 2. si irritano 3. Si infastidisce 4. si sono terrorizzati 5. si è eccitato
4-7	1. a 2. b 3. a 4. b 5. c
4-8	1. addolorato 2. arrabbiato 3. annoiato 4. imbarazzato 5. spaventato 6. preoccupato 7. stressato
4-9	1. appassionante 2. divertente 3. irritante 4. preoccupante 5. rilassante 6. stressante
4-10	1. rilassanti 2. annoiata 3. stressante 4. appassionante 5. rilassata 6. stressata
4-11	1. l(a)'ansia 2. il dolore 3. la gioia 4. l(a)'invidia 5. la noia 6. l(o)'odio
4-12	1. felice 2. sensibile 3. contento 4. costante 5. piacevole
4-13	1. b 2. c 3. a 4. c
4-14	1. la capacità, *ability/skill* 2. l(a)'irrazionalità, *irrationality* 3. la passività, *passivity* 4. la razionalità, *rationality* 5. la stupidità, *stupidity*
4-15	1. a 2. b 3. a 4. c

4-16	1. l(a)'intelligenza 2. l(o)'istinto 3. l(a)'abitudine 4. l(a)'azione 5. il sogno
4-17	1. b 2. e 3. a 4. d 5. c
4-18	1. b 2. e 3. d 4. a 5. c

5 Body care, health, and life

5-1	1. d 2. b 3. a
5-2	1. b 2. b 3. c 4. a
5-3	1. calva 2. lisci 3. grigi/bianchi 4. corti
5-4	1. Il kleenex 2. shampoo 3. l'asciugamano 4. lo spazzolino / il dentifricio 5. il rasoio / la crema da barba 6. il deodorante
5-5	1. Fai depilare le gambe?; Ti fai depilare le gambe? 2. Giovanna fa lavare la testa.; Giovanna si fa lavare la testa. 3. Piera e Luciana fanno fare la messa in piega.; Piera e Luciana si fanno fare la messa in piega. 4. Massimo e Giorgio, fate tagliare la barba?; Massimo e Giorgio, vi fate tagliare la barba? 5. Facciamo tagliare i capelli!; Ci facciamo tagliare i capelli!
5-6	1. Il massaggio 2. la chirurgia plastica 3. la depilazione 4. la permanente 5. la manicure
5-7	1. N 2. N 3. N 4. Y 5. N 6. Y
5-8	1. c 2. c 3. a 4. b
5-9	1. f 2. a 3. b 4. e 5. c 6. d
5-10	1. dal dentista 2. dalla farmacista 3. psichiatri 4. dalla fisioterapista 5. dal chirurgo
5-11	1. Gli infermieri possono curare il raffreddore, la tosse, ecc. 2. I chirurghi fanno le operazioni. 3. L'oculista mi ha fatto cambiare gli occhiali. 4. La dentista dice che la nonna deve rifare la dentiera.
5-12	1. I ate too much last night. I feel nauseous. 2. I caught a cold. 3. My mother hurt her back. 4. "Are you ill?" "No, but I'm a bit under the weather (I don't feel very well)." 5. Did you get over the flu?
5-13	1. le malattie cardiovascolari: il colpo apoplettico, l'infarto 2. le malattie dell'apparato respiratorio: il raffreddore, la polmonite, la tosse, l'influenza 3. le tossicodipendenze: la tossicodipendenza, l(o)'alcolismo, il fumo 4. i traumi e le loro conseguenze: il coma, lo shock
5-14	1. c 2. e 3. b 4. a/h 5. h/a 6. d 7. f 8. g
5-15	1. Soffre 2. rianimato 3. si è rimarginata 4. trapianta 5. si ammala
5-16	1. medico 2. mal; temperatura 3. termometro; sintomi; Mal 4. vomitato 5. influenza
5-17	1. ambulatorio 2. pronto soccorso 3. barella 4. sedia a rotelle 5. ambulanza
5-18	1. According to the ancient Greeks, gods intervened in the lives of human beings. 2. The old man couldn't read the sign. 3. Man is mortal. 4. Mental functions are less brilliant in adults than in adolescents. 5. My brother was still a virgin at thirty.
5-19	1. parto 2. gravidanza 3. mestruazioni 4. pillola 5. adozione
5-20	1. b 2. a 3. c 4. d 5. f 6. e
5-21	1. dato alla luce 2. crescono; invecchiano 3. eutanasia assistita 4. adottano 5. vergine 6. morire

6 Consumer society

6-1	1. T or F 2. F 3. T 4. F 5. F
6-2	1. apre 2. spende 3. fare la spesa 4. rendere/restituire/cambiare
6-3	1. b 2. c 3. b 4. a
6-4	1. convenienti 2. fatte a mano / fatte su misura 3. di moda 4. fatti in serie
6-5	1. lo scontrino / la ricevuta 2. l(o)'assegno 3. l(o)'affare 4. la rata 5. il resto
6-6	1. acquistato/comp(e)rato 2. consumato 3. fatto 4. pagato 5. reclamato
6-7	1. d 2. b 3. a 4. c

6-8	1. la gelateriá 2. la gioielleriá 3. la latteriá 4. la macelleriá 5. la profumeriá 6. la salumeriá 7. la tabaccheriá
6-9	1. in gelateriá 2. in tabaccheriá 3. in profumeriá 4. in panetteriá 5. in salumeriá
6-10	1. c 2. b 3. b 4. c
6-11	1. consumata 2. elegante 3. casual 4. fantasia 5. sportivi
6-12	1. l'impermeabile 2. lo smoking 3. il piumone; la pelliccia; il cappotto; il giaccone 4. maglie 5. I pantaloni corti
6-13	1. la maglietta arancione 2. i pantaloni beige 3. la T-shirt bianca 4. la felpa blu 5. il panciotto bordeaux 6. la gonna grigia 7. l'abito da sera lilla 8. le pellicce marroni 9. gli smoking neri
6-14	1. si è messa 2. ci siamo tolti/e 3. si è provata 4. Mi metto 5. si tolgono
6-15	1. la camicia di cotone 2. la giacca di pelle 3. il vestito di lino 4. le calze di nylon 5. la gonna di seta 6. il golf di lana
6-16	1. di cotone 2. di nylon 3. di cotone; di lana 4. di cotone; di nylon 5. di lana 6. di velluto
6-17	Un paio di: calze, calzini, collant, guanti, mutande, mutandine, pantofole, sandali, scarpe, stivali
6-18	1. a 2. b 3. c 4. a

7 Housing

7-1	1. a 2. b 3. b 4. c 5. c
7-2	1. sul corso 2. in una cittadina 3. in città; in campagna 4. nei sobborghi 5. in un paesino
7-3	1. d 2. c 3. b 4. c
7-4	1. Y 2. Y 3. N 4. Y 5. N
7-5	1. b 2. c 3. d 4. a 5. e 6. f
7-6	1. l'idraulico 2. il muratore 3. il decoratore / l'imbianchino 4. l'impresario 5. l'architetto 6. il piastrellista
7-7	1. perdere 2. ristrutturare 3. montare 4. costruire 5. aggiustare/riparare
7-8	1. martello; chiodi 2. cacciavite; viti 3. arnesi/aggeggi 4. corto circuito 5. tubo 6. sega
7-9	1. il muro di mattoni 2. gli oggetti di plastica 3. le colonne di cemento armato 4. i palazzi di pietra 5. le mura di pietra 6. le case di legno
7-10	1. Y 2. N 3. N 4. N 5. Y
7-11	1. b 2. c 3. b 4. a
7-12	1. lo scaldabagno / il boiler 2. l(o)'ascensore 3. una cantina 4. Il garage 5. Il pavimento 6. i soffitti 7. riscaldamento
7-13	1. accendere 2. chiuso a chiave 3. spegni 4. funziona 5. entriamo/entrate
7-14	1. prefabbricata 2. a due arie 3. di sotto 4. al primo piano

8 Domestic life

8-1	1. in/nella camera da letto 2. in/nella cucina 3. in/nel soggiorno/salotto 4. in/nel tinello 5. in/nella camera/sala da pranzo 6. in/nel bagno 7. sulla terrazza / sotto il pergolato
8-2	1. abbiamo caldo 2. abbiamo sonno 3. dormire 4. sederci 5. fare del giardinaggio / fare l'orto 6. arredato/ammobiliato 7. mangiamo
8-3	1. b 2. e 3. a 4. d 5. c
8-4	1. a 2. c 3. b 4. a
8-5	1. e 2. a 3. d 4. b 5. c
8-6	1. radio 2. frigorifero 3. elettrodomestici 4. cucina
8-7	1. l(o)'asciugacapelli 2. l(o)'asciugamano 3. il cavatappi 4. il colapasta
8-8	1. d 2. a 3. b 4. c

8-9	1. c 2. d 3. a 4. b
8-10	1. passare l'aspirapolvere / il battitappeto 2. asciugare 3. stirare 4. lavano 5. mettere in ordine
8-11	1. a 2. b 3. b 4. d
8-12	1. d 2. a 3. c 4. b 5. e
8-13	1. Fanno bollire il latte. 2. Ho fatto friggere le zucchine. 3. La mamma ha fatto da mangiare per venti persone. 4. Mia nipote mi aiuta a pelare le patate. 5. Renato ha fatto il pesce alla griglia.
8-14	1. b 2. a 3. b 4. c
8-15	1. e, *evening gown* 2. g, *wine glass* 3. c, *bedroom* 4. d, *nightgown* 5. a, *shaving cream* 6. f, *tea set* 7. b, *toothbrush*
8-16	1. il pane 2. una torta 3. la crostata 4. marmellata 5. gelato
8-17	1. e 2. c 3. a 4. f 5. d 6. b
8-18	1. b 2. c 3. a 4. b
8-19	1. a 2. b 3. a 4. b
8-20	1. d 2. b 3. c 4. e 5. a
8-21	1. vino; vino 2. liquore 3. bevanda 4. spremuta
8-22	1. macinato 2. salata 3. da asporto 4. integrale 5. mangiabile

9 Transportation, traffic, and travel

9-1	1. biglietto 2. autostoppista 3. pedoni 4. strisce pedonali 5. pendolare
9-2	1. in macchina; in aereo 2. con la moto 3. con l'aereo 4. in tram 5. a piedi 6. in bici
9-3	1. d 2. e 3. m 4. b 5. c 6. k 7. a 8. i 9. l 10. h 11. j 12. f 13. g
9-4	1. fa la coda / è in coda 2. cammina 3. noleggiamo 4. fa il pendolare 5. obliterare/convalidare il biglietto
9-5	1. a 2. b 3. c 4. b
9-6	1. b 2. c 3. a 4. e 5. f 6. i 7. h 8. d 9. g
9-7	1. b 2. b 3. c 4. a
9-8	1. c 2. d 3. e 4. a 5. b
9-9	1. a 2. b 3. c 4. c
9-10	1. d 2. c 3. a 4. d
9-11	1. a destra; a sinistra 2. d[i]ritto 3. da nessuna parte 4. a doppio senso 5. a senso unico
9-12	1. N 2. Y 3. N 4. N 5. Y
9-13	1. rimandato 2. ha/è decollato 3. imbarcare il bagaglio 4. Ho perso 5. ci vogliono 6. ci ha messo
9-14	1. bagaglio a mano 2. i trasporti a terra 3. il volo 4. Il comandante 5. finestrino 6. biglietto elettronico 7. gli assistenti di volo
9-15	1. f/e 2. e/f 3. a/c 4. c/a 5. b/d 6. d/b
9-16	1. a terra 2. andata e ritorno 3. piano/adagio/lentamente 4. in ritardo 5. presto 6. lento/piano
9-17	1. Dario is the oldest child. 2. Dario is two years older than Gianni. 3. They bought a used car at a very low price. 4. The window seat is less uncomfortable than the aisle seat. 5. The Cinquecento was a very small car, but it was a lot of fun. 6. A Ferrari is faster than a Mercedes. 7. On the highway in Germany you can drive really fast. 8. Vincenzo took an excellent trip to Patagonia.

10 Tourism

10-1	1. b 2. c 3. a 4. b
10-2	1. c, *to go camping* 2. g, *to go on a cruise* 3. d, *to be a party of six* 4. a, *to go sightseeing* 5. f, *to make a long weekend of it* 6. b, *to spend time* 7. h, *to get a tan* 8. e, *to pay the bill*

10-3	1. alla cameriera 2. l(a)'albergatrice 3. bed & breakfast 4. alla reception / al concierge 5. sistemazione

10-3   1. alla cameriera   2. l(a)'albergatrice   3. bed & breakfast   4. alla reception / al concierge   5. sistemazione

10-4   1. panorama   2. ristorante   3. chef   4. camere   5. paninoteca; ristorante

10-5   1. Mi chiamo   2. prenotare   3. biglietto   4. passeggeri   5. sistemazione   6. pensione   7. cara   8. ristorante   9. buon giorno   10. grazie

10-6   1. f   2. b   3. a   4. c   5. d   6. e

10-7   1. c   2. a   3. b   4. f   5. d   6. e

10-8   1. tintarella   2. calcetto/calciobalilla   3. spiaggia   4. lungomare   5. fare sub

10-9   1. cima/vetta   2. borraccia   3. sacco   4. alpinisti   5. picozza

10-10   1. Do you know a Brazilian?   2. Greeks learn languages easily.   3. The interpreter is translating from Russian into German.   4. The European Union has twenty-three official languages, including Maltese and Slovak.   5. I'm Italian, but my children are American.

10-11   1. Vai a Gerusalemme?   2. Elena va in Russia passando dalla/per la Polonia.   3. Sua moglie è di Stoccolma.   4. Gabriella è stata in Giappone.   5. Sua moglie ritorna da Stoccolma.   6. I miei genitori arrivano dalla Finlandia domani.   7. Vuole andare in Cina.   8. Passano dall'Olanda / per l'Olanda.

10-12   1. There are dialects in the United States, too.   2. What does *autochthonous* mean? It's not in my dictionary.   3. She's bilingual. She will become a simultaneous translator.   4. Lalla learned sign language because her son is deaf and mute.   5. My sister learned German and Russian by herself.

11   Education and technology

11-1   1. anno scolastico   2. elementari   3. superiori   4. medie   5. asilo   6. asilo nido

11-2   1. The children are in/at church.   2. My children go to the church in our neighborhood.   3. They made me wait for two hours at the clinic.   4. My husband is going to the hospital tomorrow.   5. At our country house we can host twenty people.   6. I'm in your brother's car.   7. Will you be at home tonight?   8. Are you going to the theater Saturday?

11-3   1. N   2. Y   3. N   4. N

11-4   1. tagliato [la scuola]   2. hanno passato gli   3. fa attenzione   4. frequentano la   5. impara... a memoria; senza copiare

11-5   1. ha espulso / ha punito   2. dà il voto   3. corregge   4. ha dato   5. spiega/insegna

11-6   1. Prendi tre corsi obbligatori?   2. Non è uno studente brillante.   3. Le sue risposte sono giuste.   4. Prendo due corsi facoltativi.   5. Quello studente è distratto.   6. Tuo fratello è negato per la chimica.

11-7   1. c   2. d   3. c

11-8   1. b   2. c   3. a   4. a

11-9   1. l'educazione civica   2. la matematica   3. il latino   4. la storia   5. la geografia

11-10   1. seminario   2. borsa di studio   3. preside   4. tasse universitarie   5. professore   6. crediti   7. sillabo

11-11   1. fare lezione   2. iscriversi   3. laureata   4. fa una conferenza   5. laurearti   6. fare ricerca

11-12   1. il dischetto   2. il mouse   3. il computer   4. la pila   5. il portatile

11-13   1. d   2. c   3. a   4. a

11-14   1. inserire   2. reboot   3. masterizzi   4. backup   5. cliccare

11-15   1. c   2. e   3. b   4. d   5. a

11-16   1. Giorgio è on line cinque ore al giorno.   2. Il mio indirizzo e-mail è valeria punto guidi chiocciola fastnet punto net.   3. Non risponde alle e-mail. Deve essere off line.   4. L'opzione Back ti manda alla pagina precedente.   5. Il nuovo software è davvero user friendly.

11-17   (1) internet   (2) chattare   (3) e-mail   (4) sito   (5) videogame   (6) fa il log-in   (7) internet   (8) e-mail   (9) software

12 Culture, the arts, and leisure time

12-1   1. c   2. c   3. a   4. b

12-2   1. N   2. Y   3. Y   4. N   5. Y

12-3   1. l(o)'arredatore   2. l(o)'acrobata   3. l(o)'albergatore   4. l(o)'attore   5. il consumatore   6. l(o)'editore
       7. il lettore   8. il musicista   9. il poeta   10. il regista

12-4   1. legge   2. scritto; scritto   3. intitolato   4. stampati   5. racconta   6. pubblicare

12-5   1. c   2. b   3. a   4. c

12-6   1. giornale radio   2. ascoltatori/spettatori   3. radio   4. radiocronista   5. reti

12-7   1. via cavo   2. esaurito   3. dal vivo / in diretta   4. in onda   5. registrato

12-8   1. fotografo   2. regista   3. multisala   4. macchina fotografica   5. sottotitoli

12-9   1. d   2. b   3. c   4. a

12-10 1. ritmo   2. compositore   3. gruppo   4. bis   5. direttore/direttrice   6. cantante

12-11 1. la regista   2. il compositore   3. il musicista   4. il direttore   5. un film

12-12 1. a   2. b   3. d   4. a

12-13 1. architetto   2. designer   3. modella   4. pittori; scultori; architetti   5. pittore

12-14 1. L'architetto progetta lo stadio.   2. La grafica disegna il logo della ditta.   3. La modella posa per il
       pittore.   4. La pittrice dipinge l'affresco.   5. Lo scultore scolpisce la statua.

12-15 1. a, *bathing suit*   2. d, *typewriter*   3. f, *golf ball*   4. e, *soccer ball*   5. g, *tennis racket*
       6. c, *rucksack/backpack*   7. b, *gym shoes / sneakers*   8. h, *ski boots*

12-16 1. divertire   2. giocano   3. si è divertito   4. dato scacco matto   5. bara

12-17 1. allenatrice personale   2. aerobica   3. ginnastica   4. scarpe da ginnastica

12-18 1. b   2. c   3. b   4. a

12-19 1. c   2. h   3. d   4. g   5. a   6. e   7. b   8. f

12-20 1. b, *distance learning*   2. c, *hand luggage*   3. g, *grilled meat*   4. a, *contact lenses*   5. d, *ballpoint pen*
       6. f, *oil painting*   7. e, *high-speed train*

12-21 1. il calcio / il football   2. la pallacanestro / il basketball   3. il baseball   4. il football americano

12-22 1. fatto vela   2. giocano a calcio / football   3. allena   4. pari   5. si è tuffato

13 Work and business

13-1   1. Y   2. Y   3. N   4. N   5. N

13-2   1. liberi professionisti   2. ingegnere   3. operai   4. capo/boss/principale   5. manager

13-3   1. stagionale   2. freelance   3. a tempo pieno   4. a tempo parziale   5. disoccupato   6. impiegata

13-4   1. b   2. d   3. a   4. f   5. e   6. c

13-5   1. sfruttati   2. scioperare   3. licenziato   4. prende le ferie   5. vai in pensione

13-6   1. messaggi   2. interno   3. fax   4. segnale acustico   5. operatrice

13-7   1. la consegna   2. sulla busta   3. il timbro   4. nella buca delle lettere   5. dal portalettere

13-8   1. firmare   2. telefonato   3. squilla   4. richiamare   5. riattaccare   6. restare in linea

13-9   1. fragile   2. in mutua   3. urgente   4. in ferie   5. in ufficio   6. per telefono

13-10 1. d   2. a   3. d   4. c

13-11 1. Hanno reso poco.   2. Lo sto finanziando.   3. Sto rischiando.   4. Qualcuno sta speculando.
       5. Ho avuto un profitto.

13-12 1. c   2. e   3. a   4. b   5. d   6. f

13-13 1. preso a/in prestito   2. Imprestiamo   3. fatto bancarotta   4. cambiare i soldi   5. risparmia
       6. prelevare

13-14	1. fabbrica 2. soci 3. monopoli 4. donna d'affari 5. produttività 6. robot 7. multinazionale
13-15	1. F 2. T 3. F 4. T 5. F 6. T
13-16	1. c 2. b 3. a 4. b

14 Government, politics, and society

14-1	1. bandiera 2. permesso di soggiorno 3. cittadinanza 4. frontiera 5. immigrante 6. straniero
14-2	1. d 2. a 3. c 4. b
14-3	1. deputati; senatori 2. primo ministro 3. re; regina 4. presidente 5. sindaco
14-4	1. N 2. Y 3. Y 4. N 5. N 6. N
14-5	1. e 2. d 3. a 4. c 5. b
14-6	1. presentarsi candidato 2. approvare 3. protestare 4. partecipare 5. eleggere
14-7	1. a favore 2. dittatoriale 3. contrario all' 4. pubblico 5. internazionale
14-8	(1) Rappresentanti (2) donne (3) italiana (4) politica (5) vittoria (6) voti (7) legge (8) legge (9) diritti
14-9	1. centrismo, centrista; *centrism, centrist* 2. comunismo, comunista; *communism, communist* 3. estremismo, estremista; *extremism, extremist* 4. fascismo, fascista; *fascism, fascist* 5. femminismo, femminista; *feminism, feminist* 6. fondamentalismo, fondamentalista; *fundamentalism, fundamentalist* 7. progressismo, progressista; *progressivism, progressive* 8. socialismo, socialista; *socialism, socialist*
14-10	1. anarchismo, *anarchism* 2. conservatorismo, *conservatism* 3. liberalismo, *liberalism* 4. localismo, *localism* 5. moderatismo, *moderatism* 6. radicalismo, *radicalism*
14-11	1. il comune, *town / city hall / municipality* 2. il crimine, *crime* 3. l(o)'elettore, *elector* 4. la mente, *mind* 5. la persona, *person* 6. la razza, *race* 7. lo stato, *state* 8. la tradizione, *tradition*
14-12	1. a 2. b 3. c 4. a 5. b
14-13	1. deruba 2. denunci 3. commette un omicidio 4. molesta 5. rapita/sequestrata
14-14	1. I poliziotti hanno arrestato il sospettato. 2. In Italia non esiste la pena di morte. 3. La prove presentate dall'accusa non hanno convinto la giuria. 4. Non ha un soldo: non può prendersi un avvocato. 5. Per paura della mafia, la testimone è protetta dalla polizia.
14-15	1. confessare 2. permettere 3. assolvere 4. rilasciare 5. arrestare
14-16	1. d 2. c 3. a 4. d 5. c
14-17	1. fare la pace 2. obbedire 3. ferito 4. catturi 5. tradisci 6. arrendi
14-18	1. e 2. b 3. c 4. a 5. d
14-19	1. pacifismo 2. tortura 3. rifugiati 4. diritti umani 5. asilo politico

15 Nature and the environment

15-1	1. Mercurio 2. Venere 3. Terra 4. Marte 5. Giove 6. Saturno 7. Urano 8. Nettuno
15-2	(1) Sole (2) galassia (3) sistema solare (4) pianeti (5) pianeta (6) satelliti (7) Luna (8) satelliti (9) lune (10) Giove (11) cannocchiale (12) Saturno
15-3	1. calotte polari 2. meridiani 3. paralleli 4. cielo 5. aria 6. atmosfera
15-4	1. N 2. Y 3. Y 4. N 5. N 6. Y
15-5	1. d 2. e 3. h 4. b 5. c 6. g 7. f 8. a
15-6	1. It doesn't seem true to me. 2. It's better to take the 7 A.M. train. 3. It rained for three nights. 4. It seems they will get a divorce. 5. It will snow tomorrow. 6. We need/have to talk to him. 7. "She was punished because she told the truth." "It happens to honest people." 8. What happened?
15-7	1. coperto 2. secco 3. tropicale 4. profondo 5. temperato 6. caldissimo 7. umido/afoso 8. all'ombra
15-8	1. a 2. c 3. b 4. b 5. a

15-9   1. le fonti dell'inquinamento: il carbone, i carburanti, il rumore, il petrolio, i pesticidi, lo spreco
        2. le conseguenze dell'inquinamento: il riscaldamento/surriscaldamento globale, l'effetto serra, lo smog
        3. gli strumenti per combattere l'inquinamento: la conservazione, i pannelli solari, i mulini a vento, il riciclaggio

15-10   1. accettabile, *acceptable*   2. curabile, *curable*   3. lavabile, *washable*   4. leggibile, *legible*   5. montabile, *assemblable*   6. navigabile, *navigable*   7. portabile, *wearable/decent*   8. sopportabile, *bearable*

15-11   1. incurabile, *incurable*   2. indescrivibile, *undescribable*   3. illeggibile, *illegible*   4. immangiabile, *inedible*   5. impresentabile, *unpresentable*   6. irraggiungibile, *unreachable*   7. irrespirabile, *unbreathable*   8. insopportabile, *unbearable*   9. invisibile, *invisible*

15-12   1. campi   2. fienile   3. mais/gran[o]turco   4. veterinario   5. OGM

15-13   1. addomesticare   2. domati; addomesticati   3. seminare   4. irrigano   5. fertilizzanti   6. vendemmia   7. aravano

15-14   1. selezione naturale   2. clone   3. relatività   4. adattamento   5. microscopio

15-15   cinque rose, dell'edera (*why not?*), dieci margherite, due gigli, otto tulipani

15-16   1. T   2. F   3. T   4. T   5. F   6. T   7. F

16 Measurements, time, and dates

16-1   1. addizione   2. divisione   3. sottrazione   4. moltiplicazione   5. angoli, lati

16-2   1. fare il totale   2. dividere   3. sottrarre   4. contare   5. durato   6. pesare   7. misurare

16-3   1. positivo   2. negativo   3. decimale   4. dispari   5. falso   6. unico

16-4   1. c   2. d   3. b   4. e   5. a

16-5   1. b   2. a   3. b   4. a

16-6   1. A   2. tra   3. per   4. alle   5. dal   6. [per]   7. a

16-7   1. Aprile, giugno, settembre, novembre   2. Gennaio, marzo, maggio, luglio, agosto, ottobre, dicembre   3. Febbraio   4. sabato, domenica   5. gennaio   6. dicembre   7. giugno   8. marzo

16-8   1. e mezza   2. in anticipo   3. l(o)'ultimo   4. ritarda / va indietro   5. ieri   6. un quarto   7. È mezzanotte.   8. È mezzogiorno.   9. domani   10. solo

IRCLE TIME FOR EMOTIONAL LITERACY

CIRCLE TIME FOR EMOTIONAL LITERACY

Sue Roffey

P·C·P

Paul Chapman
Publishing

First published 2006

Apart from any fair dealing for the purposes of research or
private study, or criticism or review, as permitted under the
Copyright, Designs and Patents Act, 1988, this publication
may be reproduced, stored or transmitted in any form, or by
any means, only with the prior permission in writing of the
publishers, or in the case of reprographic reproduction, in
accordance with the terms of licences issued by the Copyright
Licensing Agency. Enquiries concerning reproduction outside
those terms should be sent to the publishers.

Paul Chapman Publishing
A SAGE Publications Company
1 Oliver's Yard
55 City Road
London EC1Y 1SP

SAGE Publications Inc
2455 Teller Road
Thousand Oaks, California 91320

SAGE Publications India Pvt Ltd
B-42, Panchsheel Enclave
Post Box 4109
New Delhi 110 017

Library of Congress Control Number: 2006901649

A catalogue record for this book is available from the
British Library

ISBN-10 1-4129-1854-5   ISBN-13 978-1-4129-1854-1
ISBN-10 1-4129-1855-3   ISBN-13 978-1-4129-1855-8 (pbk)

Typeset by C&M Digitals (P) Ltd, Chennai, India
Printed in Great Britain by Cromwell Press Ltd, Trowbridge, Wiltshire
Printed on paper from sustainable resources

CONTENTS

ACKNOWLEDGEMENTS

Many people helped in the production of this book. In particular teachers and other educators were generous in sharing ideas for activities that they had been incorporating into their own Circle Time sessions. These include Carolyn Waters, Tabatha Kellett, Angie Parker, Claudia Kappenberg. Claire Finka and Fiona McCormack. I am particularly grateful to Terri Mountford and other colleagues in Canberra for their generosity in giving me copies of every Circle Time activity they had found.

I would also like to express my appreciation to all those involved in the Circle Time action research project and its evaluation in Western Sydney: Philip Ward and Liz Strasser, and all the other wonderful teachers at Penrith Public School: Melissa Jovanovitch, Christine Iokamidis, Jennifer Gunn, Julie Woodward, Sue Hitches, Konstantina Martinis, Robert Kidd, Grace Canales and Claudia Roman.

Sylvia Ruocco, Wendy McLean, Melissa Jovanovitch. Elizabeth Gillies, Peta Blood, Terri Mountford, Toni Noble and Lynette Simons read and critiqued the final manuscript and gave excellent ideas for its development.

The team at Sage is a pleasure to work with. Jude Bowen, Senior Commissioning Editor at Paul Chapman Publishing, is the personification of emotional literacy at work. She supports, consults, communicates and is forever positive (even when she disagrees with you!). Kate O'Reilly at Footprint also deserves thanks for being so helpful with the marketing and distribution of Sage books in Australia.

My own emotional well-being and resources are consistently maintained by the love and support of my family across the world, especially David. He brings me tea, switches off the computer when I've been sitting at it too long and formats the final manuscript. From him I have learned first-hand the joy of living with someone who has a positive outlook on life.

Dedication

This book is dedicated to my wonderful brothers Peter and Andrew, with
appreciation for their quick and quirky humour

AUTHOR BIOGRAPHY

Sue Roffey worked for many years as a teacher and then as an educational psychologist in the UK. She has been an academic at the University of Western Sydney since 2001, initially involved with school counsellor training and now a senior research fellow. Her projects include an investigation into the process and outcomes of establishing emotional literacy in schools. Sue works internationally as a consultant on issues related to social and emotional learning, values education and behaviour. She also offers Circle Time training. Sue currently spends about six weeks a year in the UK to get 'a necessary dose of family and friends'.

Sue is vice-president of the National Association for the Prevention of Child Abuse and Neglect NSW where she has initiated projects to develop child friendly communities. She is also a founding member of Wellbeing Australia – an organization promoting social and emotional literacy (www.wellbeingaustralia.com.au). Sue has a strong publication record showing ways in which positive relationships at all levels of the school system can promote pro-social behaviour, resilience and well being for all. More information and contact details can be found on www.sueroffey.com

This is a wonderfully lucid account of what needs to happen if Circle Time sessions are to promote the emotional literacy of children and young people.

Circle Time, Sue Roffey says, is a 'structured framework for group interaction', one that enables students to 'think reflectively and creatively, talk together about important issues, grow to have understanding about themselves and others, and over time to develop knowledge and skills they can put into practice.'

It is not, therefore, a tool for improving behaviour, even though behaviour may improve as a result of its being practised. Nor is it a therapeutic tool, even if it may have the effect of healing emotional hurt.

The power of Circle Time lies in the opportunity it provides for children and young people to experience feelings of calm that are unpolluted by the pressures of academic learning, to reflect on who they are, and to discover ways of connecting more warmly to others.

Sue lays out the theoretical arguments for practising Circle Time, but also the reasons why its value is so self-evident to her. She grew up in a family where games brought people together regularly, and as a result learned not only about being 'part of a team,' but also about 'words, numbers, feelings and thinking creatively'.

Unsurprisingly, therefore, she puts forward a vision of Circle Time as a practice that needs to become a regular and essential part of the experience we offer children and young people. That way, they will have the opportunity to make sense of their lives, and find ways of learning from and with one another.

One of the nicest aspects of this book is the way it illustrates the value of collaborative learning through the occasional insights it offers into the processes of its own composition. The cornucopia of activities that Sue describes were gleaned from many sources, from internet resources and books, but also from conversations with friends and colleagues.

A message that comes through strongly is the need for each practitioner to develop their own style of Circle Time practice, drawing on their own creativity to devise 'ever more ingenious ways of meeting the aims for social and emotional learning.' No book, however insightful and comprehensive, will be able to anticipate the particular challenges you may face, or the potential in you to come up with a fresh approach.

While many of the activities described will be familiar to Circle Time practitioners, they gain a richer resonance from their location in the framework that Sue provides. Always the attention is drawn to how they can be used to make students more insightful in understanding their emotional experience in the context of their communications, their relationships and their conflicts.

For those who feel wary about opening up emotional issues in the classroom, Sue provides a lot of advice on how to ensure that the circle is experienced as a place of safety, that tension is released and 'positive emotionality' stimulated before challenging issues are faced and serious discussions provoked. She recognizes that safety is important, but that it needs to lead towards change and growth.

Through most of the time that I have spent exploring the potential of emotional literacy to enhance the quality of teaching and learning, Sue has been one of my sanest guides. I am delighted that this book will enable others to benefit from the depth of her insights and the breadth of her understanding. I also hope that it will inspire all of us to do more to ensure that children and young people experience themselves as having a valuable contribution to make to the formation of vibrant learning communities.

James Park
Director of Antidote
www.antidote.org.uk

USING THIS BOOK

Teachers starting out with Circle Time will find everything they need here to introduce Circle Time to their class. This book is also for experienced practitioners who are seeking to further expand their repertoire of ideas.

The activities in Circle Time for Emotional Literacy are for all school age children. To make it clear, however, which age group an activity is best suited to we have given symbols as follows:

- Y is for younger children from 5–7 years old

- M is for those in middle childhood: 7–11 years

- S is for more senior students from upper primary into high school: 10–18 (these activities usually require a level of abstract thinking)

Within each chapter are suggestions and activities for students across a wide age and ability range – and many would meet the needs of an even broader range with creative adaptations.

Activities more suitable for younger children are at the beginning of chapters, followed by those that are increasingly complex or demanding. Some activities have variations and/or extensions that make them suitable for younger or older pupils.

Teachers will want to dip into sections depending on their particular needs and the age and stage of their classes. Some students may need to begin at a more basic level than their age would suggest.

Choosing activities

Although different chapters focus on specific aspects of emotional literacy there is inevitably an overlap. If you can't find what you are looking for in one chapter try another. The ideas are for you to use, develop and change according to what works for you. The important thing is to keep to the principles and general framework.

Do not be afraid to repeat activities. We often expect learners to be able to know or do something with only one or two opportunities to practise. The benefit of some activities may only be gained when students are encouraged to build on their learning in a second or third attempt. Pupils also like playing some games regularly and look forward to their favourites. Many activities are open to adaptation for thinking about different emotions or situations so you can use the same or similar games for different words, feelings or purposes.

Reinforcing learning

Emotional literacy is embedded throughout the book in the way we communicate, how we understand ourselves and others, how we promote an inclusive ethos and how we solve problems. Research (Taylor, 2003) indicates that it is helpful to mediate this understanding by making the purpose of activities explicit and adding some minimal commentary where appropriate. This helps students make connections between what happens inside the Circle with what goes on in the class generally. This is best done lightly: questions rather than statements, a phrase not a lecture. There are also additional discussion topics to extend thinking and reinforce learning.

What will you find in each chapter

The first chapter provides a rationale for Circle Time and shows the ways in which it develops emotional literacy. It covers the principles and theoretical foundations for Circle Time and stresses the importance of maintaining the philosophy in practice.

Chapter 2 covers the framework for Circle Time. There is also a section here on trouble-shooting: suggestions for what you might do when students do not conform to the rules, have communication difficulties or when sensitive issues are raised. This chapter is particularly useful for teachers starting out with Circle Time and who are not yet familiar with what happens or having some difficulty getting it off the ground.

Each Circle session has a structure with a beginning, an end and transitions between activities. Chapter 3 addresses just these aspects. In Chapter 4 we look at a wide range of communication issues from motivation and confidence to active listening skills and the rules of conversation. There are plenty of non-verbal games in this chapter to foster confidence.

Self-awareness is the subject of Chapter 5. Activities here will increase understanding of identity, personal strengths and qualities, wishes, beliefs and values. These focus on the positive and include activities to support self-esteem. Chapter 6 explores individual emotions more directly. This includes definitions, developing an 'emotion' vocabulary, understanding how feelings are felt in the body, how feelings are linked to social and cultural factors and ways to regulate and express emotions safely.

Chapter 7 is focused on building and developing a supportive class ethos. It aims to develop awareness of the feelings and situations of others and taking appropriate responsibility for one another. This is where you will find activities that encourage empathy. Chapter 8 focuses more specifically on friendliness, friendship skills and what is needed for successful collaboration.

Finally Chapter 9 addresses both challenging situations and challenging feelings. It covers problem solving for individuals and also issues that arise within the class group, including bullying. It helps readers tune into emotions to be effective problem solvers: what helps everyone feel better?

Setting the Scene

> This introductory chapter provides an overview of the history, principles and theoretical foundations for Circle Time and defines emotional literacy. Here the rationale for using Circle Time is given. The rest of the book shows you how.

Circles in History

The symbolism of circles is ageless. A circle can represent wholeness, continuity, universality, unity, inclusion, equality and protection. As with sunlight, the power within circles radiates out to all.

Using a circle formation as a means of social interaction is also historical and cross-cultural. The North American medicine wheel is just one example of how traditionally indigenous communities have used circles as a means of decision-making and conflict resolution. The 'Quality Circle' initiative, first developed by Kaoru Ishikawa in Japan in the 1960s (Ishikawa, 1985), has been used widely in a business environment. It is based on the principle that full participation in decision-making and problem-solving improves the quality of work. Circles are now also an essential feature of the restorative justice movement, involving all who have been affected by an offence, including the offender.

Development of Circle Time in Education

I first came across Circle Time in 1991 in New Jersey. The school principal told me that each class had a 'Magic Circle' session every day after recess. He was convinced that it was this that maintained a sense of calm, purpose, and mutual support.

Others have since taken up and developed the Circle Time framework and ethic. Much of this book builds on the ideas of Jenny Mosley, Barbara Maines, George Robinson, Theresa Bliss, Margaret Collins and Murray White. Jenny, in particular, is widely recognized for the significant contribution that she has made, notably for taking Circle Time into a framework for whole school quality. Like language, however, Circle Time is constantly evolving and being developed still further by authors such as Tina Rae, Charlie Smith and Andrew Fuller. Teachers and students themselves devise ever more ingenious ways of meeting the aims for social and emotional learning and some of their ideas are included here.

There are different understandings and definitions of both the terms 'emotional literacy' and 'Circle Time', so first we will clarify the meanings and foundations on which we are building here.

What Is Emotional Literacy?

Emotional literacy is a values-based concept concerned with all aspects of relationships. This includes not only the development of knowledge and skills within individuals but also the ethos of the systems and communities in which we live and work. The following is a brief summary of what this means at different levels.

Emotional literacy for individuals encompasses:

- personal awareness, understanding, knowledge and skills related to what we feel and why

- knowing how to regulate emotion safely

- having awareness of what maintains emotional resources

- having a repertoire of ways in which to express emotion safely and being able to put this into practice in challenging situations

- awareness and knowledge of others and skills in relating to them

- the ability to tune into the affective to manage situations well

- a focus on the positive

- personal and professional integrity: identifying values and acting consistently across contexts on the basis of these

- a sense of personal effectiveness and an internal locus of control

- acting thoughtfully rather than on impulse.

Emotional literacy between people promotes:

- the demonstration of acknowledgment, acceptance and value

- positive and constructive communication

- effective interactions, including appropriate assertiveness

- honesty, transparency and trust

- support and the mutual maintenance of emotional resources

- willingness to resolve conflict by negotiation and compromise

- a focus on issues rather than personalities

- exploration of competencies and possibilities rather than making judgements and attributing blame

- skills to de-escalate potential confrontation

- the ability to withdraw from situations appropriately and safely.

Emotional literacy at a systems level (classroom, school, family, community):

- enhances emotional safety
- gives agency and ownership to decision-making
- is ethical and fair
- encourages a constructive, positive and solution-focused approach
- promotes responsibility
- values diversity
- is flexible and creative
- has high expectations
- is modelled by leaders.

Emotional literacy means working in the following ways to develop social and emotional capital:

- collaborating to promote inclusive well-being rather than a blame culture
- proactively addressing underlying issues rather than reacting to and 'treating' symptoms of distress
- being reflective, listening to people and withholding hasty judgement
- focusing on the humanity we all share, respecting difference, valuing diversity and promoting a sense of belonging.

Emotional literacy is neither sentimental nor self-indulgent. It has great potential to enhance both individual and community well-being. Re-evaluating the way we think about ourselves and how we interact with others can be exciting but also challenging.

Emotional literacy is not a program – it is a way of being.
Circle Time is one way of developing it.

What Is Circle Time?

Circle Time is a structured framework for group interaction. It can be used in many different ways, but within a classroom it is focused on developing:

- self awareness, knowledge and skills
- knowledge and understanding of others
- a sense of belonging and connectedness
- a focus on the positive
- increased emotional resources and well-being
- collaborative decision making, conflict resolution and problem-solving.

Circle Time takes place *at least* once a week for approximately 30 minutes, depending on the age of the children. Regularity is important. There is little educational benefit in having Circle Time occasionally as a 'treat'.

There is a clear format in which students and teachers take part in a wide range of individual, paired, small group and whole class activities. Many activities are presented as games and participants are mixed up so that everyone interacts with everyone else.

There are three rules based on the principles of respect, safety and inclusion:

1 everyone gets a turn–when it is someone's turn to speak, everyone else listens
2 individuals may pass if they wish – there is no pressure to say anything
3 there are no put-downs at any time – this means no naming, blaming or shaming.

Principles of Circle Time

The following principles of Circle Time are the foundations of the framework.

Democracy

There are equal opportunities to participate and contribute. No one group or individual is able to dominate. Knowing that each person will get their turn promotes cooperation.

Respect

The rules emphasize respect for individuals and their contributions. The Circle will discuss problems, but not people. Students who experience respect and have it modelled to them will understand what it means and feels like, and therefore be more able to show this to others.

Empathy

Many Circle Time activities are aimed at breaking down barriers and stereotypes, valuing differences and seeking what is shared. Mixing students up so that they get to know their classmates in a variety of ways is a key feature. This actively addresses bullying, prejudice and discrimination.

Community

Promoting a whole class ethos where each is responsible for others and for creating a safe atmosphere is a central tenet of Circle Time. Although there are some team games, activities emphasize collaboration rather than competition.

Inclusion

Everyone in a class is welcomed into the Circle regardless of their ability or behaviour. Each person is given the same opportunities as every other one. Established Circles sometimes invite students from different classes or years, parents or other visitors.

Choice

No-one is pressured unduly to participate. This means that running Circles in a classroom should be a teacher's choice, not mandatory – a teacher feeling compelled to do so is unlikely to run a successful Circle. Students who regularly demonstrate they are unwilling or unable to behave appropriately in the Circle are given the choice to conform to the basic rules and stay or to leave the Circle.

Safety

As with the above, no one has to respond verbally. Students may pass if they wish for as long as they like. Students usually join in when they have the confidence or otherwise feel comfortable. Focusing on the positive helps facilitators to avoid more sensitive issues but they need to respond quickly and appropriately if these are raised.

Agency, Responsibility and Locus of Control

Circles are less about telling students what to do than providing a framework in which they take responsibility. Students are given opportunities to construct solutions for class issues themselves. Devising solutions together increases the responsibility for making them happen. Giving students agency also helps to change an 'external locus of control', where a person believes that everything just happens to them (good things happen by chance and bad things are someone else's fault) to an 'internal locus of control', which is a belief that a person's own actions and efforts can effect change.

Reflection

Many of the games and activities are designed to encourage discussion and reflection. This includes definitions of more abstract concepts such as feelings, values, rights and responsibilities. Even very young children can talk and think about what is fair, friendly or kind.

Creativity

There is a wide scope for creativity in Circle Time activities. Imagination underpins the ability to problem-solve, have compassion for others and think laterally.

Positive emotionality

Many activities are structured so that individuals experience positive emotions. When people feel better about both themselves and others they have more emotional resources to cope with challenges (Frederickson et al., 2000).

Having fun

The focus is on feeling good in a safe and supportive way. This increases the sense of belonging in a class, which in turn raises resilience. Students are highly motivated to participate in Circle Time because it is fun.

The actual content of Circle Time is varied. Teachers may determine activities or students may suggest topics: these may arise as issues which need addressing.

Circle Time is an indirect teaching tool. The aim is for students to think reflectively and creatively, talk together about important issues, grow to have understanding about themselves and others, and over time to develop knowledge and skills that they can put into practice. If Circle Time is run with too didactic an approach, where teachers tell children what to think and do, it may not be so effective in the long run. The skill lies with the facilitator asking the best questions and making the links for students.

Although Circle Time can serve a therapeutic purpose it is not intended to be group therapy. Similarly, although behaviour is likely to improve, Circle Time is not intended to be a behaviour management strategy.

Why We Need Circle Time for Emotional Literacy

Many children today face major challenges in their everyday lives. Although poverty is a reality for some families, economic disadvantage is not the only reason that children are vulnerable. There is less stability and more stress in families, increased mobility as a result of social and political unrest, more mental illness and addiction, high levels of social exclusion and a competitive ethos which interprets success in terms of money and status, which are denied to many. Racism, violence, fear and greed are on the rise while lower standards of ethical behaviour are evident across all strata. Global conflicts are dealt with in ways that sometimes seem archaic when seen in the light of what we know about effective conflict management. Bullying behaviour and hypocrisy is rife.

It is not surprising that people get the idea that it is everyone for themselves. The importance of strong communities has been systematically eroded. Children may have few good models from which to learn how to work in collaboration with one another or develop constructive ways of dealing with difficulties. Even children from traditionally 'good' homes may believe that they have no responsibility towards others.

That's the bad news. The good news is that there is a resurgence of belief in cooperation, working together and the vital importance of community. There is also a growing awareness that values in education matter.

Professor Fiona Stanley, Australian of the Year 2003, says this:

> There is abundant evidence that the 'me first', individualistic, materialistic approach to life pathways doesn't lead to happiness. Rather, a focus on the quality of our human relations and the collective good or a sense of 'outer directedness' brings much greater individual as well as community well-being. (Stanley et al., 2005: 184)

To develop and learn optimally children need stability, loving and nurturing relationships, acceptance of difference, strong communities and a sense of agency. All of these foster social inclusion and well-being. Where this is lacking in the home and neighbourhood, an emotionally literate school can provide a community with structures and relationships that facilitate and support positive change in individuals. It gives them a sense of belonging that is the cornerstone of resilience. Schools can build community values from the inside out.

Impact of the Social and Emotional Climate of Classrooms and Schools

There is now a wealth of research that highlights the importance of a caring supportive ethos for both well-being and academic outcomes (Cohen, 2001; Zins et al., 2004). Schools that have a strong focus on the welfare of students, and a culture that promotes inclusion, benefit not only the more vulnerable children but everyone. Circle Time is a 'universal' intervention. It is not just about meeting the needs of targeted individuals but developing relationship knowledge and skills for all.

Teacher–Student Relationships

Circle Time has the potential to develop the positive relationships that teachers have with their students in the same way that it changes peer relationships. Many have commented that the intervention has changed the way that they see individuals and increased their enjoyment in teaching their class. Any behaviour management strategy will be more effective when implemented by a teacher who has established a positive relationship with a student (Roffey, 2004; 2005b).

Effective Approaches to Reduce Bullying

Interventions have moved away from focusing exclusively on students who bully and those who are bullied to a whole school approach. Bullying has an impact on everybody and can thrive only in a culture that condones it, either actively or passively. Fear, anxiety, discomfort, anger and disempowerment can thread through a school, undermining positive relationships. Motivating and empowering bystanders to discourage bullying incidents is one of the more promising approaches (Rigby and Bagshaw, 2006). Circle Time can change how students perceive one another and create an ethos in which bullying behaviour is challenged more easily. It also provides an ideal framework to address bullying when it occurs.

Developing Pro-social Behaviour

Reward and sanctions have limited effect in changing behaviour, especially when strong emotions are involved. Although Circle Time is not a behaviour-management strategy, it does provide a place for reflection on behaviour and helps individuals to explore their emotional reactions in situations. If a student is given structured opportunities to establish positive relationships with others in their class, they also have more motivation to behave in pro-social ways.

A Community Approach to Reducing Violence/Restorative Practices

There is a growing interest in addressing conflict between individuals and groups based on building self-respect and relationships and mending what is broken between people. Circle

Time is congruent with the 'alternative to violence' and 'help increase the peace' workshops which have been run in several countries and evaluated as making a positive difference (Phillips, 2002).

Mental Health and Resilience

There are many excellent initiatives taking place to promote mental health in young people and to help them cope with the myriad difficulties that they face in life. These include anger management strategies, peer mediation and social skills programs. However, research indicates that all such initiatives need to be integral to the life of the school to maximize their effectiveness, otherwise the positive effects can wear off (Murray, 2004). Circle Time is not a 'one-off' program but an intervention that is embedded into school life. One of the strongest protective factors in resilience is a sense of belonging. The inclusive ethos of Circle Time actively promotes this.

Democracy and Citizenship

What happens in schools has an impact on what happens in societies. Where there are demands for unquestioning conformity to imposed rules and expectations, young people have no experience of participating in decision-making. Even when there is a school representative council, not everyone has their views represented. Circle Time gives all students the opportunity to express their opinion. This 'agency' develops a sense of ownership and responsibility, not only for students as individuals but also for what happens in their class.

Values and Human Rights

Many education authorities have mission statements about values such as respect. Circle Time provides a space for reflection and deconstruction of these values: what do they mean and why are they important for both individual and communities? Circle Time itself is a values-based framework with a foundation based in both rights and responsibilities.

Promoting Acceptance and Reducing Prejudice

Racism and intolerance of difference is the basis of much conflict in the world. Circle Time actively promotes acceptance by helping students to know one another in ways that break down stereotypes and exploring the many things that individuals and groups have in common. It also celebrates differences and the uniqueness of each individual.

Social Inclusion

There has been much discussion about the impact of social exclusion on the health of the community and ways to address the issue. Social exclusion can be mediated or exacerbated by what happens in schools, and Circle Time is one way of mediating the risk for young individuals by providing a motivation to be engaged in something positive.

Theoretical Foundations of Circle Time

The philosophy of Circle Time is based in several ways of thinking about learning, human interaction, well-being and the development of pro-social behaviours. Many books have been written about each of these. The brief summary provided here is intended to support eclectic practice and enable people to explore these theories more deeply if they so wish.

Positive Psychology and Solution-focused Approaches

This comparatively new branch of psychology focuses on the empirical study of positive emotions, character strengths and healthy institutions. It moves away from the traditional model of psychology that deals with deficit and pathology, in an attempt to discover what actively makes people happier and more fulfilled (Seligman et al., 2005). The evidence so far indicates that meaningful and engaged lives are more important than pleasurable experiences in determining well-being.

Circle Time seeks to help students to identify their strengths, competencies and potential. It encourages collaboration to construct possible solutions to everyday issues. Often it is not a direct approach that works best but an indirect one focusing on the positive. Instead of talking about bullying, we can talk about safety; instead of discussing stealing, we talk about trust and how trust develops.

Social Learning Theory

Much of our learning occurs in a social context, including watching and hearing others. Circle Time provides many opportunities for both active and reflective learning and collaborative problem-solving. It supports the attention skills necessary to maximize observational learning, strongly advocating that the facilitator models the behaviours that they want the children to learn (Bandura, 1986).

Eco-systemic Theory

Each person lives and works in nested systems, all of which have an impact on the other in both directions (Moen et al., 1995). This theory, originally developed by Urie Bronfenbrenner, emphasizes that there is rarely a simple cause and effect in human relationships and behaviours but that events, the context in which they occur, interpretations and responses interact in an accumulative and circular way to produce an outcome at any given time. Circle Time is intended to make a positive difference within context: for individual students and teachers, groups and classes and their thinking, being and doing both inside and outside the Circle.

Social Constructionist Theory

This emphasizes the power of language: how what people say and the way that they say it create 'realities' for their worlds. Circle Time actively changes the discourse in order to construct some alternative ways of seeing the world. This theory says that what much of what we feel is also socially constructed. If the dominant culture promotes success as having high grades then people will feel proud or ashamed of their results: if the dominant culture dictates an obligation to defend your family against any abusive remarks, you are more likely to experience anger if someone says something nasty about them (Potter, 1996; Vygotsky, 1978).

Choice Theory

William Glasser (1997) says everyone seeks to have their needs met in whichever ways are available to them. These needs are for love, freedom, power, belonging and fun. Glasser emphasized the importance of schools exploring ways in which to meet these needs within a whole school framework. He also emphasized the need for respectful relationships and for everyone to take appropriate responsibility for the choices that they make. Circle Time puts choice theory into practice in several ways.

Attachment Theory

People need to feel a sense of belonging, inclusion and safety in order to function well. Attachment theory usually refers to the relationship that infants have with their immediate carers and the impact this has on their future functioning (Bowlby, 1982[1969]). However, we know that a sense of belonging can be developed by people outside that immediate group and provide a buffer of resilience for children who are otherwise very vulnerable. Circle Time supports this sense of inclusion in a class setting.

Moral Development Theories

There are different theoretical approaches to moral development, with different emphases on justice, fairness and the 'ethic of care' (Gilligan, 1982; Kohlberg and Turiel, 1971). However, being 'good' needs to develop from simple obedience to authority and conformity to social norms, to understanding why we make the choices that we do, and what is involved in responsibility towards the self and others. Circle Time provides an opportunity for reflection on these issues, so that moral values can be internalized with a sound personal rationale rather than be imposed from without.

Summary

There are many reasons to consider using Circle Time in your classroom. The next chapter details how to successfully establish the framework with your students – how to get it going.

CHAPTER 2

The Circle Time Framework and Getting Circle Time Going in Your Class

The chapter describes what happens in a circle session and the specific processes that maximize effectiveness. There are also suggestions for: getting Circle Time going with a class – working on the basic rules and philosophy; what to do when students struggle with expectations and do not conform to the rules; adaptations for children with additional needs and/or language difficulties; and sensitive situations.

The Circle Format

The importance of having everyone sitting in a Circle is both symbolic and practical. A Circle symbolizes inclusion. It brings people into a whole, where each person is important. In a Circle, no one is isolated or left out. A circle symbolizes connection. There are evident links between everyone – it encourages wholeness rather than fragmentation.

A Circle symbolizes equality. Everyone is at the same level and has the same right to participate. Everyone has the same responsibility to the others in the circle. The boundary between teacher and students is weakened, as the expectations are that the facilitators are also participants and must abide by the same rules.

When people sit in a circle each individual can see everyone else. This makes it easier to hear what someone is saying. You can see what they are communicating by non-verbal means. No one is looking at someone else's back and there is nothing between the speaker and listener. Because no one is hidden there is limited opportunity to speak behind someone's back. Disrespectful behaviour such as making negative comments or gestures is less likely to occur. If they do happen it becomes obvious to everyone in the circle.

In a Circle it is easier to focus attention on what is happening – distractions are less possible and less powerful. Sitting in a circle together with the Circle Time framework reduces domination of discussion by a small number of people. This both encourages participation from everyone and inhibits the development of a dominant view perpetrated by a powerful faction. The space in the middle of the Circle is valuable for everyone to either mingle together or see clearly what is going on.

Moving Furniture

Getting everyone into a Circle can sometimes be challenging. Organizing students to move furniture might appear to be more trouble than it is worth. However, once a routine is established so that everyone knows what they are supposed to do, it becomes less of a problem. As students like Circle Time they are usually motivated to get on with it. Plan where the tables are going to go, who is going to move what to where and how to put it all back together at the end. Some teachers have arranged their classroom layout to make Circle Time easier, or have found that Circle Time has changed their pedagogy and students no longer sit in rows.

There is no doubt that Circle Time works better on chairs – participants can move about more easily. However, some teachers have established Circle Time by using small pieces of carpet for children to sit on; others draw a chalk circle on the floor. One imaginative teacher has the children doing a conga dance to music until the front of the line catches up with the end and then everyone sits down in the circle they have formed.

Role of the Circle Facilitator

The way in which Circles are run is central to their effectiveness, therefore the skills of the facilitator are crucial. An effective facilitator aims to:

- guide the process so that it is coherent with the underlying principles and values

- participate fully in all activities and model expected behaviour – this means listening respectfully and not putting students down

- emphasize the need for respect and safety for all

- be positive and optimistic

- be sensitive to the needs of the class and choose appropriate activities

- repeat rules to everyone as much as possible, rather than singling out individuals

- introduce activities so that everyone understands what to do and give opportunities for questions and practice where appropriate

- comment briefly on the aims of activities and summarize what has been achieved

- acknowledge all contributions, especially feedback from group activities

- be aware of time issues and maintain an effective pace

- ensure that people move physically – no Circle Time should be all sitting

- be creative and prepared to be flexible if the need arises

- be sensitive to individual circumstances where possible

- offer opportunities to students to take a lead when they are familiar with the framework

- offer choices to students who resist conforming to the basic rules – they can choose not to participate in the Circle but this is their choice.

The participation of the facilitator is of particular importance. In silent statements, for example, the facilitator can show that they also experience some difficult situations or emotions and this will encourage others to acknowledge similar events for themselves.

The emotional and social learning that Circle Time activities promote requires the facilitator both to model these skills and to help students make connections between what they are doing, what they are learning, how they are feeling and the changes in the class ethos. Using 'I' statements is helpful. This means using phrases such as: 'I need one person to speak at a time so I can hear what is being said', rather than: 'Stop talking all at once'. Also, an element of enthusiasm makes a big difference. Even the best games can fall flat with a half-hearted introduction.

You will notice throughout this book that 'teacher' and 'facilitator' are interchangeable terms but that activities may have a 'leader'. This is deliberate as students may take the role of leader and, as they become familiar with Circle Time, are encouraged to do so.

Resources

Many of the activities in this book require little in the way of additional materials. However, a facilitator would be advised to have a selection of resources kept separately for use in Circle Time. These might include some or all of the following:

- a 'talking piece' to show whose turn it is to speak

- separate emotions on cards: words and/or pictures depending on the age and ability of students

- books, stories and pictures which can be used as stimulus material

- 'strength' cards or similar

- rolls of paper and coloured pens

- old cards for cutting up into jigsaw pieces for getting groups together

- music, visualizations and meditations

- materials for favourite games

- eye shades, such as those given to passengers on long flights, which make good quick 'blindfolds'.

(A list of published and Internet resources is given in Chapter 10.)

What Happens in Circle Time?

A Typical Half-hour Circle Time Session

- Reminder of the rules (1 minute)

- Introductory game (2 minutes)

- Mix-up activity (2 minutes)

- Pair share with feedback or passed interviews (2 minutes for pair share, 5 minutes for feedback)

- Whole group activity or game (5 minutes)

- Small group activity or discussion (10 minutes with feedback)

- Calming activity to close the circle (3 minutes)

Each Circle Time is different. Although the content can be flexible, the principles of safety, respect and inclusion are consistent.

Reminder of the Rules

Once everyone is in the Circle there is a statement of the rules by either the teacher or students.

- everyone has a turn and when one person is talking everyone else listens.

- you do not have to say anything; you may pass

- there are no put-downs – only 'personal positives'.

An Introductory Game

This can be a greeting, name game or energizer (See Chapter 3 for ideas)

Introductory games can also be sentence completions. Here the facilitator provides a sentence stem, which is completed by each person round the Circle – ideas in Chapters 4–9. This activity ensures that everyone has the chance to say something but keeps contributions brief. It helps individuals to feel they are being 'heard', supports listening skills and increases emotional resources by reducing feelings of isolation. Silent statements have a similar effect but also maximize safety. A sentence stem can double up as a check-in: 'Today I am …'

Mix-up Activity

This is an essential feature of Circle Time as it provides opportunities for individuals to interact with others outside of their usual social network.

Pair Share with Feedback

This is a structured conversation that draws out what people have in common. It is helpful to ask for two items for feedback so that each person in the pair has something to say to the group. Partners may need to be reminded to swap around.

Paired Interviews

Each partner finds out something about the other. This promotes questioning and listening. If there is to be feedback, each partner is asked what information may be shared with the whole circle. This demonstrates an important element of respect.

Whole Group Activity or Game

Do not leave this out: it is where students have most fun and is a great motivator for Circle Time.

Small Group Activity or Discussion

Small group work is particularly valuable for collaborative activities and for problem-solving. Discussions should provide brief feedback to the whole group and may be recorded if they are ways to address class issues. Stimulus material such as stories, pictures, music or film clips can be useful here.

Calming Activity to Close the Circle

Relaxation, visualization, meditation or quiet reflective activity – this is particularly necessary if the Circle has been very lively and will be followed by a return to more 'academic' activities. Also, a 'check-out' can provide a reflection on the session: 'In this circle I learned/enjoyed … .'

Planning Circle Time Sessions

There are different ways to think about how to plan Circle Time in your class. It is useful probably to have a general idea of what you want to address throughout the year, but be prepared to do this flexibly. You could devise your own structure to focus on areas in a certain order but follow the lead of your students when appropriate and work with the issues that seem most relevant to your class at the current time. It is useful to establish familiarity with the framework and enthusiasm for Circle Time before attempting more challenging topics.

Work across chapters in this book: you may be choosing activities that address self-awareness, a sense of belonging, emotional skills and communication in one Circle session. Issues such as bullying can be approached from different perspectives. Themes can be revisited in consecutive years, as there is plenty of scope for development. Friendship, for example, has different meanings for four, seven, 10 and 13-year-olds.

Another way is to use a curriculum base on which to structure activities. Social and emotional competencies have an increasing profile in education internationally and there are stated outcomes in many curriculum documents related to personal, social and health education, values in schools, safe schools frameworks and citizenship education. In the UK, Appendix Five of the *Excellence and Enjoyment: Social and Emotional Aspects of Learning* (SEAL) document

(Department for Education and Skills (DfES), 2005) says that Circle Time is potentially an effective vehicle for classroom delivery of this SEAL program. The National Framework for Values Education in Australia (Commonwealth of Australia, 2005) addresses many of the same issues that Circle Time does, including respect, compassion and responsibility. Many activities are multidimensional and meet several criteria at once, including a broad range of communication skills, personal development and health education.

The Importance of Process – What You Need to Make it Work

Students need to know clearly what to do – if necessary, break down instructions into small manageable chunks. Demonstrate if it is a new game. Activities need to be mostly short, not too complicated to explain and enjoyable. Encourage brevity in activities such as sentence completions and use energizers to help maintain a good pace. These are activities that require people to get up and move around. Sometimes time restrictions make it difficult for everyone to give feedback, so a student from the small groups may be nominated to do this on behalf of the group. Any other group member has a chance to add a comment if they wish.

Circle Time is a regular, not an intermittent, intervention: once a regular routine is established, students look forward to that particular time slot and unless there are really exceptional circumstances, Circle Time should not be jettisoned in favour of something else. Students may take time to become familiar with the framework but are usually highly motivated once they realize how enjoyable it can be.

The framework allows both teachers and students to develop their own content, and although this book contains many ideas to choose from there are other many other resources available. Sometimes students will create their own games together or bring in new ideas from home. Stimulus materials can be very helpful. Stories and pictures enable students to discuss emotions and difficult issues without referring to themselves. Asking children to discuss 'What might a child your age think or do?' can help to create psychological distance and safety. Comments on the learning gained in Circle activities and games make the Circle not just fun but meaningful.

Most significantly, the teacher needs to facilitate Circle Time rather than control the proceedings. It requires a high level of skill to do this well but it has great benefits in building positive relationships with the class and increasing group responsibility for individual and collective well-being.

You know that Circle Time is really effective when you see changes in the students at other times in the school day. The following are comments from teachers in an evaluation of Circle Time:

> One kid will say, 'I get lonely in the playground sometimes' and people who have never seen this kid before will say 'Oh well, I'll be with you at lunchtime if you like.'

> I found that the whole positive rephrasing, not using 'put downs' has rolled over into every day.

And, from a student:

> You think about when you've done bad things and you want to make up for it. (Roffey, 2005a)

Students may welcome acknowledgement that they are making changes to develop a positive, supportive class – *their* ideas and actions are making a difference.

Why Games?

I come from a family who have always played games together. Every Christmas afternoon as far back as I can remember we have played 'the drawing game' or 'in the manner of the word'. As I grew up and became a teacher, a mother and then a psychologist I realized what a blessing this game playing has been. I learned so much about being part of a team, what is needed for everyone to have a good time and that it is not fun when someone cheats, sulks or dominates. I learned about words, numbers, feelings and thinking creatively. These games bring all ages together in shared fun and laughter. Winning or losing does not matter much, it is the process that counts.

It would seem that children today have fewer opportunities to enjoy such games together. They no longer routinely play out in the street and are not allowed in parks without the watchful eye of an adult. Privileged young people spend their lives being ferried from one activity to another. Less advantaged children may live in an increasingly passive world where they watch others do things on TV rather than doing them themselves. Games often mean solitary computer games or hand held battles which hone eye-hand coordination or at least eye–thumb coordination as various enemies are slaughtered to accompanying dramatic sounds. Alternatively, games mean competitive sports where the importance of winning at all costs dominates interactions.

In this book there are new activities developed from Circle Time training, ideas collated from my own history including teaching both young children and teenagers and activities remembered from youth groups. Friends and colleagues have shared games they have been using and I have surfed the Internet and identified other books as a resource. There is a plethora of creative possibilities out there and I have picked a few which fit the Circle Time format and philosophy well. Activities will be successful if they are clearly understood, timely, appropriate to the particular needs and characteristics of your class, engage all students positively – especially by not singling out individuals to lose – and can be linked to one of the aims of Circle Time. If one thing falls flat, try another: there are plenty from which to choose.

Getting Circle Time Started in Your Class

For some students Circle Time is a very different way of being in school. Most love it and take to it immediately with great enthusiasm. Others take time to get used to being given a voice, being given choices and being asked to respect and listen to others. For classes where students do not conform it is useful to think about both preempting difficulties and how to respond to challenges when they do occur.

Clarifying the Rules

Everyone gets a turn and when one person is speaking everyone else listens

Many Circle Time facilitators have incorporated a physical symbol – a 'talking piece' – that indicates whose turn it is to speak. This is especially useful for younger students but is acceptable for any age. It could be a magic wand, 'rainstick', shell, puppet, soft toy, or a laminated card with a picture or words. Some older students like the idea of a microphone but others find this a little intimidating. One class uses a large plastic yellow flower and the more shy children hide behind this. The advantages of a talking piece are many:

- it reinforces the principle of equality in the circle

- it ensures that everyone knows who has the right to speak at any given time

- it encourages thinking before speaking

- it encourages the contribution of the quieter students

- it increases peer pressure to listen

- it shows how close it is to each person's turn

- it helps as a reminder of who started the round

- it reinforces the safety of passing as someone can simply pass the talking piece.

No Put-Downs: Personal Positives Only

Defining what this means may need to be done over several sessions. These are examples of activities that you might incorporate to do this:

*Sentence completion:

- A personal positive might be …

- To me a put-down would be …

- I would feel putdown in Circle Time if …

- A put-down feels …

- Circle Time needs to feel …

- If someone gave me a personal positive I would feel …

*Ask your students to interview one another about what a put-down is and how it makes them feel about themselves and the person who does it.

Summarize what the students have said and reinforce as necessary. You may also want to ask small groups to decide on an appropriate response to put-downs if they happen in the Circle.

Passing

This rule ensures psychological safety. Everyone has the choice to say something or not. Even when students appear to use the pass rule as defiance, this can be interpreted as a statement that they do not yet feel safe enough to participate fully. Some students pass all the time when they are not used to Circle Time. Smile and nod to acknowledge their presence and ask them again at the end of the round if they wish to say something now.

Teachers sometimes find it difficult to accept that students choose not to contribute. Remember that they are watching and learning from others and that this is a legitimate way of gaining knowledge and skills. Usually, they will be taking part in the whole group and non-verbal activities. Experience indicates that peer pressure and wanting to be part of the group means that all students eventually contribute, even though this may take a long time for some individuals.

Choosing Activities and Maintaining Pace

When you first introduce Circle Time, choose activities that are motivating and simple to understand: 'When the Warm Wind Blows' (Chapter 7) is popular with primary-aged children, and 'Guessing Good At' (Chapter 5) is a simple way to acknowledge strengths. Many of the activities in Chapter 7 are intended for a class to begin to get to know one another and are fun to do at all levels.

Attention to pace is important, especially when establishing a Circle Time routine. Ensure that all individuals are engaged quickly either by having their turn to speak or being involved in a large group or small group activity. Alternate sitting activities with energizers that require participants to get up and move about; whole group games with actions can have the same effect. Try to have quick rounds so that no one has to wait long for their turn. Encourage brief answers in sentence completions.

Monitoring and Evaluation

This not only helps the teacher know how Circle Time is going, but also supports those students who want it to go well but might be 'shouted down' by a powerful and negative minority. This can be done in several ways, for example, by sentence completion:

- The best thing about Circle Time is …

- Circle Time is best when …

- My responsibility in Circle Time is to …

or silent statements:

- Stand up and change places if you like having Circle Time in this class/want Circle Time to continue/don't want to have Circle Time anymore.

or small group activities:

- Which games do we like the best?

- What three things would make Circle Time even better?

Making Circle Time Inclusive

One of the principles of Circle Time is that it is an inclusive activity. Everyone gets the chance to be involved. This means that adaptations will need to be made on occasions for individuals. Some suggestions are made below.

Check-In

Some facilitators have found that a 'check-in' activity at the beginning of a Circle session can be valuable, especially for older students. This is a brief round that gives everyone the chance to say how things are for them at the moment. This could be sharing one good thing that has happened since the last Circle or perhaps just one word to describe how things are going this week.

Students Who Find it Difficult to Take Part in Circle Time Properly

All of the ideas given below are strategies that teachers have put in place when some students struggle with the expectations for Circle Time, especially at the beginning:

- stopping an activity and saying: 'We are just going to wait until everyone is ready'

- stopping the activity and simply repeating the rules to everyone so that no one student or group is singled out

- mixing students up to break up negative groups.

One teacher has said that if an individual continues to disregard the rules she quietly asks them to leave the Circle – they can choose to return when they can feel capable of joining in appropriately. If it happens a second time then they are asked to leave the Circle for the duration of that session.

Occasionally students will leave the Circle but continue to disrupt from outside. Special arrangements may need to be made for such individuals, but they need to know that they will be welcomed back into the Circle whenever they think they can manage this. Asking students if they would like to join in for the last five minutes and then increasing that time might help.

In another class a child with social and behavioural difficulties is given things to do at a table just outside the Circle. He chooses the activities that he could join in with, and when he is in the Circle he has to conform, like everyone else.

One teacher found that very short, fun Circles that got gradually longer were successful in accommodating a seriously traumatized child.

A high school teacher uses a check-in activity at the beginning to give older students the chance to opt out if they so choose.

An outline of the Circle session on the board with an option to change an activity also increases commitment.

Having Circle Time at the end of the day is helpful when students find it difficult to calm down to resume normal class activities; focusing on small group activities rather than whole Circle games might also reduce such problems.

One teacher analysed why her class was resistant to Circle Time and found that not having tables made them feel exposed and vulnerable. She moved Circle Time sessions outside for a while, where students stood rather than sat and played 'sporty' non-verbal games. The talking component was gradually reintroduced with non-threatening topics, then mix-up games and fun collaborative activities. It took a term to get the class back inside with a traditional Circle Time format but eventually this happened.

Another teacher asked students to come up with suggestions to help those who could not conform so that they could all have a good time.

Persistence and involving students usually pays off. If the Circle is lively and fun then most students will not want to miss out and will have a vested interest in it continuing; the serious stuff can come later. The general view is that in some classes it can take a while before everyone settles to a positive Circle Time routine. Some students get into a run either of 'passing' or repeating what someone else has said. This stops in time and individuals become more creative and innovative in their contributions. Younger children sometimes respond positively to the teacher using a puppet as the Circle Time 'facilitator'. Encouraging students to take turns in leading some structured activities may increase confidence in shyer individuals and provide opportunities for students who are dominant to use their abilities more constructively.

If you have a serious difficulty with several students in Circle Time, first, simply ask the group to sit down and discuss what is happening and ask for their ideas for how it might be made better so that everyone can join in: you may wish to do this in small groups initially. As a last resort, rather than give up altogether, consider making this a voluntary activity for whoever wishes to attend.

Some teachers have divided larger class groups into two to make it more manageable at the outset. You will not get all the benefits of Circle Time in developing a whole class ethos, but when clearly a group is having fun it motivates others to join in.

Students with Learning Difficulties

Circle Time caters for many different learning styles – visual, auditory, kinaesthetic, experiential, individual and cooperative – so there is something here for everyone. Circles are not overly dependent on academic skills such as reading and writing, and therefore are usually suitable for a wide ability range. However, you may wish to have activities at the beginning of the Circle that include everyone and then do one or more of the following:

- ask a partner or small group to support a particular child so that they are always part of what is going on – this should not always be the same people, so that everyone gets a chance to be a supporter

- amend more challenging activities so that there is a specific role for an individual which they can manage.

(For communication difficulties see the suggestions below.)

Students with Language Difficulties

Circle Time is an excellent place to develop language skills, as it does not undermine confidence and supports social development in a structured way. There are many non-verbal activities here that ensure that everyone is included. Students who have fewer language skills than others in the group are likely to need more opportunities to watch and listen rather than actively participate. They need to be aware of the 'pass rule' so that they can feel safe at all times.

However, there are several ways to increase participation for children with language difficulties in Circle Time. Maximize visual support so that there are models to copy, pictures to reinforce words and alternative communication opportunities such as miming or drawing. Peer support and encouragement to participate include limiting the amount of language given at any one time, speaking slowly, using simple terms supported by gestures and expressions and offering to speak for someone. Where students are learning English as an additional language, other more fluent students may be paired with them on occasions to help out. This needs to be planned carefully so that the responsibility does not fall consistently on one person.

Circle Time is also a place where other languages and signing might be introduced, so that children perhaps learn songs from other countries or how to use simple signs to aid communication. Circle Time is ideal for students with hearing impairment as they can see one another's faces and can therefore lip-read more easily.

Sensitive Issues and Confidentiality

Circle Time focuses primarily on strengths and positives, but for some students inevitably there will be times when the issues under discussion touch on harsh realities in their own lives. The skills of the facilitator are crucial here, as well as the knowledge that the teacher has about their class. This supports intuition about what is appropriate or not. Let students know that if there is an activity that makes them feel uncomfortable in any way they may step out of the Circle and do a quiet activity on their own. Re-emphasize the 'pass' rule. It can be helpful to remind students, especially older ones, that they must take responsibility for what they choose to say and that they can only speak for themselves. It makes discussions safer if the group stays with issues and the third person rather than asking for personal information. In this instance, you may choose to limit the use of the word 'I'.

Many classes have discussed ground rules for their own Circle Time, including: 'What is said in the Circle, stays in the Circle'. It is hard to guarantee that this will always happen, but if the confidentiality of the Circle is broken in a damaging or hurtful way this needs to become an issue that everyone addresses (see Loss of Trust, Chapter 9).

If a facilitator realizes that a student is disclosing very personal information then gentle intervention would be appropriate. It is vital that this is done by giving the impression that what they are saying is too important for Circle Time rather than dismissing it. They may be encouraged to speak afterwards with the teacher and perhaps to write or draw for their Circle Time file (see Chapter 3). If there is someone in the school who takes responsibility for listening to students then it might be appropriate to refer to this person. Disclosures that indicate serious harm for any individual require mandatory reporting. All students in a school should be aware that this is the case, whether in Circle Time, a counselling session or an informal conversation with a teacher.

The Basics

In this chapter you will find a wide range of activities for opening Circle Time, managing the transition from one activity to another, different ways to mix participants up and calming activities for the end of a circle session. Unless there are indications otherwise, all activities in this section are appropriate for all age groups.

It is useful for everyone to have their own Circle Time file in which they can collect things about themselves that they draw or write in Circle Time such as cloud dreams, shields and life maps. This can also double up as a place to write or draw about more personal and/or difficult issues that are less appropriate for Circle Time discussion.

Opening and Greetings

As previously mentioned, all Circle sessions begin with a reminder of the rules, either given by the teacher or students:

- everyone has a turn–when one person is speaking, we all listen

- there are no put-downs

- you may pass.

Silent Greetings

For all of the following activities, one person carries out the action towards the person sitting on their left or right. The activity then goes around the circle until it reaches the person it started with:

- Pass the Smile

- High five–right hand to right hand to the person on the left is easiest

- Handshake–right hand to left side again

■ Mexican Wave—everyone stands up in turn and throws their arms in the air and sits down again. This forms a 'wave' around the circle. You can do this calling out your name as your turn comes around

■ Pass the Wink

■ Pass the Hand-squeeze—once the class can do this smoothly, you can add sound. When the squeeze is going to the left you say 'Ooh', and when it is going to the right you say 'Aahh'. Send a couple of squeezes around, speed it up and change direction from time to time!

Spoken greetings

■ My name is …

■ Each person says their name and the rest of the class echo it back three times, starting loudly and ending with a whisper

■ You say the name of the person on your right, your own name and then the name of the person on your left

■ Ways of Greeting—go around the circle with as many different ways you can think of: 'Hi', 'Hello', 'Good morning', 'Nice to see you', 'How's it going?'

■ I am [positive adjective] name: 'I am smiley Sam', 'I am terrific Tom', 'I am amazing Abdul'

■ Say your name and then a feeling starting with the same letter: 'I am Geeta and I am feeling great', 'I am Wahid and I am feeling wonderful', 'I am Cherie and I am feeling cheerful'.

■ Say your name backwards – maS, neB, enaJ, arimaS, ahpatsuM.

Name Games: Combined Words and Actions

■ Stand and sit again as you say your name

■ Stand and sit again as your name is spoken (doing this with the person on your left and right is much more difficult than you might think–it requires a lot of concentration)

Soft Balls   **YMS**

One person throws a soft ball at someone and says their name as they are doing it. This person throws to another and then puts their hands behind their back to show they have had a turn. When everyone has been named you can reverse the sequence. Each person throws the ball to the person who threw it to them: again saying their name. Let everyone know this is what will happen so they focus on remembering who threw the ball to them.

Variations

(For the following you do not put your hands behind your back when you have had a turn.)

- When you drop a ball you play with a 'forfeit', for example, with one hand only then down on one knee. You can 'regain' this loss with a subsequent catch so the aim is for others to help you out and get you back on your feet again.

- With music: the aim is to not be holding the ball when the music stops.

- Add a second or third ball.

Bunnies

This needs good attention skills. The game begins with someone putting both hands up on their head as 'bunny ears', waggling their fingers. The person on their right puts up their left hand as an ear; the person on their left puts up their right hand. The middle person 'passes the bunny' by calling out the name of another person in the circle and pointing at them with both their hands. This person becomes the 'bunny' with those on either side also putting up the nearest hand. This is a great game for concentration, especially for those on either side of the bunny. Continue until everyone has had a turn. When you have had a turn you sit on your hands (on your bunny ears). You can play this as a 'silent' game without names too.

Names on a Train

A student volunteers to be the train conductor. They go up to someone in the circle and say: 'What's your name?' This person says their name, e.g. 'Wayne' and the conductor repeats it and then says 'come on board, Wayne'. Wayne then goes to the front of the train and approaches another in the Circle, asking: 'What's your name?'. He repeats the name, the 'conductor' behind him repeats the name and says 'come on board ... '. This game continues with each successive person coming onto the front of the train. As names are said they have to go down the line until they reach the 'conductor' at the back who welcomes them 'on board'. When the last person has been picked up the conductor says: 'Everybody off the train', and everyone goes back to a chair in the circle. Students can lift their arms up and down or make train noises as they go around the circle 'picking up passengers' to add to the energy. The facilitator should be 'picked up' last.

Good Morning Captain

(This is a good game for a class who know one another well.)

One person is blindfolded in the middle. The leader indicates someone in the Circle who says 'Good morning Captain'. If the person in the middle can identify who it is they say 'Good morning' (and their name). They then become the 'Captain'. If the person in the middle cannot do this the first time the person says again

'I said Good morning Captain'. If they still cannot identify who it is, the whole group says: 'Captain, Captain, that was [person's name] – now who is this?' Another person says 'Good morning Captain' and the game continues. Disguising voices makes this more fun.

Name Chain
YM

Each person finds another who has at least four letters in their name that are the same (less for the youngest children). They hold hands. Now each of the pair find others which connect with them. Within a short space of time everyone should be linked together.

Autographs
MS

(A good activity for students who do not know one another well.)

Everyone has a copy of the class roll. They take this around to each of their classmates and everyone signs next to their name. You could ask people to explain how their name is pronounced if it is unusual, or whether they prefer to be known by a shortened version or nickname. This means that each individual has a brief interaction with every other individual in the class.

Transitions

After a paired or small group activity the facilitator needs to regain everyone's attention. The best way to do this is to negotiate it with your class. They will come up with a whole range of different ideas. Here are a few you might like to suggest or try in the meantime:

- clapping rhythm and then hands on knees – everyone copies

- fingers on noses – everyone follows suit and looks at the teacher

- hand in the air – everyone copies as soon as they see the action (this one is particularly useful for younger children)

- folded arms, or hands in laps – each person follows suit as they notice

- pass the message quietly round the circle

- counting down from five–as people hear the facilitator count they join in, and when everyone gets to one then there is silence

- a small tinkling bell, hooter or other sound.

If students are involved in an intensive small group activity or discussion it is good practice to give them warning that their time is nearly up. If people are going to feed back to the group, ask them to sort out who is going to say what at this point. Even if one person is nominated to speak, all others in the team should have the opportunity to add something if they wish.

Mixing Up

Mixing individuals up so that they interact with different people in the class is a central feature of Circle Time. This can be done in many different ways.

Personal Categories

Have categories that are as innocuous as possible and do not highlight differences in a potentially hurtful way. What is comfortable would depend on the circumstances of people in the class.

Stand up and change places:

- everyone who has blue eyes (brown eyes, green eyes, grey eyes)

- everyone who has a sister (a brother, a pet)

- everyone who likes ice-cream (chocolate, bananas, chips, orange juice)

- everyone who can ride a bike (climb a tree, whistle a tune)

- everyone who can speak more than one language

- everyone who likes football (tennis, cricket, swimming, running)

- everyone who saw (a film, a match, a TV programme)

- everyone with a birthday in …

- everyone who has had measles (mumps, flu, chicken pox)

- everyone whose name begins with (ends with, includes …)

Given Categories

Here the facilitator gives names or numbers to everyone in the circle, then asks everyone whose name or number is called to swap places. There are many possibilities. The simplest is to give everyone in the circle a number: then you could ring the changes – all even numbers change places, (specific) numbers change places, all numbers which are in the five times table change places. Other categories could be:

- seasons

- months

- colours

- alphabet

- shapes

- types of cake–chocolate, ginger, iced, fruit, sponge

- names of planets, cars, countries, states or counties, flowers, trees, animals.

Mixing Up Games to Form Small Groups or Find Partners

Students quickly get used to the fact that they will be working with a wide range of their classmates rather than in friendship or ability groups. Although you may get initial objections, this is one of the things that students like best about Circle Time.

- Cut up paint-sample cards so that groups find those with the same colour (quick and easy).

- Cut up old birthday cards, postcards or similar into the same number of pieces as there are in a group. Jumble the pieces up and give one piece to each person. They find their group by putting the pieces together.

- Put the names or pictures of animals onto cards. Four cards are the same: dog, rabbit, elephant, cat, fish and penguin are good ones. The leader gives each person a card – they memorize it and give it back. They then find the rest of their animal 'family' using only animal noises and actions. (You could put the names of musical instruments, swimming strokes, feelings, sporting teams.)

- Find your family – for groups of five. Each person is given a paper with 'Mr', 'Mrs', 'Brother', 'Sister' or 'Baby' and the family name (or variations on this – grandma, mum, daughter, cat and dog – the important thing is the family name at the end). This paper is folded in half. Everyone mingles in the middle, passing on their paper as many times as possible. When the leader calls out 'Find your Family', everyone looks at the paper they now have and seeks others in the same family. You could ask students to do this without words or to line up in a certain order.

- On separate cards put names or pictures of things that go together, such as knife and fork, pencil and paper, hat and coat or phrases such as 'Happy Birthday' or 'Prime Minister'. When all students have their card, they find their 'pair'.

- Half the cards have capital letters and the other half have lower case. Students find their matching half.

- Words with two syllables: car-pet, hon-ey, break-fast, morn-ing, sun-shine, pan-cake. The pictures on the other side help those who are not yet able to read. This takes time to prepare but then can be used many times.

Closing the Circle

The final activity in a circle session needs to be a calming one. Students often get excited by playing the games and need something that will settle them. There are many ways to do this.

Relaxation Exercises

Deep Breathing

It is useful to teach children to breathe deeply for many reasons. It is a strategy to reduce stress, ease tension, increase calm and improve feelings of well-being. Ask the Circle to sit comfortably with their feet on the floor and their hands resting in their laps. They concentrate on their breathing and then take a few normal deep breaths. Ask them to breathe out so that their lungs are empty and then breathe in slowly for a count of six, hold the breath in and then breathe out for a count of six. Do this several times.

Deep Breathing with Visualization

Each time a deep breath is taken the person imagines that they are filling up with light or peacefulness and that this is passing into their bloodstream, being taken to all parts of their body to give them a feeling of calm or good energy.

Tense and Release

In this exercise the students tighten muscles in different parts of their body and then release them. You can do this in different parts of the body separately or start with the feet and work up and then release gradually, so that everything becomes very floppy, the head rests on the chest and the arms hang loosely. Hold this very loose position for a minute. You may find that lying on the floor is better than sitting on chairs.

Sounds

Everyone closes their eyes and sits comfortably. Begin by raising awareness of all the sounds that they can hear outside of the room, then bring them inside and listen for any sounds in the room. Finally they focus on sounds inside themselves, their own breathing and even heartbeat. Do not worry if you get a tummy rumble: a good laugh is relaxing too.

Stretching

For this activity, students stand with their feet slightly apart. They begin by reaching with both arms high over their head. Bring their arms down level with shoulders but then reach out far in front. Now come down and bend from the waist so that they are trying to touch the floor with their fingertips without bending the knees. Now ask them then to stand sideways so that they are facing the back of the person in front. Ask them to stretch as far out as they can, as if they are trying to touch the walls on either side. Now they face the front again and this time go very loose and shake out their hands and arms.

Stories

A short story or poem with a gentle theme – nothing too exciting or sad. The aim is to leave the circle with a positive feeling.

Visualization

Children can respond surprisingly well to the idea that they can create imaginary worlds in their head and enjoy being guided in this. Keep your visualizations short enough to maintain concentration for the age group in the class. Bring them out of the visualization slowly. Ask the children to sit comfortably with their feet on the floor and their hands in their lap. Ask them to close their eyes and imagine:

- a peaceful place

- a safe place

- a magic place

- a place where there are no crowds, no noise and where they feel comfortable–help them to imagine what they see there, any gentle sounds they might hear

- take an imaginary journey

- create a safe place–sitting around this place are people who will take care of them.

One Minute Massage

This takes a little training (see Chapter 10: Resources) but when done correctly, helps everyone to feel calm and relaxed. The facilitator shows everyone how to do a one-minute neck, shoulder and back massage by demonstrating with a volunteer and talking through what makes a good massage. Everyone turns to their left and massages the person whose back is now in front of them.

Check-out

This activity summarizes the learning and/or how participants feel at the end of the Circle. This can be a simple sentence completion, pair share or the use of a picture that represents the learning in some way.

Sleeping Lions

(A favourite with teachers.)

All the students lie on the floor. They have to stay very still as if they were 'sleeping lions'. When the leader sees someone moving they tap them gently and say which part they saw moving. That student then quietly finds a seat back in the circle. Students, who are 'out' can help the leader by pointing to someone who is wriggling but must stay silent. When there are only two or three people left on the floor, the leader says 'lions alive' and these children join the rest of the group in the Circle.

Circle Activities to Promote Communication

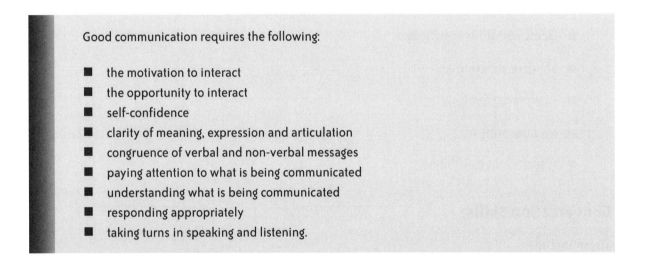

Good communication requires the following:

- the motivation to interact
- the opportunity to interact
- self-confidence
- clarity of meaning, expression and articulation
- congruence of verbal and non-verbal messages
- paying attention to what is being communicated
- understanding what is being communicated
- responding appropriately
- taking turns in speaking and listening.

Concentration span depends on age and development – younger children cannot manage more than a few pieces of information at any one time. This means that the younger the child, the shorter and less complicated the interactions and the more visual support they need. Children benefit from opportunities to interact with one another, even if they cannot use words yet. Those who have very little social confidence or poor language skills may join in readily with non-verbal games which promote interaction, even when their spoken language skills are minimal.

Circle Time activities in this chapter are focused on developing the following.

Attention Skills

Before we can listen we need to be able to attend to the appropriate stimulus. We live in a world beset by distractions, and sometimes focusing on just one thing is hard to do. There are many excellent games here to help children tune into a stimulus.

Motivation and Confidence

The incorporation of non-verbal or minimally-verbal games is intended to promote social confidence. Children are motivated to speak about things that are of real interest to them, where they feel safe, so activities are structured to incorporate these criteria.

Speaking Skills

People talk to one another for many reasons. These include:

- asking for something that is needed

- asking for information or clarification

- finding out about someone

- explaining something

- demonstrating knowledge

- sharing experiences

- expressing feelings

- seeking support

- responding to others.

Conversation Skills

These include:

- taking turns

- responding to what others are saying

- having congruent body language.

Listening Skills

This is more than just hearing what someone is saying. Active listening requires focusing on another person and responding to acknowledge or clarify what has been said. It is a powerful confirmation of the self to have someone really listen to you, which is something that not everyone experiences in their everyday lives. Share pairs and interviews in particular are opportunities both to practise listening and to be heard. (There are no small group activities in this chapter.)

Sentence Completions

- A good thing to talk about is …

- Talking is easiest when …

- I don't feel like talking when …

- I like talking to …

- I like talking when …

- It is difficult to talk when …

- I know someone is listening to me when …

- When someone listens to me I feel …

- The person who listens to me best is …

- I like it when someone says …

- When someone doesn't listen to me I feel …

- It is difficult to listen to someone when …

- I need someone to listen to me when …

- My favourite word is …

- The nicest thing anyone ever said to me was …

Silent Statements

Stand up and change places if:

- you think you are a really good listener

- you have ever been at a loss for words

- you have said something you wish you hadn't

- you would like people to listen to you more.

Activities with a Partner

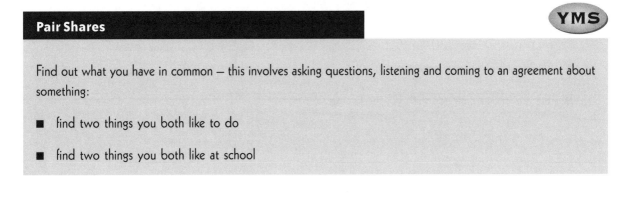

Pair Shares   **YMS**

Find out what you have in common — this involves asking questions, listening and coming to an agreement about something:

- find two things you both like to do

- find two things you both like at school

- find two things you both like to eat

- find two television programmes you both like to watch

- find two things that both of you would like to have in your ideal school.

My Favourite Things

YMS

(Focusing on the positive and practising listening skills. Check what is OK to be said in feedback to the Circle.)

Each person interviews the other about their favourite things. These can be:

- favourite things to do

- favourite places to be

- favourite people to be with

- favourite animal

- favourite experiences in the last year

- the best day of your life

- favourite book

- favourite film

- favourite music.

Extension Discussion

- What feelings are associated with some of these favourite things?

Variation

- Sometimes people are bonded by talking about things they really don't like. What is:

  - the worst thing you have ever eaten?

  - the most boring sport you can think of?

  - the TV programme you wish you hadn't seen?

At the Movies

M

(Focusing on body language.)

Using sounds and gestures but not words, communicate something that has happened to you to the other person. Don't tell them what this is. See if they can guess what you are trying to tell them. Then swap around so that the other person has a turn. Here are some examples:

■ the journey to school this morning

■ going to a see a scary film

■ what it is like to have a new baby in the house

■ learning to ride a bike

■ going to the park and finding a broken swing

■ not getting what you wanted for your birthday.

Discussion

■ What helps you to understand what someone is trying to communicate in real life?

■ What do you pay attention to?

Variations

S Show a film clip with no sound so that the class can see all the different ways that there are to communicate without words. Make lists of body postures, gestures, facial expressions.

MS Cut out pictures from magazines of people interacting. What can you see being communicated?

Active Listening Skills

MS

(It can be distressing when someone 'tunes out', so it is important that the topic under discussion is a positive one.)

Each person chooses an experience they have enjoyed, such as a holiday, party or outing. Each one takes it in turns to tell the other. The listener begins by focusing on what is being said and responding by nodding, asking questions or commenting. At a given signal they stop listening, look away, interrupt or talk about themselves. After about 30 seconds another signal is given and they start listening again. Then the other person has a turn with the same sequence of listening, not listening and listening again.

Discussions

■ What did it feel like to be listened to? What happened?

■ What did it feel like not to be listened to? What happened?

- How can you tell that someone is really listening? What messages are given in the body, face, verbal responses? What are these?

- What do you agree are the two most important skills in a good listener?

- Feedback to the Circle.

Encouragement

MS

The pair makes a list of things to do or say to encourage someone to continue telling a story about themselves. They then try this out on each other.

Discussions

- What did this feel like?

- Did it work?

Extension Activity

- Make a list of things that teachers might say which encourage students in their work.

Good news

S

There are four ways of responding to good news (Gable et al., 2003):

1   active constructive – showing real pleasure for the other person and giving them credit

2   passive constructive – minimal comment such as 'that's nice'

3   active destructive – belittling the good news and finding something negative to say

4   passive destructive – talking about something else all together.

The pairs take it in turns to tell each other about something they have achieved which has really pleased them. Each responds first in one of the last three ways and then in an active constructive way.

Discussion

- What difference was there is the way you felt?

- What do you think that this would mean for a relationship?

- Why might someone choose to respond in a negative or passive way?

Monologues and Dialogues

The same subject under different conditions highlights what it means to have a conversation and the skills involved.

Monologues

One of the pair has to speak for 30 seconds on a topic without repeating themselves or having too many pauses. The other person times them and notices if they are repeating themselves. Then they swap around. Ideas for monologues:

■ spiders

■ football

■ going to the emergency department in a hospital

■ grandparents

■ changing a nappy

■ making a cup of tea.

Conversations

Using the same category as before, the partners talk about the subject together for one minute, sharing experiences, ideas and views.

Discussion

■ What is different about a monologue and a conversation?

■ Which is easier?

■ Which is more enjoyable?

Extension Activities

■ The pairs are given a subject, but this time one person only asks questions and the other one only makes statements. Then swap around.

■ Each time someone says something, the other must respond to what has been said by asking a question about it.

All Change

(A paired game for focusing visual attention and awareness of others.)

Pairs face each other and study what each is wearing for one minute. They then turn their backs to each other and change five things about their appearance: undo a button, put a watch on a different wrist, comb their hair differently, fold a sleeve up, etc. They turn back to each other and see how many of these differences they can identify.

Whole Group Games

Clapping Rhythms

(This builds confidence in being part of a Circle without having to say anything.)

The leader begins by clapping a simple rhythm and the children follow suit. The leader does this two or three times, then points at one of the children who does one clapping rhythm for the others to follow and then passes it along to someone else.

Bear Hunt

(This is a whole group action and mirroring game which helps to focus attention and is a fun energizer. The children can do this sitting or standing.)

The leader asks the group: 'Do you want to go on a bear hunt?', and all the Circle shout 'Yes'. This is the script with actions.

First we go through the short grass [small chopping movements with hands]. Then we go through the long grass [bigger swooshing movements]. Now we reach the mud swamp [the children lift their feet one at a time, making squelchy sounds]. More long grass. Here is the river, but there is no boat [hand shading eyes looking left and right]. We'll have to swim [swimming arm movements]. And now we come to the dark, dark forest [walk through carefully, looking to left and right].

Not sure if we are going in the right direction, have to climb a tree [climbing movements]. There's a cave [pointing] halfway up the mountain. It's hard work climbing the mountain [trudging steps]. Here's the cave at last. Shall we go in? [whisper] And what's inside the big dark cave? It's a bear! [Everyone screams and goes backwards through the journey as fast as they can with the movements as before.] Down the mountain, back through the long grass, run through the forest, swim across the river, through the swamp, more long grass, now the short grass and *home*. [Collapse in relief.] Who wants to go on a bear hunt? No!

Fruitbowl

(Developing listening and attention skills.)

One person is in the middle. Each person in three in the Circle is given the name of a fruit such as pear, grape, kiwi, apple, mango, orange, plum, cherry, lemon. Someone starts by saying the name of their fruit and the name of another fruit, e.g. kiwi mango. The person in the middle tries to touch the second person (the one named mango) before they can say their name and another one, e.g. mango apple. When someone is touched they swap with the catcher. At this point everyone moves one place to the left so that the second third of the Circle can participate. Each person takes over the name of the fruit that was in the vacated chair. This is then repeated for the third section.

Variation

■ Vegetable basket — this time people have to say the names of vegetables but not show their teeth while doing so.

People Music

(This is a noisy but non-verbal activity which creates a sense of community and is a great energizer.)

We can make music in many ways with our voices, hands and feet. The teacher, with the students' help, chooses a song that is familiar to everyone and each person thinks for a moment what they are going to use as their 'instrument'. They can hum, whistle, clap with their hands or on their knees, stomp with their feet, click their fingers or tongue or just sigh! No words. Everyone applauds at the end.

Birthday Lines

(Asking and answering simple questions and tuning into others.)

Everyone lines up according to their birthday, with January at the front. When this is done, everyone sits down again. Now ask people to line up again this time with the last birthday in the year in the front. This time they do this without speaking.

Variations

(Beware using anything which may be more sensitive, such as height.)

■ Longest to shortest hair.

■ Smallest to biggest feet.

■ Living nearest to furthest from school.

■ Longest to shortest name.

■ Names in alphabetical order.

Catch the Train

(Another non-verbal game to develop attention skills.)

Everyone holds hands. Three (or more) people are nominated as 'stations'. The 'train' is the hand squeeze. This is passed around the Circle with the 'stations' calling out 'toot toot!' as the hand squeeze goes past them. The direction of the squeeze can be reversed by anyone at any time. Once the Circle has had a chance to practise the 'train' going around, someone stands in the middle to see if they can 'catch the train' by saying where it is. If the student gets it right, the person caught with the 'train' becomes the catcher.

Mirroring

(A silent game to improve concentration and make good eye contact. It also raises awareness of others.)

In pairs students form two concentric Circles, with students in the inner Circle facing their partner in the outer Circle. One person is the leader and the other is 'in the mirror'. The leader makes movements with hands, head and upper body which the 'mirror' aims to copy as if they were in a mirror. The aim of the game is for each couple to be so in tune with each other that there is virtually no difference between the person leading and the person who is 'in the mirror'. The leader can help the 'mirror' by using smooth rather than jerky movements. Looking at eyes is more useful than looking at hands. The facilitator can develop this game by asking the mirror and leader to change roles without any noticeable difference, or for the outer Circle to take three paces to the left so that everyone is with a different partner.

Social Bingo

(This game provides opportunities for structured, brief conversations with a wide range of people. It also gets participants up and moving around.)

Each person is given the same 'bingo card' with nine squares and a pencil. For each square they have to find a different person fitting a particular category, write down their name and the answer to the question, if there is one. Some examples follow.

- Find someone who has seen the same film as you — what film?

- Find someone with a birthday in the same month as you — which month?

- Find someone who has a dog — what is the dog's name?

- Find someone who can speak two languages — what languages?

- Find someone who has a name beginning with the same letter as you — which letter?

- Find someone who likes the same music as you — what music?

- Find someone who has been to the same place on holiday as you — where?

■ Find someone who is left-handed.

■ Find someone who has been to the dentist in the last month.

(See the blank bingo sheet, Appendix 3.)

Killer

MS

(Making eye contact.)

Everyone is given a card, they look at it and give it straight back to the facilitator so that no one else sees. One card a picture of an eye on it. That person is the killer. He carries out his evil deed by winking at people. If he winks directly at you, you count to five and then play dead. The aim is for someone to identify who it is before he 'gets' too many victims.

Heard You!

YMS

(Focusing auditory attention. This is also a calming activity.)

One person chooses to be blindfolded. They stand in the middle of the Circle. The other children pass round something such as a bell, a bunch of keys or a 'rainstick'. When the person in the middle points accurately at the person holding the item, that person is then blindfolded (they can nominate someone else if they wish or have already had a turn).

Fizz Buzz

MS

(A game in the round which gives everyone a quick turn and is good for concentration.)

The students say a number in turn. Every time the number has a five in it, the student says 'Fizz' instead of the number: if it has a seven, the student says 'Buzz'.

Variations

■ For more able students you could add anything that is divisible by five or seven.

■ A fizz buzz poster could be made by students to help those who need some visual support.

Going to the City

(Enhances attention, memory and class support.)

Each person finishes this sentence with a phrase and an action. 'My friend went to the big city and she brought me back a ...' For example, if the word is 'kite,' the student mimes flying a kite; if it is 'kitten,' then the action might be a stroking movement. On each person's turn they list everything that went before, also doing the actions, adding their object last. Other students help one another by doing the actions but not saying the word.

Variations

■ You could change the first sentence:

   ■ I'm going on holiday and in my suitcase I have packed a ...

   ■ I'm off to the country and with me goes ...

   ■ We went to the moon and with us we took ...

Stand up, Turn Round, Sit Down Stories

(These are good energizers as well as focusing attention on an auditory stimulus.)

Give everyone in the group a part in a short story. This can be either a character or an object. With a large class some students might be asked to do this in groups, e.g. you can have a several beans in *Jack and the Beanstalk* or several mice in *Cinderella*. When each person hears the name of their part said they stand up, turn around and sit down again. Stories need to be suitable for the age and interest of the participants and short enough to hold interest. You may like to give your most energetic students the characters who are mentioned most.

Kim's Game

(Focusing visual attention.)

Put several small objects onto a tray. The number depends on the age of the children. This could include the following: A key, pencil, marble, whistle, toy car, coin, balloon, toothbrush, small ball, pair of scissors, elastic band, candle, eraser, bar of chocolate, button, earring, watch, box of matches, bus ticket, ribbon.

Name all the items and then let the children look at the tray for 30 seconds. Cover the tray and out of sight of the children take one item away. Take the cover off. The children look to see what is missing. Either you can let them call out immediately or say that they must wait until you have counted to 10 and then say it all together. An older group might like to write them down. This could be done in pairs as a collaborative activity.

Guess the Leader

(Focuses on body movements and enhances group cohesion.)

One person leaves the room and someone in the Circle is nominated as 'the leader'. This person starts an action such as tapping a foot, rubbing their head, clapping. Others follow suit. The person outside comes back and sees how quickly they can work out who is the leader as the actions change. Once they have been 'caught', the 'leader' becomes the one to guess. It is important for children to not look directly at the leader but to copy actions quickly.

Birds Fly

(To focus attention on meaning.)

The leader flaps her arms and says 'Birds fly'. She continues with other sentences and actions such as 'Fish swim', 'Cats purr, 'Snow falls', and so on. The rest of the group follow suit unless the leader says something incongruent, such as 'Penguins climb'. Those who continue with the actions are 'out'.

Variation

- A simpler version of this game is to continue with other things that fly and everyone has to flap their arms until the leader says something that does not fly.

Hello Goodbye

(Learning different greetings and farewells and making contact.)

The class wander around the centre of the Circle. At a given signal they have to say a greeting word to the person nearest to them. If both say the same greeting they are 'out' and sit down in the Circle. The game continues until everyone is sitting down. When there are small number of people – perhaps about six – any are out if they say the same as anyone else. Now play the game with words for 'goodbye'.

Variations

- Include non-verbal greetings and farewells such as a handshake or wave.

- Teach the various greetings for different cultures:

  - in Paris they kiss four times on alternate cheeks

  - in Russia they give a bear hug

  - Germans have a very strong handshake with a hand on the arm as well

  - the Japanese put their hands together at chest level and bow from the waist

- Thai people put their hands together at forehead level and bow their head

- the Spanish and Portuguese kiss on alternate cheeks

- the British give a simple handshake

- the Americans give a 'high five' if they know each other well

- Maoris and the Inuit rub noses.

■ Get everyone to go around and, at the whistle, the leader shouts out a country. The pairs greet each other in the appropriate way.

■ Half the class represents one country, and the other half another country.

Extension Discussions

■ How does it feel when you meet someone from another culture who offers a different greeting to you?

■ What must it be like for those who are in a different country?

Whispers

Send a phrase or sentence around the Circle, whispered into the ear of the next person. No repeats. Is it the same when it gets back to the beginning? Here are some examples.

- I like marshmallows for breakfast.

- Red lorry, yellow lorry.

- Pass the pickles, please.

- Theo has lost three teeth.

- The chocolate is in the desk drawer.

Two messages going in different directions is even more challenging.

Extension Discussions

- Are whispers about people always true?

- Might stories get changed in the telling?

- Does a whispered 'rumour' miss out information that might make you think differently about a person?

I See You

(Making eye contact.)

Everyone stands in a Circle – everyone looks down. The leader counts to three. On three, everyone looks up and looks directly to the person on their left, or their right or straight ahead. If they make eye contact both shout 'Yes' and sit down. The game continues until everyone is sitting.

Sea, Shore and Sharks

(This game is a good active one which requires limited but focused attention.)

The leader indicates a line in the middle of the Circle, on one side of which is the shore and on the other is the sea. The leader calls out 'In the sea' or 'On the shore' and the children jump to whichever side of the line is the right one. When the leader calls out 'Sharks!' everyone runs back to a seat in the Circle. You can develop this game by removing one chair so that the person left without a seat is 'out' or becomes the next leader.

The Drawing Game

(This game involves every form of communication except speech. It can be adapted to all age levels. Flexible and lateral thinking are encouraged.)

The Circle is divided into groups of four or five, who gather in far corners of the room so that they cannot hear each other easily. Each group is given some scrap paper and pencils. The leader has a list of 10 items or phrases suitable for the age and ability of the students. Someone from each group comes to the leader in the centre of the Circle and is secretly given the first item. They then communicate this to their group with the aid of drawing and mime. No words, either written or spoken are allowed. When the group guesses correctly, someone goes and tells the answer to the leader very quietly and is given the next item on the list. The group to finish the list first is the winner.

Phrases may need to be communicated one part at a time, or words one syllable at a time, so it is useful to indicate how many words or syllables are required by drawing lines on the paper. Older students might need to resort to charades-type clues such as touching their ears for 'sounds like' and miming messages such as 'shorter' or 'you are on the right track'. Students will enjoy being given the opportunity to devise their own lists and be leaders in this game. Examples of lists:

- ■ **Y** sunhat, shopping trolley, ice-cream, black cat, shell, Christmas tree, birthday party, rainbow, aeroplane, whistle

- ■ **M** bus ticket, bar of chocolate, lipstick, lawnmower, storm, school assembly, bad dream, spider's web, glass of water, hot shower

- ■ **MS** horror film, winning a match, surfing the net, pantomime, exhausted, skiing holiday, breaking the speed limit, burst balloon, wet weekend, tantrum

- ■ **S** personal best, magic spell, alarm bells, peace and quiet, protest march, flat battery, big favour, frantic, lost in thought, storm in a teacup.

One Word Games

(Listening skills and paying attention to meaning.)

This is a game played in the round. Everyone claps on their knees three times and then on the fourth stroke claps or snaps their fingers. At each clap the person whose turn it is says a word in a category that no one else has said before.

These categories could be animals, colours, football teams, countries, stations, things to eat, feelings, an item of clothing, makes of cars or something beginning with a particular letter or the last letter of the previous word. If that word has already been said by someone before or the person cannot think of anything, that person is 'out' and sits in the middle of the Circle. The game ends when one person is left.

Single Word Stories

(This pays attention to sequence and meaning and gives everyone a quick turn.)

Each person in the Circle says one word of a story so that the developing narrative makes sense, even if it stretches the imagination.

Extension Activity

■ Record the Circle stories and then write them up for display, perhaps with illustrations, so that the class can see what they have created.

Who Am I?

(Structured questions and answers.)

The names of well-known people are pinned onto people's backs. These could be real people such as a famous footballer or actor, or fictional such as cartoon characters or from a book. Each person asks questions of others to work out who they are. These could be questions such as: 'Am I male?', or 'Am I real?' The only answers allowed to the question are 'Yes' or 'No'. Once someone has given a yes answer the student moves onto someone else. When they have guessed who that person is, they sit down in the Circle. When there are just one or two people who are finding this very difficult, the rest of the group can give them clues to help. Where there are individuals with additional needs or language difficulties or may not know the 'famous' people, do this activity in pairs. No looking at the back of your partner!

CHAPTER 5

Self-awareness and Self-esteem

Self-awareness in this chapter encompasses identity, values, dreams, desires and goals. Activities are aimed at helping students to identify and celebrate their histories, competencies and qualities. In addition, some areas for change and development are addressed.

More vulnerable students often experience low self-esteem. This means that they believe that they are not worthwhile, that they cannot do very much or be successful and that they are not liked, loved or valued. They may seek ways to feel better about themselves which involve putting others down, or reinforce this negativity by living up to their own expectations.

This chapter helps students to seek, acknowledge and develop the positive in themselves and in others.

Sentence Completions

- I can ...

- I am good at ...

- I like ...

- I am proud of ...

- I am grateful for ...

- When I was very little, I ...

- One of my first memories is ...

- The best thing that ever happened to me was ...

- When I grow up ...

- My hero is ... because ...

- If I was an animal, I would like to be ...

- I would most like to be able to ...

- Someone I really admire is …

- The most important thing to me is …

- The best day of my life …

- This week I have achieved

- My resolution is to …

- I am inspired by …

- I am fascinated by …

- I would like to know more about …

- Something I've done this year is …

- I believe that …

Silent Statements

Change places if:

- you know something you are good at

- you are pleased when someone pays you a compliment

- you have a dream about your future

- you are taller/stronger/know more than last year

- you are learning about yourself

- you are learning about other people

- you know something you are aiming for

- you are a bit scared sometimes

- you have met someone you admire

- you believe that we are all capable of change.

Activities with a Partner

Pair Shares

- Find two things that you like doing outside school.

- Find two things the same about your family.

- Find two places you have both been to.

- Find two things that are similar about your appearance.

- Find two things that you don't like doing.

- Find two things that are very important to both of you.

- Find two things that you both would like to change about the world.

- Find two things that you are thankful for.

Introductions

Names are an important part of our identity.

In pairs, the students interview their partner about their name. Where did it come from, is there anything special or unusual about it? Do they like it? The students introduce their partners to the Circle, saying something about their name.

Variation

■ Interview your partner about any scars they may have and the stories connected with this.

Aladdin's Lamp

Each partner takes a turn to be the genie in Aladdin's lamp and says that they will grant three wishes to the other person. For older students, you may like to define these wishes as one thing to have, one thing to do and one thing to be.

Extension Discussions

■ Give three reasons why each wish is important and then choose the most important reason.

■ If you could only have one of these wishes, which one would it be and why?

■ Would you wish for the same things for your family or your best friend?

For Older Students

■ How have your wishes changed since you were young?

■ Do you think they will change again?

■ There is a saying: 'Be careful what you wish for.' Why should you?

Personal Bests

(Encouraging competition against oneself rather than others.)

A personal best can be in anything from a sporting endeavour to a level of reading to not losing your temper. If personal bests are not already part of class talk, students will need time to think about the concept before introducing this activity. Interview each other about:

- the personal best each is most pleased with

- the personal best they are going for this year.

Dream Time

(Thinking about goals.)

Give each person a piece of paper shaped like a cloud. This is where they place their dreams or wishes in pictures and/or words. Each person in the pair talks about their dream to the other person. Do they have some similar dreams, or are they very different?

Extension Discussions

- What will you do to reach your dream?

- Draw a ladder with the dream at the top and fill in the steps you might take to get there. What is important about the sequence of steps?

- Do you think your dreams might change as you get older?

Personal Shield

Each person is given a piece of paper or card that is shield-shaped. On this they draw all the things and people that help to keep them from harm. They then share what they have done with a partner.

Life Map

(This provides awareness of history.)

Each person is given a piece of paper and something to write with — they draw a road from one side to the other. They then mark the most important events in their life, starting with being born. Each person in the pair share talks about their life map to the other person.

Future Map

(This provides a space for reflection on multiple goals.)

This time the road begins with where the student is now and each person uses their imagination to plot a possible future for themselves. They may choose to draw several different roads, as there will be many possibilities. They share this with their partner and choose one goal to share with the Circle.

Me in the Future

Give each person a cut-out shape of a person. They draw the person they would like to be in 10 years' time. Each talks to their partner about this person. How are they different from the person they are now?

Success Stories

(This provides an opportunity for students to reflect on what is really important.)

Can you agree on a definition of what makes someone successful? Find one thing that has made each of you feel successful.

Extension Discussions

■ What do advertisements tell us about being successful? Why do they do this? Should we believe them or not?

■ Is someone always successful if they have fame and/or fortune?

■ Are success and happiness always the same thing?

This is me – and me – and me

(We all have many roles and behave differently in each role. This activity raises awareness of this.)

Each person is given a piece of paper, which they divide into six sections. Each section has one of the following headings:

■ Me at school

■ Me as a son or daughter

■ Me as a brother or sister (or grandchild)

■ Me as a friend

- Me as part of a team

- Me by myself.

Students draw and write down three things about themselves in each role. They then share with their partner and look for what is the same or different for each of them. You may wish to do this in two parts, so you discuss three roles each time.

Extension Discussions

- What other roles do we have or might we have in the future?

- In which role do you like yourself most? Why is this?

Whole Group Games

Personal Positives

YM

(Positive comments about others need to be genuine and specific and based on character and actions rather than possessions and physical attributes. With practice, students get the idea and stop saying 'nice'.)

Each person becomes 'Star of the Day' in turn. It needs to be planned carefully so that everyone knows when their turn will come. This can be done around birthdays or simply a class list. Having this displayed is useful.

The 'Star of the Day' goes out of the room. In the middle of the floor is a large piece of paper (A1 size). The group brainstorm everything positive that they can think about the person outside, while the teacher writes this down. Examples of these qualities are even better. The person is invited back inside to hear what people have said about them. They are given the paper to take home or to place in their Circle Time file. It is essential that every child has the opportunity over the year to be the Star of the Day and to know that their turn will come.

Variations

YMS Each person writes their name on a paddlepop or ice-lolly stick and puts it in a pot. Everyone picks a name from the pot. They have a week to identify something positive about this person, something they do or say that they can tell the circle about — the circle might brainstorm the sorts of things to try and find.

MS Pin a piece of blank paper to the back of each person in the room. Give each person a coloured pen. The group mingles in the middle of the Circle and individuals write on the backs of their classmates (and teacher) anything about them that they value. Students are encouraged to comment on those they know less well rather than special friends. When someone has written the fifth thing they tell that person who returns to the Circle. The facilitator ensures that no one is left out.

S Each person puts their name at the bottom of a piece of paper. They hand the paper to the next person on their right. This person writes something that they value about the person and folds the paper over so that it cannot be seen. All the papers go around the circle with the same activity until they reach the person to whom it belongs.

Special Me

Y

(Becoming aware of being unique.)

The leader passes around a box with a lid and a mirror pasted on the bottom. The children are told that in this box is a picture of a very special person but they are not to tell anyone else who it is until the box has gone all around the Circle. When the round is completed, the leader says 'You can now all shout out who the very special person is.'

When all the children call out 'Me!' the teacher uses this opportunity to say how very special each person in the class is because there is nobody else like them. They are unique and Circle Time will help everyone to understand what is the same about people and in which ways they are special and different.

Alliterations

YM

(Increases awareness of likes and abilities.)

In the round, everyone introduces themselves with a statement that begins with the same letter as their name. This can be phrased as 'I like … ', or 'I can … ':

■ I am Pedro and I like pasta.

■ I am Fenella and I like films.

■ I am Brad and I can ride a bike.

■ I am Rosie and I can read.

Circle Unique

YM

This takes a little planning, as the facilitator decides on which person or people will be identified as unique and special today and therefore needs to have several facts about them available. The idea is for participants to drop out as categories do not belong to them, so the game starts with something that applies to everyone. Everyone should have a turn throughout the term. For example:

■ Stand up and enter the Circle if you are aged seven or eight (or are at school today).

■ Stay in the Circle if you are a girl.

■ Stay in the Circle if you have brown hair.

■ Stay in the Circle if your birthday is in March.

■ Stay in the Circle if your name begins with …

■ Say: '[Name], you are unique and special and there is no one else like you.'

Everyone applauds.

Guessing Good At

(This acknowledges strengths.)

One person turns to the person on their left or right and says: 'This is [name] and she is really good at [takes a guess — for example, reading, football, belly dancing, climbing trees].' The person then says: 'Yes, I am good at ... ', or 'No, I'm not good at ... but I am good at ...' [saying something that they are good at]. They then introduce the next person in the round and so on until everyone has had a turn.

Strength Cards

(Identifying positive qualities and abilities.)

There are some wonderful materials on the market that identify different strengths or abilities for different ages. These include I Can Monsters, Strength Cards for Kids and Reflections (details of these are in Chapter 10: Resources).

You can also make your own or get students to make them as a separate Circle Time activity with their own illustrations. Here is a list of strengths: you may want to phrase some of these differently depending on the age group that you are working with, but also you may want to use this as an opportunity to develop children's vocabulary and understanding:

happy, kind, helpful, friendly, truthful, good at sport, loving, careful, generous, calm, polite, good at literacy, good at numeracy, cuddly, hardworking, fair, interested in things, strong, tidy, well-organized, funny, good at making things, energetic, trustworthy, imaginative, persevering, honest, reliable, flexible, willing to try new things, understanding of others, brave, fast, affectionate, independent, thoughtful, considerate, forgiving, patient, active, creative, fun to be with, supportive, a good team player, sensible, artistic, quiet, adventurous, chatty, resilient.

The following are ideas for using these cards in Circle Time activities.

■ Lay all the cards out on the floor in the centre of the Circle and ask the students to pick one each about themselves. They then tell the group or a partner why they chose this one.

■ Lay all the cards out on the floor in the centre of the Circle and ask students to pick a quality or skill that they would like to have or develop. They tell the group or a partner why they have chosen this.

■ In pairs, each student is given a card and they tell each other how the qualities on this card apply to them. Each tells a story about how that strength was demonstrated.

■ In pairs, each student is given a card and they tell each other the ways in which they might develop this quality for themselves.

■ Students are asked to choose a strength that they admire in another person. Who is this person and how do they know they have this quality?

Me as a Baby

Each person brings in a photo of themselves as a baby with their name on the back. If not all children can do this (some families may be refugees, or children may be fostered or adopted and the information lost) then either do not play these games or give everyone the choice to draw themselves as babies, if they want. The children find out about themselves as babies from their parents or others in their family by asking the following questions. Point out that not everyone has access to this information, so some questions will not have answers. The class may suggest more.

- Which day of the week were you born on?

- What time of day were you born?

- How much did you weigh?

- Where were you born?

- Were you the first child in your family to be born or the youngest?

- What was your favourite toy?

- What did you like most to eat as a toddler?

- What were your first words?

- Do you live in the same place now?

Other questions:

- What is your first memory?

- Did you remember having a special person when you were little? What was their name? This can be a grandparent, other relative, carer or family friend.

Variation

(You may want to do the following activity over several Circle Time sessions as it is quite time-consuming. Remind everyone of the 'pass' rule if they either do not know or do not remember.)

- Photographs are attached to plain cards and put in the centre of the Circle. A person in the Circle chooses a card and guesses who it is. If they are correct, they can ask the person one question about themselves as a baby. If they are wrong, the next person has a guess about the same photo. After three turns the person in the photograph says who they are and says three things about themselves as a baby.

Extension Discussions

(In small groups)

■ Is it better to be a baby or to be the age you are now?

■ What is the difference?

■ Do rights and responsibilities change as you get older? In what ways?

■ Make two lists for people your age – a list of rights and a list of responsibilities.

■ What do babies need to grow healthy and happy?

Small Group Activities

Time Capsule

YMS

(A self-awareness activity that runs over time between Circle Times.)

Each person in the Circle is given a box the size of a shoebox. They are to imagine that this will be their time capsule which will be buried for 100 years. In this box they place anything which will tell the person who finds it all about them and the age in which they lived. This can include photos, drawings, favourite music or evidence of something that they like to do. Each person brings their time capsule to Circle Time and small groups share the contents with each other.

Beginnings, Middles and Ends

(This activity is to begin to show students who think of themselves as having no concentration that in fact they can complete many activities.)

In groups of three, one person draws the beginning of an activity, the second person the middle and the last person the end. If there is a group of four they draw two middle sections. Give scenarios the first time and then let groups think about others. In their feedback they show their 'cartoon', saying what they feel when they have completed the activity and what helps them get from one end to the other. Possible activities include:

■ eating a meal

■ watching a film

■ walking the dog

■ an outdoor game

■ doing a puzzle

■ reading a book

■ swimming the length of a pool

Me in My Family

MS

(What are the advantages and disadvantages of each position in a family?)

Students divide themselves into four groups:

1   only children

2   oldest children

3   youngest children

4   middle children.

Each group makes a list of what they like about being this person in their family and what they do not like. How much do they share as a group? Share the lists with the whole Circle.

What Is Open to Change?

MS

(There are some things people can change and some they cannot. Some changes depend on what you do and some changes are out of your control. This activity looks at possibilities.)

Give small groups the following list:

■   your history

■   your looks

■   your fitness

■   your skills

■   your 'race'

■   your age

■   the way you see things.

First, the group decides what it is impossible to change. For the rest they give three ways in which they can have some control and what they might do to change things for the better.

Extension Discussions

■   What things might happen to people that they have little or no control over? What do you think they feel about that?

■   Do people sometimes get blamed for being poor, ill, refugees or being a different race or religion?

■   Has anything like this happened to you? Is this fair?

Values

MS

Spread out a large number of assorted photographs on the floor — these can be cut out from magazines or bought for the purpose, such as photolanguage cards. Each person chooses one photograph to illustrate one of the following:

■ what is important to me at the moment

■ my hopes for my future

■ my hopes for the world

■ my fears

■ my passion.

Each person explains why they have chosen this picture.

Postcards

S

(Representing and talking about the self.)

If you live in a city you can often get free cards from cafés, galleries and entertainment centres. Put out a number of postcards in the middle of the Circle and ask students to choose one to represent one of the following:

■ life now

■ struggles in the past

■ challenges ahead

■ this is what I feel today

■ people around me

■ hopes and wishes.

Students show their card to the Circle and say why they chose this picture.

Stories of Strengths

Each group chooses or is given a strength card. They make up a short story that illustrates this strength. Then they draw it in a cartoon strip and share with the Circle.

I Believe

(Faith can be an important part of someone's identity. This is an activity best suited to multicultural classrooms and with students experienced in Circle Time.)

The facilitator asks the students to group themselves according to what they believe or do not believe. Examples are:

- Christian

- Muslim

- Jewish

- Buddhist

- Hindu

- Humanist

- Atheist

- Agnostic

- Sikh

- Rastafarian.

If there are some individuals put these together in a group. Each group then agrees on three things that they would like to tell the Circle about what they believe. For some groups this will not be so much about a for- mal religion but about a philosophy of how to live life. After the feedback to the circle, mix up the groups so that there are some people of different beliefs in each group who discuss the following.

- Did you find out anything you didn't know?

- Why do you think there is so much hostility around the world between different religions?

- What might help to reduce this?

- What one thing will this group do to promote tolerance in this class?

Each group feeds back to the Circle.

Future World

S

(In this activity the small group takes on the role of future parents. It encourages reflection and discussion on the connection between now and the future.)

Each small group has a large piece of paper. On this they draw and write what they hope for in the future world for their children.

■ What would they like their children to learn?

■ What do they hope their children will be able to experience?

■ What would they like to be different for their children?

■ What qualities do they hope for in their children?

■ What would they like their children to feel about themselves/their family/the world in which they live?

■ Is there anything that each person can do now to make these things more likely in the future?

CHAPTER 6

Emotional Knowledge: Understanding and Managing Feelings

Here we explore the wide range of feelings that are part of our sense of self. The activities are intended to provide students with opportunities for talking and reflecting on emotions so that they can understand them more fully. This includes:

- the ability to recognize and name emotions

- tuning into the physical sensations of emotions

- knowing what stimulates certain feelings, including interpretations of events

- tuning into the positive

- knowing about emotional regulation – what makes us feel better

- acknowledging feelings without letting them become overwhelming and 'in control'

- increasing the repertoire for management strategies – how we safely express what we feel.

Talking about feelings can be challenging, so a safe and supportive Circle is crucial. Facilitators may choose to focus on positive feelings at first if some students are likely to struggle with more difficult ones. In a class where you anticipate difficulties, start by keeping to the third person rather than expecting students to acknowledge personally how they feel. (Problematic situations and feelings are dealt with more fully in Chapter 9.)

There are several activities here that are designed to increase 'positive emotionality' in the group: to release tension and foster feelings of well-being by having a good laugh. There are also more serious discussions to introduce when the Circle is well established.

The lists below are feelings that you might want to work with depending on the age and stage of your class. The following is a general guide only. You will want to repeat some of the early words as children get older as meanings develop with more complex cognitive abilities. Many of the activities given in this chapter can be adapted to specific emotions.

Feelings in the Early Years

- happy, friendly, loving, cuddly

- excited, surprised

- warm, cosy, comfortable, special, safe, loved

- unhappy, sad, hurt, sick, bad, funny

- cross, grumpy, cranky, fed up, tired

- bothered, scared, frightened.

Additional Feelings for Five to Seven-year-olds

- pleased, cheerful, sparkly, lively, bouncy

- interested, curious, able

- lively, caring, cared for, concerned, fair, unfair

- muddled, confused, worried, unsure, silly

- shy, gentle, quiet, thoughtful

- disappointed, upset, tearful, sorry

- miserable, bad-tempered, angry.

More Feelings for Seven to 11-year-olds

- delighted, enthusiastic, thrilled, fascinated, enjoying

- energetic, confident, keen, determined

- proud, thankful, relieved, amused, generous, affectionate, grateful

- included, important, trusted, valued, heard, cared for, understood, respected

- trusting, responsible, patient, brave, forgiving, sympathetic, understanding

- left out, ignored, rejected, let down, doubtful

- anxious, moody, irritable, frustrated

- flat, bored, down, exhausted, selfish

- shocked, horrified, disgusted, crazy, envious, furious, wild

- lonely, uncomfortable, embarrassed, stressed

- reluctant, indecisive, hesitant, helpless.

Increasingly Specific Feelings for 11-year-olds Onwards

- satisfied, joyful, ecstatic, spirited

- serene, centred, appreciative

- acknowledged, supported, involved, appreciated

- independent, energized, motivated, anticipating

- courageous, resourceful, fearless

- in control, efficacious, absorbed

- empathic, altruistic, compassionate, apologetic

- apprehensive, ambivalent, fretful, awkward, distracted, disturbed, ashamed

- misunderstood, victimized, excluded, gutted, empty

- outraged, appalled, chaotic, desperate, frantic, overwhelmed, out of control

- rejected, marginalized, defensive, envious, jealous, arrogant, complacent

- depressed, despairing, hopeless, isolated, impotent, impatient

- indifferent, apathetic, disengaged.

Sentence Completions

- A good feeling is …

- Today I am feeling …

- People feel [emotion] when …

- I like it best when I feel …

- I don't like it when I feel …

- Something that would make me feel [emotion] would be …

- I am most absorbed when I am …

Silent Statements

Stand up and change places if:

- you have ever felt proud of something you have done

- you are happy when you are totally involved in doing something

- you are confident about being able to do one thing well

- you are an optimistic person – you see things positively as much as possible

- something has excited you in the last year

- something has made you sad in the last year

- you have ever felt sad for someone else.

Activities with a Partner

Pair Shares

- Find two things that make you both feel [emotion] …

- Find two things that someone might do or say that help you to feel good about yourself.

- Find something that has happened to both of you that has made you feel …

- Find something that helps both of you feel better when you are [angry, upset, disappointed].

Feelings in Pictures

(Talking about personal feelings.)

Students draw how they are feeling today and share this with their partner — can each guess what the other is feeling? How can they tell?

Extension Discussion

- Does talking about feelings make any difference to the feelings?

Special People

Who and what makes us feel good? Our special people are not necessarily the same all the time. A footballer who scored a goal for our team last Saturday might be the person who makes us feel happiest all week. Students interview their partner about someone who made them feel good recently, what did they do or say? Is there anyone who does this a lot – do they have one special person, or are there several?

Extension Activities

- Students draw a person (anyone or a particular person they can choose) and write down all the things they can think of that someone else does and says that make them feel good about themselves.

■ Students draw themselves and write down all the things they can think of that they have done or said that have made someone else feel good about themselves.

■ Students interview each other about their pictures.

Mirrored Emotions

YMS

(Focusing on how emotions are expressed in the body and on the face.)

One person is the leader and expresses a given feeling, the other person mirrors this, copying as exactly as possible the body language and facial expressions of the other.

Extension Activities

■ The emotion is made larger or smaller by the mirror partner.

■ Opposites — the mirror tries to do the opposite of their partner.

■ This game can be played in concentric 'double' circles where pairs stand opposite each other and then the outer circle moves on so that they are with a different partner.

Extension Discussions

■ When you are mirroring the emotion, do you feel differently according to what your body is doing? Does smiling make you feel happier, for example?

Good and Bad

MS

(Linking events with feelings.)

One of the pair says as many negative things that they can think of, while the other says positive things at the same time. They do this for 30 seconds and then change over.

Extension Discussions

(For more senior students.)

■ Which was easier or more difficult to list, and why that might be?

■ Did thinking about and listing negative or positive things make a difference to your feelings?

■ How much of what you listed is personal and how much to do with others or the world in general?

■ Do world events such as disasters, war, famine or injustice affect your feelings? In what ways?

- Does it make a difference how events are reported? For example, hearing about personal stories rather than statistics?

- Can emotions such as sadness and anger be good to experience sometimes? In what ways?

Extension Activity (Small Group)

- Make a poster of positive events, experiences and the emotions associated with them. Use magazine pictures, drawings and words.

Dreams and Nightmares

MS

(Realizing that you can have strong feelings about things that are not real.)

Students interview their partner about their dreams. Do they remember what they dream about? Do they remember their dreams or do they fade quickly? Do they wake up with strong emotions in their body sometimes? What happens when they realize that these are based on a dream? Is it possible to have strong feelings sometimes that are generated by thoughts rather than by what is actually happening? What can be done about this?

Extension Discussions

- What do filmmakers do to get us to feel strongly about a story?

- How can people work up feelings of fear, anger, sadness and happiness in others?

- Make a list of the strategies that are used. Can you think of instances where this has happened?

Shadows

S

(Looking at feelings from different perspectives, and raising awareness of others.)

Every feeling has a shadow side. For example, if you were very happy this might be difficult for others who were dealing with a tragic event in their life. If someone was very angry about something, others might be frightened. Someone being sad gives others the opportunity to show concern. A highly confident person can undermine someone else's confidence.

Each pair is given or chooses a feeling word. They talk about its shadow side and share this with the Circle, giving an example.

Whole Group Games

If You're Happy and You Know It

Y

A song for younger students that will be familiar to many early years teachers. The actions follow the words:

If you're happy and you know it clap your hands,

If you're happy and you know it clap your hands,

If you're happy and you know it and you really want to show it,

If you're happy and you know it clap your hands.

More Verses

■ angry — stamp your feet

■ friendly — smile and wave

■ sad — say boo hoo (rub eyes)

■ scared — hide your eyes

■ hungry — rub your tum

■ sleepy — close your eyes

■ excited — yell hooray (raise arms overhead).

The Smile

Y

Another rhyme for young children (use faces on cards for each expression).

A scowl and a smile

Met each other one day.

But somehow the scowl

Was not able to stay.

Facing the smile,

It just melted away.

Variations

- To be said in pairs with one child doing the scowl and the other the smile.

- Using faces on balloons and popping the 'scowl' at the end.

Simon Says, Look Happy
Y

(To focus in on facial expressions in feelings.)

Play 'Simon Says' with the children substituting feeling phrases for the usual directions. For example, say: 'Simon says, look happy'; 'Simon says, look tired'; 'Simon says, look friendly'. Children can learn quickly to be leaders in this game.

Faces
Y

(Tuning in to what we feel in different situations and learning that it is not the same for everyone.)

Have a series of pictures that depict faces looking grumpy, sleepy, happy, sad and surprised. Hold up one of the pictures and ask the children how this person feels. How can they tell?

- Hold up one of the pictures and go round the circle with this sentence stem: 'I think this person feels grumpy/sleepy/happy/sad/surprised because ...'

- The children change places if they feel the emotion being held up on the card:

  - when they wake up in the morning

  - when they go shopping

  - when they go to a birthday party

  - when they are asked to tidy their room, etc.

Inside Outside
Y

(To raise awareness of emotional hurt and to think of what helps. This is quite a serious activity.)

This game is best played with pictures to illustrate, but words will do. The teacher explains that there are 'inside hurts' and 'outside hurts' Outside hurts are when it is a part of your body that is damaged even though this might be invisible, like a headache. Inside hurts are when your spirit hurts, when something happens that makes you feel angry or sad. Some things are both inside and outside hurts, like someone kicking or hitting you. The teacher then calls out a variety of 'hurts' such as a broken leg, a bump on the head, a grazed knee and being left out, being laughed at, being ignored for a long time. The students call out if it's an outside hurt or an inside hurt.

Talk to the students about how our bodies sometimes hurt to tell us that we need to pay attention to something and look after ourselves. There are things that help with outside hurts, plasters, ointments or pills, etc. The most effective thing, though, is time. Sometimes we need to pay attention to inside hurts as well. They might help us to understand what is important, what we need to do or how other people might feel.

Ask the children to talk to each other in pairs about the sorts of things that might help with 'inside hurts'. What has helped them not feel so bad? The pairs decide on two things, and give feedback to the group. Make the connection with time.

Pass the Banana

(This is a fun activity about controlling facial expressions and paying close attention.)

One person (the guesser) is in the middle of the circle and keeps their eyes closed until the game starts. Everyone else has their hands behind their back. The facilitator walks around the outside of the circle, puts a banana (a squishy one is good) into someone's hands and says that the game has begun. The banana is passed round the circle behind backs and the guesser tries to find where the banana is by the expression on people's faces. The aim is to get the banana around to the first person again without getting 'caught'.

Catch Me if You Can

(This is a similar activity to the one above.)

Three people close their eyes or are blindfolded while three marbles are passed quietly and separately around the circle. At a given signal, everyone puts their closed fists on their knees. The people in the middle open their eyes and try to work out who has got the marbles by looking at people's faces. When they make a guess they tap that person's fist, who opens it up to reveal either the marble or an empty hand. Each person has three attempts at finding a marble. Those who still have undiscovered marbles at the end become one of the next finders.

Angry Alex

(Thinking about what triggers certain emotions.)

The students sit in a circle and one is given an apple to start the game. A piece of music is played by the teacher and whoever is holding the apple when the music stops becomes 'Angry Alex' and yells, 'Aaaarrrggghhh!!!!' (an angry sound). The Circle asks the student in chorus: 'What makes Angry Alex angry today?' and the student gives an answer. The apple then continues around the circle until several students have had a turn. If the music stops at the same student more than once, they can hand the apple to another student to be Angry Alex.

Variations

- Happy Henry

- Miserable Michael

- Stressed Samantha.

Mad, Bad, Sad and Glad

All of the emotion words given at the beginning of this chapter can fall under one of these headings. Choose the section(s) that fit the class, put these words on cards and share them around pairs in the circle. They have to choose into which of the four categories their words will go. This provides an opportunity to talk about more complex aspects of feelings: when does excitement become mad instead of glad? When might they experience feelings that are sad and glad at the same time?

If You Really Love Me, Won't You Please, Please Smile?

(This is a great game for raising positive emotionality in the group and awareness of how good feelings can give everyone more resources. Some students are very uncomfortable about the word 'love' – this gives them an opportunity to practise saying it in a safe setting. A teacher model at the beginning is particularly helpful here.)

One person turns to the person on their left and says: 'If you really love me, won't you please, please smile?' The other person replies: 'You know that I love you but I just can't smile.' This is said in as straight a voice as the person can manage. Few people are able to keep a straight face.

Extension Discussions

- Does it make you feel good inside when you can't help laughing?

- Was it difficult to stop laughing? What made it even more difficult to keep a straight face?

- Does it make you feel more positive towards everyone else?

- Is it a different feeling when you are laughing at someone in a hurtful way or with someone in shared fun?

The Laughter Chain

(This also shows how infectious emotions can be.)

Half of the class lie in the centre space with their heads on each others tummies forming a circle. One person starts by laughing. As you laugh your tummy wobbles. When the person feels the wobble they also start laughing and so on, until the laughter chain reaches around the circle. Ask the rest of the class if they could see the laughter chain moving. Now the other half of the class does the same thing. This time, they have to try not to laugh until they feel the tummy wobble of the person before them.

Variation

■ You could try this with the whole Circle together if you have enough space.

Won't You Buy My Donkey?

(You could try this with teenagers but they would need to be extraverts and not too image-conscious.)

A donkey seller and his 'donkey' are in the centre of the Circle. The donkey is on all fours. The donkey seller approaches an individual in the circle and asks them: 'Won't you buy my donkey?' The person says: 'No thank you', keeping a straight face. The donkey seller then says: 'My donkey can do really cool things, like ... [tap dance, juggle, sit up and beg for a carrot].' The 'donkey' carries out these actions. The donkey seller asks again: 'Won't you buy my donkey?' All those in the Circle now have to say: 'No, thank you' without laughing. The first one to laugh becomes the next donkey, the donkey becomes the seller and the seller joins the Circle.

In the Manner of the Word

(How our bodies reflect emotions and how we might 'read' these in others.)

One person (or a pair) leaves the room. The Circle chooses an adverb such as happily, grumpily, frantically, thankfully, serenely, depending on the age of the students. The pair come back in and ask individuals to mime actions 'in the manner of the word'. If they cannot get the word the first time, someone else is asked to carry out another mime. There are many possibilities for mimes, such as:

■ ride a bike

■ brush their teeth

■ change a nappy

■ fly a kite

■ play drums

■ take a maths test

■ wash a car

■ skateboard.

You may wish to put these ideas on cards. Alternatively, all of the Circle could be asked to mime the action. When one adverb has been guessed correctly, another pair leaves the room and another adverb is chosen.

Energy Pots

MS

(We all have a pot of energy that we use up when we are active and replenish when we rest and eat healthily. This is also true of emotional resources.)

A container such as a wastepaper basket is put in the middle of the room. Each person has a piece of paper and writes or draws something that particularly raises their emotional resources, something that cheers them up when they are tired or down or helps them keep their anger under control so that it does not hurt anyone. It must be something that does not reduce emotional resources in the long run. They then screw up their 'resources' and throw them into the 'energy pot'. Each person in turn takes out one a piece of paper and reads it out to the group.

Extension Activity

■ These ideas could be divided into groups: things to do, ways to think and the support of other people.

Extension Discussion

(For more senior students)

■ What do people use or do to make themselves feel better that only has a short-term effect and often makes them feel worse afterwards?

Freeze Frame

MS

(Emotional management. A useful way to manage difficult emotions is to distance yourself temporarily until you can get a handle on what to do for the best. One way is to imagine that the situation that is happening is in a film and that you are standing outside, looking at what is going on. Role play gives students an opportunity to practise this technique.)

Students are put in to groups of three. Each group is asked to devise a three-minute scene for one or more to act out which gives rise to one of the following emotions: anger, fear, despair, panic. Scenarios could include:

■ just missing a bus which will make you very late for something important

■ being caught doing something that will get you into trouble

■ being teased about your haircut

■ getting your exam results today – you expect them to be really bad

■ arranging to meet a friend who does not turn up.

At a suitable point when the emotion is getting stronger, the leader calls out 'cut!' and everything stops. The group are asked to replay the scene so that it has a different outcome.

Extension Discussion

■ What might you say to yourself in these situations that would help you manage it better?

Guess the Feeling

(In this activity students discuss the meanings of different emotions.)

Each group of four is given a different emotion. Which one will depend on the age and ability of the group. They are asked to decide the following.

■ If this emotion was a colour, what would it be?

■ If it was an animal, what would it be?

■ If it was an item of food, what would it be?

■ If it was an item of clothing, what would it be?

Each group says what their colour, animal, food and clothing are, and the rest of the class guess which emotion is being represented. (You could think about this emotion as a car, type of weather, shape, plant, sound, machine or place.)

Variation

■ Each group is given a word as above, but this time they have to make a statue representing the feeling and the rest of the class have to guess. The students can make a still statue or a moving one.

History and Culture

(This activity highlights that emotions are not separate from the world we live in and that the values of the society we live in have an impact on our feelings.)

Begin with sentence stems around the Circle.

■ My family are proud of me when …

■ My family would be ashamed if I …

Small groups discuss the following.

■ How do we learn what is important?

■ Is this the same or different from one generation to another?

■ Is this the same or different from one family and community to another?

■ What does this tell us about where some of our feelings come from?

Now and Then

S

(This also shows that some values and the associated emotions are dependent on social context.)

The Circle is given one the following words:

- humility

- modesty

- fidelity

- honour

They will debate the following motion: 'This circle believes that [this value] is still important in today's world.'

The Circle divides into two groups; one will develop arguments to support the motion and the other will speak against it. Each group has 10 minutes to prepare their argument (they may need a dictionary). The debate takes place with two speakers representing the group's view. The teacher asks at the end: 'Which people have been swayed by the arguments and have changed their mind from their original position?'

Small Group Activities

Patterns

YMS

(Talking about feelings.)

This game requires a wide selection of different pieces of wrapping paper or cloth in different colours and patterns (and textures) and can be played in a number of different ways.

- Each group is given five different pieces and is asked to agree which emotion each represents.

- Each group is given a list of emotions and asked to choose a piece that represents each of them.

- Each group or individual chooses the piece that best represents how they are feeling now.

- Each group or individual chooses a piece that represents how they would like to feel.

- Each group chooses a piece for the feeling in the class today.

I Feel it Here!

YMS

(The embodiment of emotions.)

Each group is given an outline of the human body and a feeling. The group talk about where that feeling is felt and write on the body what changes occur. They then write all around the body the stimulus to these sensations: what things happen that increase the chance of the body responding in this way.

Extension Discussions for older students

■ Is it what happens that causes the feelings or what we think is happening?

■ Could we put arrows from the external stimuli straight to the head and then from the head down to other parts of the body?

■ What influences how we think?

Little Mr or Miss

YM

(This game is based on the well-known children's books.)

Each small group is given a word describing a personal quality such as kind, generous, gentle, determined, helpful, lively, truthful, etc., and a piece of paper which is folded into four, concertina style. One person draws the head, the next the body and arms, the third the legs and feet. The last person gets to write what the person would say or some object in the picture. The group can offer ideas to the person who is drawing or writing. The group shows it to the class and they have to guess which 'Mr' or 'Miss' it is.

Extension Activity

■ The children do individual drawings of their own little Miss and Mr in small groups and talk about what happens when this person gets into their lives. For example, what happens when Mr Cheerful arrives or Miss Worried? If this is a negative quality, does this get in the way of having a good time? How do they get them to go away? If this is a positive emotion, how do they make life better – how can they be encouraged to stay around?

What Would You Notice?

MS

(This presents a narrative approach to emotions that enables people to look at them from a different perspective.)

Give each group a piece of paper. This represents a large room. At the moment there are people but no feelings in the room. Students begin by drawing in some people.

■ What would you notice if happiness/helpfulness/respect/thoughtfulness/support/friendship/acceptance were present in a room?

   ■ How would people talk?

   ■ What might they be saying to one another?

   ■ What would their voices be like and the expressions on their faces?

   ■ What might be happening?

- What would people be feeling?

- Would the room be somewhere where people would want to be?

The group writes and draws on the paper to illustrate their report back to the Circle.

Variations

- How might you know if negative feelings like anger, fear, intolerance, bad temper, anxiety crept into a room?

- How might you encourage them to leave? What is more likely to work?

Where Is the Feeling Now?   MS

(This introduces thinking about the different strengths of a particular emotion.)

Each small group is given one of these series of words, which are all muddled up. Each is on a separate card. They are asked to put them into order from the mildest to the strongest:

- comfortable, content, pleased, happy, joyful, elated, ecstatic

- down in the dumps, sad, miserable, depressed, hopeless

- bothered, annoyed, irritated, cross, upset, angry, furious

- uncomfortable, worried, anxious, scared, frightened, terrified

- uneasy, concerned, embarrassed, guilty, ashamed

- interested, engaged, fascinated, absorbed, obsessed.

When the group have done this they lay them out on the floor explaining to the whole group why this is the right order and the differences that are noticed as feelings get stronger or milder.

Over the Top and Back Again   MS

(Expressing emotions.)

Half of the Circle stands up and approaches the centre of the Circle slowly. They begin by expressing an emotion in a mild way but build up to demonstrating this in an extreme way. Then they turn around and the emotional expression diminishes as they return to their seat. The other half then do the same.

Extension Discussion

- Was there a point where your over-the-top expression made you want to laugh at yourself?

Who's in Charge Here?

MS

(The same activity as the two above but with additional discussions about emotional regulation and management.)

The group decides where they are in control of the feeling and when the feeling might be in control.

■ What happens when feelings get out of control?

■ How might they stop feelings getting out of control?

■ Feedback – produce a list of things they might try to stop a feeling getting the better of them.

Extension Discussions

■ Some people seem to seek out extreme feelings – for example, some want to take part in extreme sports – why might someone want to do this?

■ Can you feel strongly without this being unsafe in some way?

Ambushed

MS

(Sometimes feelings seem to come from nowhere. What happens then?)

Each small group is given one of the following feelings:

■ anger

■ fear

■ anxiety

■ embarrassment.

The group answers the following questions.

■ Are there any events (triggers) that make it more likely to happen?

■ Do you get any warning that this feeling is about to pounce? If so, what gives you the warning?

■ What sorts of things happen to your body?

■ What makes it more likely that you will be able to keep the feeling at a manageable level?

■ Each person, think of a situation in which they might experience this feeling; what things might someone do to:

    ■ prevent such situations arising?

    ■ deal with the feeling when it attacks?

■ What are protective factors – what are one's shields against this attack? These can be words, thoughts, people or actions. Make an ambush shield showing what helps.

The Mask

(Sometimes we present a different person to the world than the one we might feel we are inside.)

Each person is given a paper plate, string or ribbon and coloured pens. On one side of the plate they draw how they like to be seen by others. Inside they write or draw how they sometimes feel different to their 'public' persona. In small groups, each individual puts their mask up to their face and the others say what they see. They do not have to speak about their 'inner self' unless they choose to do so.

Extension Discussions

■ Is there a similarity between individuals in the ways they want to be seen?

■ What happens to the more difficult feelings inside the mask?

Catching Feelings

(This activity shows how infectious feelings can be.)

Divide the class into small groups of about four or five. They are given a simple task to do, such as plan an end-of-term party or draw a plan of the room. One person is secretly given a feeling and joins the group, demonstrating the feeling in the way they talk, the expressions on their face, their body language and their general demeanour. This can be either a positive emotion (enthusiasm, interest, calmness) or a negative one (boredom, misery, irritability). The others copy these 'symptoms'.

Extension Discussions

■ What difference does this make to the group?

■ What did group members feel?

■ Did it make a difference to completing the task?

■ How might you stop a negative emotion infecting the whole group?

Collages

(Talking about feelings.)

Each group has a large piece of paper, magazines and things with different textures such as balloons, fake fur, feathers. The aim is to represent an emotion by making a collage of it.

Moods and Music

(These activities are about how things around us affect how we feel.)

■ Each small group is given a good-sized piece of modelling material. A two-minute piece of music is played while they listen. The group are then given two minutes to decide how they are going to mould the clay to express how the music makes them feel. The music is played again while they mould the clay. Each group shows their sculpture and explains why they made it that way.

■ Each small group is given a piece of paper and some coloured pens. (The same activity as above but this time, creating a picture.)

Extension Discussions

■ Does music change the way we feel?

■ Who uses music as a mood changer?

■ What else in our environment can change our mood?

CHAPTER 7

Feelings of Belonging: Tuning into Others

This chapter specifically addresses one of the main aims of Circle Time – promoting class cohesion and a supportive group ethos. The activities here are aimed at encouraging people to know one another in different ways, to discover what individuals have in common, explore the different groups to which we all belong, break down stereotypes and weaken 'cliques' in the class. They are intended to foster a sense of connection. This includes defining trust and support and exploring how we might value diversity both for ourselves and for others.

Sentence Completions

- The best thing about my school is …

- This class is great when …

- The best day I had in this class was when …

- I feel welcome in this class when …

- I look forward to coming to school because …

- Valuing someone means …

- I feel valued when …

- When someone smiles at me I feel …

- The best thing anyone said to me in school was …

- When someone says something positive to me I feel …

- When someone asks me to join in I feel …

- When I am having a hard time it helps when …

- We all need help when …

- For me respect means …

- I feel supported when …

Silent Statements

Stand up and change places if:

- you have ever asked someone to join a game you are playing

- you have ever offered help to someone who is stuck on a work problem

- you have been able to ask for help

- you have been willing to lend something of yours to a classmate

- you return borrowed things

- you have ever asked someone who is left out to join your game

- you have ever stuck up for someone who was being bullied

- you have been invited into a game

- you know people who jump to conclusions about someone based on their looks/'race'/religion/what they are wearing/ability or disability/family/voice/accent

- you have met people who are different from you, who treat you with respect.

Activities with a Partner

Pair Shares

Ask pairs to check with each other what they are happy to have fed back to the class group.

- Find two things you both like doing at school.

- Find two things that you both like doing at home.

- Find two things that you both like about this school.

- Find two things that you both like about this class.

- Find two things that you could say or do to make someone feel they belong here.

- Find two positive things that you have said at home about this class.

- Is there one thing you both would like to change about this class (no naming – issues only)?

- Interview each other about the things you might do on a Sunday.

- Interview each other about your favourite place and what is in it – this could be a room at home, somewhere at school or a holiday destination.

Whole Group Games

The first activities here are designed for people who either are getting to know one another or who have just started Circle Time.

Alphabet Groups

Put all the letters of the alphabet on the floor. Each person goes to the letter that their name begins with and introduces themselves to others in that group, saying one thing about themselves. The leader can choose a category or let students choose what they say. Then they go to the letter that is the first letter of their family name, street name, their mother's name, or their favourite colour.

Picture Me

Each person has a piece of paper and something with which to draw. In pairs, each person interviews the other, finding out what their interests are. They draw these on the paper — the only writing is the person's name. After five minutes the pieces of paper are sent five places around the circle. The person with the paper then has to introduce the person and talk about their interests. The person has a brief right of reply to correct any inaccuracies.

Guess What

MS

(This shows how well we do know or do not know one another.)

Everyone passes one another in the room, they make eye contact and give a greeting every time they walk past someone. At a given signal they stay with the last person that they greeted. The teacher calls out a question and each person guesses the answer for the other. Examples of questions follow.

- Is this person an only child?

- Does this person like eating rhubarb?

- Does this person wear something around their neck?

- Is this person religious?

Was the guess right or wrong?

Odd Fact Out

(Can you tell which is truth and which is fiction?)

Each person writes four things about themselves on a piece of paper: three are true and one is made up. You can change this for younger children to one thing true and one not true: they say it, not write it down. Everyone goes into the middle of the Circle and shares the information with others in pairs. Who can guess which is the odd one out, what is true?

When the Warm Wind Blows

(This is a good energizer and shows that we have many things in common.)

One chair is moved from the Circle. The leader of the game says: 'The warm wind blows for everyone who …' and chooses a category that many children share. Students change places (including the leader), leaving one person without a chair. They become the leader and choose the next category saying the same phrase. Categories that many share might be:

■ likes chocolate

■ has a brother

■ is learning to swim

■ is [x] years old.

Have You Ever … ?

(To show what we share, celebrate difference and get to know one another.)

Give a statement to the group. If the statement applies to a person, they run to the middle and do a 'high five' with the others who share this experience. If someone is the only individual with this experience, the circle applauds. The following are examples.

Have you ever:

■ ridden a horse

■ surfed in the sea

■ slept in a tent

■ owned a dog

■ played the drums

CIRCLE TIME FOR EMOTIONAL LITERACY

- seen a snake

- sung karaoke

- broken your leg

- had a relative who lived to 100

- eaten snails.

People to People

(Making limited physical contact.)

Each pair stands up in the middle of the Circle facing each other. One chair is removed from the Circle. The leader calls out actions such as:

- hand to hand

- finger to thumb

- hand to head

- back to back

- nose to nose

- toe to toe

- right hand to left knee.

The pairs make the appropriate actions. When the leader calls out 'People to people', everyone rushes back to their seat, leaving one person without a chair. They become the next leader.

Footsie

(Group cooperation.)

Everyone sits on the floor with their legs stretched out in front of them towards the centre of the Circle. Two or three soft toys are placed on ankles and at a given signal the group attempts to move these around the Circle without touching them with their hands.

Extension Activity

- You could play rabbit and fox by trying to get one animal catch up with (or escape from) the other.

84

Mirror Wave

(A version of the Mexican wave that involves everyone in a physical activity – also great for concentration.)

Each person stands up and turns so that they are facing the back of the person in front. One person is designated the leader and makes a simple movement such as swing their arm to the side. The person behind waits one second and then copies, so that the movement goes all around the room. When it reaches the leader, the person behind starts a different movement which goes all around the room. You may want to ask some students to watch from inside the Circle from time to time to rate how well the group has done as a team.

Class Web

(This uses a ball of string to demonstrate that we are all important and each is responsible for what happens in our class.)

Everyone stands up. The person holding the ball of string holds one end and throws the ball to someone else saying their name. This person holds onto the string, the connection is tightened and they throw the string ball to someone else. This continues until everyone is included and the web has been made. The facilitator comments on the importance of everyone in the group being part of the web that has been made. If time is an issue, do this in several small groups.

Extension Activities

■ The Circle sits on the floor rather than stands. One person starts a story with one sentence. They then roll the ball of string to someone else who continues the story with another sentence.

■ One person says: 'I like … because …', and rolls or throws the ball of string to that person who says: 'I like … because … ' this continues until everyone is included. The facilitator might wish to be the last person.

Circle Knot

(This is an activity demonstrating that sometimes whole groups of people get themselves into knotty situations and that it is up to everyone to work out a solution.)

Everyone stands up, and joins right hands. Then they join left hands with a different person. They all then move anywhere they want so long, as they do not let go. After 20 seconds the group will be in a knot and now have to try and untangle themselves, again without letting go of one another's hands. If this works, the circle will reform with some people facing in and some facing out.

Hoop Game

The group holds hands around the Circle. The Circle is broken in one place and a large hoop is placed on the hands before they join up again. The aim is to get the whole hoop around the Circle without anyone letting go. You may want to split large Circles into smaller ones and turn this into a race.

Guess Who?

(This is for when the class really knows and feels safe with one another.)

One person volunteers to be blindfolded. They then sit on a chair in the middle of the Circle. Another person then comes and sits on a chair opposite. The first person has to guess who their classmate is. They do this by touching the person's face and by asking questions of the Circle.

Find Your Match

(Looking for similarities between people.)

Everyone stands up and walks around the room, greeting one another without words. Each person then finds someone:

- with the same colour eyes

- with the same hair length

- with the same size feet

- with a first name starting with the same letter

- with a last name starting with the same letter.

Variation

- Find all the people who share the named characteristic.

Thanks in a Hat

(This activity focuses on respecting others by acknowledging them.)

This is in two parts. The first is a sentence completion in the round to raise awareness of possibilities: 'I could say thank you for …' Suggest that people are specific: not just for 'helping me', but 'helping me with …'; not just 'being a friend', but 'being a friend by …' Each person puts their name on a piece of paper and puts it into a container. The container is shaken up and then everyone takes a name out. Each person reads out the name and says: 'I would like to thank … for …'

This Class Says Thank You

(Promoting acknowledgement and respect around the school.)

The Circle brainstorms all the people who do things for the class in any way. This could include the caretaker, administrative staff, cleaners and so on. Each small group takes one of these people, discusses what this person does, how they help the class and the difference that they make. The group then makes a card that expresses the thanks of the class. Also, they take responsibility for delivering it to that person.

Purple World

(This builds on an activity for younger children suggested by the UK's Qualifications and Curriculum Authority to address racism.)

The teacher tells a story about a world where everything is purple – clothes, food, cars, houses and schools. The only food is purple soup, which everyone eats at the same time. Students talk in pairs about what it would be like if everything was the same – would they like it or not? This activity is followed by sentence completions:

■ if everything was the same ...

■ being different is good because ...

The children then talk in pairs and find one thing that is the same about them and one thing that is different.

In or Out?

(This illustrates that we all belong to a variety of groups.)

Students are asked to come and sit in the middle of the Circle; they will enter or leave this group depending on whether the given category applies to them. Many different categories can be used – here are a few.

Those who:

■ have moved house/town/country in the last year

■ had a shower this morning

■ have a brother/sister/new baby

■ love to dance/play football/go fishing

■ have blue/brown/green/grey eyes

■ are wearing socks/jewellery/hair band/wristwatch

- had toast/cornflakes/tea/coffee for breakfast

- like reading books/watching TV/playing football

- like maths/history/art/English

- walked to school/came by bus/came by car/rode a bike

- have seen the latest *Harry Potter* film

- pray/take exercise/watch the news every day.

Knee Race

YM

(For groups who feel comfortable with this level of physical contact.)

This is an alternative way of playing the above game. All those who fit a category (like football, are wearing blue, have a cat) move one place to the right. If there is someone on that seat, they sit on their knee. If there is someone already on that person's knee, they must stay where they are. The game ends with the first person to get around the Circle and back to their own seat.

Sticky Popcorn

Y

The children 'pop' about the room as individual pieces of popcorn. When they touch someone else (or are touched), they 'stick together'. Eventually all the group are stuck together like a big ball of popcorn.

Extension Discussions

- What does it mean when people 'stick together'?

- What is good about this, what might not be so good?

- Sentence completions:

  - Sticking up for someone means ...

  - I want my friends to stick up for me when ...

Here Be Monsters

YM

(This demonstrates how we can all help one another to overcome obstacles and get through difficulties to reach goals. Success depends on support from the whole class group.)

Two people volunteer to be the travelling adventurers. They will cross the land of monsters and dangers to reach the land of sweet dreams and treasure. They will be supported by a team of guides (the whole class), who will show them the way and keep them safe.

Each adventurer is blindfolded. There is an empty chair at each side of the Circle and several 'monsters' and dangers are placed across the Circle. Plastic dinosaurs, sharks, toy lions, etc. can be used as well as boxes for mountains and pieces of paper for lakes. The students might like to make their own 'monsters' and other obstacles for this game. On each chair is placed a bag of treasure. This could be stickers, gold chocolate coins or other small items. There must be enough for everyone. The aim is for both adventurers to negotiate the dangers and collect the treasure from the other side of the room and for the class team to help them succeed. The aim is to get them to the treasure at about the same time. It is not a race.

The whole group helps in the negotiation of monsters and dangers by giving instructions of where to move, how far to move and when to stop. It is the responsibility of the class to ensure that the person is safe. There are several ways to do this. Either each person takes it in turns to give an instruction about how far to move and in which direction, or the class can shout out when the adventurer is in danger and tell them which way to go. Also, you may use signs, perhaps a whistle for stop and clapping for going forward. You may like to start the game by asking the class, together or in small groups, what the best strategy would be. The 'treasure' is shared with the class in a gesture of solidarity and thanks.

You could give each adventurer seven lives, which means that they lose a life each time they come into contact with a monster. Alternatively, you could give other members of the team spells or special powers to use when the monsters get too close, such as a disappearing spell, a charm offensive or a cuddly spell. The creative options are endless.

Escape!

YM

Extension Discussions

■ What sorts of difficulties or monsters might someone in this class face?

■ How might people in the class support someone who is having a challenging time?

(Fun, contact and support.)

A small group of five to eight students volunteers to be quackers. These are rare birds who stand bent over with their hands behind their knees. They only walk backwards and cannot see in daylight. The others form a 'pen' by holding hands in a Circle. There is one place where the Circle is broken, which is the escape route for the quackers. The quackers start off by huddling in the middle of the Circle with their heads towards the centre. With their eyes shut they move backwards trying to find the exit, quacking from time to time. The rest of the group gently keep them penned in until they find their escape. When one has escaped the pen they can stand up but keep quacking to help the others out. Escapes can be timed to introduce an element of competition as well as cooperation.

Who Is Missing?

YM

(This game increases awareness of individuals in the group.)

One person is blindfolded in the centre of the room. All the other children change places and one child leaves the room. The person in the centre takes off the blindfold and tries to work out who is missing. If they cannot say straightaway who it is, they can ask questions of the group which have a yes or no answer: 'Is it a girl?', 'Does she have brown hair?' Once identified, the person outside then becomes the blindfolded one in the centre.

Rescue!

M

(Students have to work together to get everyone to safety. This activity is worth doing several times consecutively to improve outcomes.)

Three students are in the original rescue team. Everyone else is unconscious in the burning building (lying motionless in the middle of the Circle). No one can help to rescue anyone else until they have been rescued themselves and taken to a safe place outside (a point outside the circle). Once they have been rescued, they join the rescue team. The building will blow up in four minutes. Can all the class get to safety before it does? Aim for class bests and talk about what worked well and how to do it better next time. You may want to talk about fire safety as a conclusion to this activity.

Walking a Mile in Someone's Shoes

This is a phrase that suggests that once you know what life is like for someone, you will have more empathy with them. These activities help students to understand how things might be for others by imagining and/or experiencing some of their situations and challenges.

Shoes

MS

(This activity encourages imagination.)

Have a collection of different interesting shoes. These can be for men, women, children, in good condition or scruffy. Each group of three or four students is given one of the shoes and is asked to write a profile together on the person that may have worn that shoe. This includes physical attributes such as age and gender, likes and dislikes, what they might have done for a living or for a hobby, what made them really happy or sad and the best thing to happen to them when they wore the shoe. Each group then presents their character to the Circle.

Variation

You could do the same activity using hats.

Extension Discussions

■ How much can you tell about someone from what they are wearing or look like?

■ Is there always a 'story' for each person that you don't know about?

■ Could their 'story' affect how they feel about things?

Extension Activities

■ Put each character in a setting and discuss or act out how they may react to given situations: knowing their background, how they may feel and react. For example: they are in a car accident, they are bullied at work or school, they have a disagreement with their best friend.

■ Give each group a card with a single additional piece of information about their 'character' such as 'this person is deaf' or 'this person has just won the lottery'. How does this single piece of information change how you see someone?

Give Us a Clue

MS

(This activity is intended to develop empathy with those who cannot read well or have a struggle with understanding language.)

Ask everyone in the Circle to try and work this out. They do it by themselves for the first two minutes then in a pair for five more minutes then in groups of four for a couple more minutes.

■ ☆ ●❈❊❊ ❊❑❈❊❈ ❊❊▲❊❊■❊❧ ☆ ❊❑ ◗❈▼❈ ○❋ ▲▼❊❑⬣❊❑❊ ❖■❊ ○❑❑❖❊❊❑ ▲❑❑❊▼❋○❊▲❧ ❊❊ ▲❈▼ ❖■❊ ❊❖❊❊ ❑◆❑ ●◆■❊❊ ❑◆▼ ❑❊ ❖ ◗●❖●▲▼❊❊ ○❋ ❖■❊ ❊❑❈■❊ ❊❊■❊❊❑ ❖❊❊❑❧ ☆ ❖○ ◗❊❖●●❋ ❊❑❑❊ ❖▼ ❊❊▲❊❊■❊❧ ☆ ●❈❊❊ ❊▼ ○❑❑❊ ▼❊❖■ ◗❊●❊❊■❊ ❖■❊ ◗❊❊▼❊■❊❧

They also should be given these clues:
| = |

●❈❊❊ = like

❊❊▲❊❊■❊❧ = fishing

❊❖❊ = dad

○❑❑▼❊❊❑ = brother

❊❑❑❊ = good

❖■❊ = and

❊▲ = is

When the time is up, show the answer.

■ I like going fishing. I go with my stepdad and brother sometimes. We sit and have our lunch out of a plastic box and drink ginger beer. I am really good at fishing. I like it more than reading and writing.

Students can then brainstorm:

- what did they feel when they were working this out?

- what helped them feel better?

Point out that for some individuals, tasks are hard like this all the time.

Extension discussions

- What other situations are there where it is a real struggle to understand communication?

- Has anyone in the Circle got a story that illustrates this?

The next two activities give students a taste of what it is like to be visually impaired.

The Jelly Wobble Game

YM

(A messy game perhaps for the end of term.)

One-third of the group at a time (an even number) takes part in this game. Each needs to volunteer to be blindfolded. Pairs sit opposite each other in the middle of the Circle and are covered with protective clothing (oversize old shirts put on backwards work well and long strips of plastic to cover legs and feet). Each person is given a bowl of jelly and a spoon. The aim of the game is each person to feed their partner the jelly until the bowl is empty. The first pair to do so wins. If noise isn't a problem, the rest of the Circle can call out helpful directions.

In the Dark

YMS

(This game also develops trust.)

Students are in groups of three. In the Circle a number of obstacles are placed. Two students lead the blindfolded student slowly around the Circle, not tripping over anything or bumping into other groups. Each student in the trio has a turn of being blindfolded and takes a turn around the Circle. You may want to do this with a section of the Circle at a time if space is very limited.

In your groups, discuss the following.

- What did it feel like not to be able to see where you were going?

- How did you feel about the two people who were guiding you?

- What helps to trust somebody?

- What can you imagine are the difficulties for someone who can't see properly?

- What sort of things might they need to live as near normal a life as possible?

- Can you always tell if someone can't see properly?

Hearing Impairment: Seeing Is Hearing

Partners cover their mouths with a scarf and engage in a conversation about something that has happened at school in the last couple of days. How easy is it to hear someone when their face cannot be seen properly? Then each person places a piece of blutac about the size of a marble in both ears. How easy is it now to make out what someone is saying? Then teacher plays some loud music (or even better, a tape of playground noise) Does this make a difference to their ability to understand?

Discussion

■ What does this tell you about what people with a hearing impairment need?

Physical Difficulties: the Drawing Challenge

This is a paired activity. Each person has a piece of blank paper and a pencil. They draw a picture of their partner with their name below it but they draw with their non-dominant hand.

Variation

■ Draw or paint a picture holding the pencil or brush in your toes or mouth.

Relay Race

Students are placed in groups of equal numbers. Each person has to keep one arm by their side and not use it, or put it in a sling. The students are in a line. Some way in front of them are chairs on which are placed a shirt with buttons, a hat and a pair of boots. At the signal the first person in each team runs to put on the clothes, runs back around the line back to the chair, takes off the clothes and runs back to touch the second person in their team. The first team to finish the relay wins.

Discussions

■ What was different from the way you usually do things? What did you have to think about? What feelings did you experience?

■ Do you know anyone who has a physical disability? What adaptations do they have to make in their lives?

■ Imagine not having the use of your legs and being in a wheelchair. Check out how many slopes and steps are there from your house to school or in your local shopping centre.

Visiting Strange Lands

MS

(To appreciate the difficulties that newcomers might have.)

Divide the circle into two groups. One group is the Maxis and the other the Minis. The Maxis:

■ greet each other by putting out their tongue and wagging their hand behind their head

■ are very interested in all watersports and often want to talk about this

■ think that people with brown eyes are the most important

■ avoid touching one another in public in any way

■ have a great sense of humour.

The Minis:

■ greet each other by grabbing the other person's arm with both hands and looking deep into their eyes

■ are very interested in all ball games and often want to talk about this

■ think that people who are short or wear glasses are especially wise

■ avoid laughing in public

■ breathe very deeply when they are upset about anything.

Each group is told only about their ways of being. The separate groups then spend five minutes with their own 'people'. Then they start to 'visit' each other in small groups. This cultural exchange is to foster good international relations. Everyone needs to visit the other group until everyone has been.

Discussions

■ Did you feel some affinity with your original group?

■ Did you feel confused when you went for a visit?

■ How did you learn what to do?

■ Did you mind trying to be different from your first group so you could 'fit in'?

■ List what you have learned from this activity.

Extension Discussions

■ What experiences have some people had before they arrive in a new country?

■ What difference will this make to how they feel about being there?

■ What do you think people miss about their old country?

■ What might help them to settle in?

Small Group Activities

Our Class Shield

(Deciding how to represent this class.)

Small groups are given a large piece of paper in the shape of a flag or shield and some coloured pens. The groups talk about what they would put on such a shield to represent their class. They then draw and/or write what they have agreed. Each group shares their shield with the Circle.

This Class Cares

(Small group discussions to raise awareness of actions that might be taken to promote an inclusive atmosphere in the class.)

■ What can we do to welcome someone new to this class?

■ What can we do to help someone new to fit into this class?

■ What would we want a new person to think about this class?

■ What can we do to welcome someone back when they have been away for a long time?

■ What can we do to learn about one another and one another's families?

■ What might help someone who is always left out?

■ What might help someone who struggles to understand what to do?

Absent But Not Forgotten

(To support students away from school.)

Sometimes an individual is absent from the class for a length of time because of illness, bereavement or even suspension. Showing that person that they are still part of the class not only makes them feel supported but also promotes an ethos that everyone matters here. Groups are given card, stickers, and felt pens. They discuss what is going to go on the card for the student to show them that their classmates are thinking of them. What words will go on it, and who will write them, What illustrations will there be? The teacher takes responsibility for sending the cards to the student concerned.

CHAPTER 8

Friendship and Cooperation

Here we explore aspects of both friendliness and friendship. On the one hand, friendliness is defined as 'contextually appropriate' social behaviour and positive responsiveness towards others – often referred to as social skills. On the other hand, friendship is the establishment and maintenance of a supportive relationship. You can have friendliness without friendship but not the other way round. A friend is someone who helps you to feel good about yourself. However, the definition of a friend changes with age and, to some extent, by gender.

This chapter contains activities to reflect on what it means to be friendly, the qualities that we seek in friends and the skills involved in becoming and being a good friend. This chapter also addresses group behaviour – group collaboration and valuing diverse skills and abilities.

There are several ideas here that require student involvement between Circle sessions. These might be particularly useful at the beginning of a year to maintain focus on friendship development and class cohesion.

Sentence Completions

- A friend is ...

- Friends are important because ...

- A friendly person would ...

- This class school is friendly because ...

- My friends and I like to ...

- A friendly thing that happened this week was when ...

- The name of my first friend was ...

- My oldest friend is ...

- What I value most in a friend is ...

- My best quality as a friend is ...

Silent Statements

Stand up and change places if:

- you know someone who is really friendly

- you know someone who is shy

- you know that some people are lonely sometimes

- you think that people sometimes find it difficult to join in a game

- you think that some people don't know what to say sometimes

- you think that friends have to agree with each other all the time.

Activities with a Partner

Pair Shares

- What are two reasons to have friends?

- In what two ways might a friend help you to feel OK?

- In what two ways could you help a friend to feel OK?

- What are two things you need to do to stay friends with someone?

- In what two ways could you show a friend that you value their friendship?

- If you could go anywhere with your friend, where would you like to go?

- What are two things that might spoil a friendship?

- What two things might mend a friendship?

- Interview each other about the best friend you have ever had. Why was this person your friend?

- Interview each other about the activities you enjoy with your friends. Is there one you both share?

Joining In　　　　　　　　　　　　　　　　　　　　　　**YM**

(Many difficulties are caused by children barging into games.)

In pairs, students talk to each other about what they might do if someone wants to join in a game in the playground. Ask students:

- what would you say and to whom?

- What would you say to someone who asks to join in your game?

- In the feedback, one person says the first sentence and the other the second. Role-play joining in a game.

Acrostic Poem

(This encourages discussion about what these words might mean.)

Give each pair a piece of paper, and a word with five to eight letters such as:

- friend

- respect

- safety

- sharing

- trust

- loyalty.

This word is written down the page with one letter on each line. The pair agree a word or sentence beginning with each letter which is about the word. What they end up with is an acrostic poem. For example:

Fun to be with
Ready to help
Interested in other people
Especially nice to me
Never mean
Does kind things.

One way of sharing this is for both to have a copy of the poem. The tallest of the pair stand in a circle facing out and their partner faces in. The person outside steps three people to their right; then they are facing another partner. Both share their poems. The outer person takes another three steps and shares and so on until they have been around the circle reading their poems and hearing several others.

Extension Activity

- This could be done in small groups with one person writing each line while the others give suggestions.

Whole Group Games

If students try to interact only with their good friends, then do these next two games as paired activities once you have mixed everyone up.

How Are You Today?

(Conversation openers.)

Students stand in pairs in concentric circles, — one facing in and one facing out. The game starts by pairs saying to each other: 'How are you today?' They then ask one question that could be asked of anyone in the class, such as: 'What did you watch on TV last night?' When both have had a turn, the outer circle takes three paces to the left and faces another partner to repeat the activity. Encourage different questions.

Extension Discussions

■ What sorts of questions are good ones to ask?

■ What is the difference between an open question (one that encourages people to talk) and a closed question (one that has a one-word answer)?

How Did it Go?

(This game is for students who have been together a while. It encourages conversations that tune into others.)

Begin with pairs in concentric circles. This time students ask a specific question of the other that shows an interest in them as a person. When both in the pair have had a turn the outer circle moves around three places and repeats the activity.

Extension Discussion

■ What might you say if you find that you cannot think of what to ask?

Beware Crocodiles

(A game to encourage contact and communication.)

Each pair has a piece of paper (a large sheet of newspaper will do). They walk around together until the leader calls out: 'Beware crocodiles'. They put the paper on the floor to make an island and stand on it. They then fold the paper in half and walk around again. Each time the paper gets folded again until it is so small that pairs have to decide how they are going to stay on the island best. If a pair loses their balance and falls into the 'billabong', they are deemed to have been attacked by crocodiles and are 'out'. They return to a seat in the Circle. The winner is the pair who manages to stay on the island longest.

Warmer ... louder

(For group cooperation and support.)

One person leaves the room and an item (treasure) is hidden (chocolate gold coins make good 'treasure'). The group decide on a familiar song — the closer the person gets to the treasure the louder the song becomes, and when they move away it becomes softer.

Variation

- An alternative version of this is just to say 'hotter', 'warmer', 'cooler', 'colder' — but the singing is better.

Flour Cake

(A good turn-taking activity.)

The teacher puts a gold chocolate coin or something similar in the centre of a bowl and fills the bowl with flour, packing it down firmly. The bowl is turned upside down onto a plate to form a 'cake'. The cake is placed in the centre of the Circle and one person in the circle is given a teaspoon. The idea is for each person to take a teaspoon of flour from the cake and put it in the empty bowl. The whole Circle applauds each person who manages to do this. The aim is to get around the group at least once before the flour cake collapses. The person holding the teaspoon when the flour cake collapses has to retrieve the coin with their teeth. This means that they get their face covered with flour.

Nursery Rhyme Alphabet Song

(A cooperative turn-taking game.)

Divide the circle into two halves. One side begins by singing the alphabet — by the time they get to the end, the other half will have decided which nursery rhyme to sing. As soon as they have finished the nursery rhyme they sing the alphabet, and then it is the turn of the other half of the circle. This goes on until one side runs out of nursery rhymes to sing or the time limit is up. No repeats allowed.

Variation

- It is also possible to do this with other songs that the group may know.

Snowball Fight

(Defining the qualities of friends.)

Each person has a piece of A5 size paper. They write down the quality that they most like in a friend. Each person screws up the paper into a ball. At the count of five, each person throws their 'snowball' across the circle. The paper must stay within the circle, not be thrown outside. Participants pick up a snowball and throw it again. This continues for up to 30 seconds. Then at a signal everyone keeps the last 'snowball' they picked up. Each person open ups this up in turn and reads what is written inside.

Extension Activity

■ People guess who wrote what.

Elephant, Giraffe, Palm Tree

(Collaborating in groups of three. Give students a chance to practise this first. Then play the game fast as an energizer.)

The leader in the middle points to someone in the Circle and says one of the above three words. The elephant is formed by the central person making the head and trunk with their head and arms and the two either side holding their arms at either side of the middle person to represent the elephant's ears. The giraffe is the centre person standing with their arms aloft and hands pointed forward as the giraffe's head. The two either side put their hands around the person's waist and form the four legs of the giraffe. The centre person forms the palm tree by putting their arms above their head and spreading their arms and fingers out. The two at the side do the same but lean out from the centre.

As soon as the animal or palm tree has been formed, the leader points to someone else. The aim is to keep this moving quickly. The leader should ensure everyone has a turn.

Secret Friend

(Practising friendship skills and making links with feelings.)

Each person puts their name on a piece of paper. They then fold the paper up into four and place it in a container, preferably a cloth bag so it is impossible to see inside. Each person then takes out a name. That person is their 'secret friend' for the week and they have to do some things in school that make that person feel good.

Extension Activities

■ The next week a sentence completion could be: 'I felt good this week because ...' or silent statements:

  ■ stand up and change places if you found out who your secret friend was

  ■ stand up and change places if your week was especially nice.

Compliments

(Compliments are best when they are genuine and specific. Body language needs to match the words.)

In small groups talk about the following.

- The nicest things that anyone has ever said to you?

- What might you compliment someone on?

- How might you respond to a compliment?

- What makes a compliment worth having?

The group makes a list of possible compliments that they might give someone. Then, as a circle activity, each person says the name of the person next to them and offers them a compliment. The person thanks them and turns to the next person in the Circle, doing the same.

Extension Discussions

- What do people prefer: compliments about the way they look, about the things they have, something they have done or about themselves as people?

- Some people find it very hard to hear good things about themselves. Why is this? Does it make a difference who is saying the compliment?

The Chocolate Game

(This is about taking turns and appreciating that many games can be fun for everyone only if they are played according to the rules.)

In the middle of the circle is a bar of chocolate on a breadboard, a hat, gloves and a knife and fork. Each person in the circle takes a turn of rolling a dice. When someone gets a six, they run to the middle of the circle, put on the hat and gloves and begin to cut the chocolate into small squares with the knife and fork. They can eat as much of the chocolate as they can, one square at a time, until the next person throws a six, at which point they have to pass on the hat and gloves and return to the circle.

If you have a large Circle and some very lively individuals, you may wish to divide students into smaller groups so that they do not wait too long for their turn.

Feelings in Pictures

(Turn-taking and team support. This is a game of carefulness as well as speed – if you are using water it is best done outside, if other materials have a dustpan and brush ready for clearing up afterwards.)

Teams are put into a line from front to back. Each person has a plastic teaspoon. The person at the end of each line has a container of water, sand, lentils or other 'spoonable' material. At a given signal they take a spoonful and pass it into the teaspoon of the second person in the line and so on, going into every teaspoon until it reaches the person at the other end who pours it into a container such as an egg cup. The winning team is the one who has the most in their front container at the end of five minutes or when it reaches a given level.

Extension Discussions

■ How can teams encourage each other?

■ Does it help the team if people get angry with someone who has a spill?

Small Group Activities

Drawing a Friendly Person

YM

(Definitions of what is friendly.)

The Circle is put into groups of four. A piece of paper is folded into three sections and given to each group. The first person draws the head of a friend and says what is friendly about this head. This part of the picture is folded again so the next person is given the middle section on which to draws the body and arms and says what is friendly about this; the third draws the legs and feet and says what is friendly about these legs and feet. The last person writes or says something that a friendly person might say. Each group does a 'Show and Tell' about their drawing to the Circle.

Silent Construction

YMS

(What is involved in a collaborative activity?)

Each group is given some construction materials in a plastic bag. They are not to open the bag but decide in discussion what they are going to make. After two minutes they are asked to open the bag, take out the pieces and make their model, but without speaking to each other. Each group shows what they have made to the rest of the circle and talks about how they made decisions and who did what.

Variations

■ Simple jigsaw puzzles.

■ Making the tallest building that will stand up, using cardboard, straws, newspaper and sticky tape.

■ A get well card or congratulations card for someone.

Desert Island

(What different qualities in a person might you want for different situations?)

Each group is given a piece of paper in the shape of an island. They are told that they have been shipwrecked on this island and there is no one else there. After three weeks another ship is wrecked and there is one survivor who turns up on the island. Ask students: what qualities would you want in a companion to share the island with you? Share this with the circle.

Extension Activities

What qualities are helpful in the following:

- you need to build a shelter

- you need to eat

- you need to stay well

- you need to stay happy

- you want to escape.

Extension Discussions

- Are all our friends the same?

- Do we have different friends for different reasons?

- Do we do different things with different friends?

- Why is it a good idea we are not all the same?

Matchbox Scavenger Hunt

(A collaborative activity.)

Each group is given a matchbox. They find as many things they can in a given time that will fit in the box. You may wish to introduce this activity in one Circle Time and give groups until the next Circle Time to produce the filled box. Feedback is in the form of questions from the facilitator.

- How many items have you got?

- What was your plan?

- Who did what?

- Was it the best plan or could you have had another one?

MS

Scavenger Hunt

(Teamwork. This activity structures group communication over a week. This has the added advantage of helping less integrated students establish closer relationships with others in the class.)

The groups are all given the same list of about 12 to 15 items, such as a:

- bus ticket between named places
- homemade biscuit
- picture of a whale
- magnet
- certain song
- purple sock
- shell
- fan
- group photograph
- map of the school
- wooden animal
- foreign coin.

The group have to decide how they are going to collect the items, where they are going to keep them and how they will communicate with one another about how the hunt is going. They have a week to gather everything together. In the circle in the following week each group talks about what they did, how they felt it went and what skills they used to get to their goal.

MS

Newspaper Game

(Decision-making in a group. Making sense out of disorder.)

Each, team is given a newspaper that is all in the wrong order, with some pages upside down. The teams are given one minute to decide how they are going to work together to put them in the right order. At a given signal they get to work — the first team to hold up the completed paper wins. Feedback: how did the groups organize themselves? Did everyone have a role to play?

Variation

- Choose different leaders.
- Choose only one person who can speak.

Extension Activities

- Find a picture of …
- Find an advertisement for …
- Find an article about …
- Find the name …
- Find a headline that says …

Instant Treasure Hunt

YMS

(Team communication.)

The circle is divided into small groups who sit together. The leader stands in the middle of the circle and calls out: 'Bring me …'. This could be:

- a pair of shoes with the laces tied together
- a leaf
- a picture of a pink elephant
- someone whose mother's name begins with …
- the oldest person in the group giving the youngest one a piggy back
- a knot
- a sharp pencil.

The team who gets there first with each item wins a point.

Limbo

MS

(An excellent game for demonstrating the importance of individuals to a team effort.)

You need teams between five and eight people. Each group is given either a long piece of wood, such as a six-foot cane, or a hula-hoop. This rests on the index fingers of every team member. The aim is to lower the cane or hoop to the floor. It is not as easy as you might think as sometimes the direction is reversed. The first team to the floor wins.

YM

Body Letters

(Another game to practise cooperation.)

The teacher calls out a letter of the alphabet and the group has to make themselves into that shape. Then another letter is called out. The teams can do this upright or on the floor, whichever is easiest. Then get the whole class to make a word with the same number of letters as groups.

Discussions

■ How did everyone do that?

■ What worked, what would they do differently next time?

■ Who wanted to tell everyone what to do?

■ Who wanted to be told what to do?

■ Did people build on one another's ideas?

Variations

■ Do this using sign language only.

■ Make it into a race or making the neatest letter.

MS

Body Words

This requires larger teams of six to eight people. The leader calls out a short word, such as 'book' or 'nose' and the team forms the word with their bodies.

Variation

The leader gives each team a word secretly and the rest of the Circle has to guess what this is.

MS

Points

(An activity that requires the full cooperation of everyone, problem-solving, agility and balance.)

This takes place in teams of four to six. The leader calls out a number. This is the number of points of contact with the floor for each team. When the number of 'points' called out is small, the teams have to work out quickly how they will do this. For example, for a team of five people, the number seven could be two people having their feet on the floor and three standing on one leg. They have 20 seconds to decide how to do this and then have to 'hold' their position for a count of three to stay in the game.

Lists

(This illustrates that one person's idea can spark off ideas for others.)

Three people are in the middle of the room. An object such as a ball or toy animal is given to one person in the circle. The leader calls out a group name such as:

- animals

- colours

- feelings

- cities

- sports

- underground stations

- furniture

- football teams

- countries

- things that fly

- cars.

The group of three names as many as it can before the object gets round the circle.

Alphabet Lists

(This is a variation on the above but involves everyone at the same time with one person in each group as the scribe.)

Each team is given about 12 categories on paper similar to those above. The leader calls out a letter of the alphabet and each team has to write down something in each category that begins with that letter within a given time limit, such as three minutes. If this is run as a competition you might wish to give one point for getting an item in that category and an extra point for finding something that is different from everyone else. This encourages creativity.

Variation

- Each group is given a different letter of the alphabet. They have two minutes to list everything in the room beginning with that letter.

MS

Unusual Objects

(This fosters creative thinking in a group.)

Give each team an everyday object such as a hairbrush or a coat hanger and ask them to work out a completely different use for it. They can be as imaginative as they like. They have to present this to the rest of the group in a convincing way — stories are welcome.

MS

Team Play

(How we are treated in a group makes a difference.)

This activity done in full might take up most of a Circle Time session, so it may be better divided into two for consecutive Circle Times. It needs teams of five to seven and can be played several times, with different people having different labels.

On each person's forehead, place a sticky label. These say the following (or something similar depending on the age of the students):

■ ask me

■ ignore me

■ laugh at me

■ thank me

■ listen to me

■ criticize my ideas

■ build on my ideas.

The team are given an imaginary task such as the following:

■ plan an end of term party

■ re-organize the playground

■ organize a sports day

■ think up a fundraiser for charity.

The team are given five minutes for their task. As they do this, everyone treats each person according to the label on their forehead. Each person then guesses what might be written on their head, then takes off the label and tells rest of the team what it felt like to be treated in this way. What difference did it make to their contribution?

Then the teams are given five to 10 minutes to complete their set task where everyone focuses on positive cooperation and participation. Each team feeds back to the group on their task, the process and the feelings generated.

CHAPTER 9

Challenges and Solutions

This chapter deals with difficult issues and the painful feelings that often result. Sometimes challenging situations are short-term for students, but for others they are continuous and part of life. Some individuals deal with one difficulty; others face multiple stresses. These issues are often at the root of many of the social, emotional and behavioural outcomes that are manifested in school.

The aims of Circle Time strategies in this chapter are to:

- provide an opportunity to talk about challenging issues safely

- show students that others have similar experiences and that they are not alone

- help students to learn the skills involved in effective problem-solving

- devise ways forward, collaboratively either to address a problem or cope with it

- explore difficult feelings and how to stop these from becoming overwhelming

- develop a supportive framework in the class

- reflect on individual and collaborative responsibilities.

It is wise to familiarize students with the philosophy and practice of Circle Time before moving on to some of these more challenging topics. Some teachers may not feel confident or comfortable facilitating some of the following activities in Circle Time; in a few cases they will not be appropriate for a particular group. No one should feel obliged to do anything about which they are unhappy.

Introducing Problems Safely

Circle Time is not intended to be group therapy, so individual disclosures are not sought except in silent statements to illustrate commonality. The use of puppets, stories and games engage students in addressing issues without personal risk. However, should students become distressed in any way, the facilitator needs to give them the opportunity to opt out or use their Circle Time file. It is essential to follow this up with a conversation that demonstrates concern and, if appropriate, a referral onward.

Puppets

Creative teachers can use puppets to motivate young students to be thoughtful problem-solvers. Give puppets names and characters and make them regular visitors to the Circle. Puppets can talk with the teacher and the children about problems such as being teased or left out, not being sure about something or being frightened. The puppets ask for suggestions as to what they could do. The students can discuss the puppets' problems in small groups and give feedback in the Circle. A follow-up in the next Circle Time reinforces the learning.

Stories

(Stories are a very useful means to engage students and stimulate discussion. These are available both in books and other media for a wide range of ages and abilities (see Chapter 10: Resources) and, as with puppets, they free up individuals to talk about issues rather than themselves. Stories illustrate that the more information we know about something, the more our thoughts and feelings about it change. We need to avoid making hasty judgements about someone and their situation based on incomplete knowledge of their 'story'.)

The leader reads a short story to the group that focuses on an issue or difficulty. A paired or group activity follows the reading in which the following discussions or activities may take place. These are general suggestions; stories may give rise to more specific questions.

Discussions

This can be in pairs, small groups or in the Circle, depending on what suits the class best.

■ What did you feel hearing this story?

■ Did your feelings change as the story went on?

■ What do you think were the feelings of the characters in the story?

■ Without giving any names, do you know anyone who might have had similar experiences?

■ Has this story made you think or feel differently about their situation?

■ Is there anything you would do differently after having heard this story?

■ What does this story mean for our class?

Extension Activities

■ Small groups act out the story and then talk about the thoughts and feelings of the characters.

■ Small groups make up and act out a story that is about the same issue but different from the one that has been read out.

MS In pairs, one person takes on the role of the main character and the other interviews them about what happens in the story.

MS Small groups make a strip cartoon of a similar situation.

MC Each small group has a large piece of paper with the long side at the top and a line drawn across the middle. The beginning of the line on the left represents the beginning of the story and the end of the line on the right represents the end. The group plots the story, marking the places where there were alternative choices and decisions to be made. Choices that might have changed things for the better are written on top of the line and choices that would have made things worse are written at the bottom.

Detective

(This activity is designed to work through the steps in making a decision about a problem.)

Discuss with the group how someone can tell if they are uncomfortable about something. This feeling is telling them that there is a problem that needs to be addressed. These are hypothetical situations that might make someone feel uncomfortable. The students may have other examples:

- someone with the reputation of being 'tough' has taken something of yours without asking

- you have heard that someone is going to 'get' one of your classmates after school

- your friend is spreading rumours about another girl which may or may not be true

- you borrowed something from a teacher and can't find it now

- you join in with laughing at someone, even though it really upsets them

- you owe your brother some money and he needs it tomorrow to buy a ticket for an important match — you don't have it

- you have agreed to go to see a film with someone but then get asked to a party, which would be much more fun.

Ask students to come to an agreement about what the problem really is, and brainstorm all the possible solutions, listing the positives and negatives of each, including the potential consequences. The group chooses the solution that they think is the best. Why do they think it is the best? Feedback to the Circle.

True or False

(Discussions show that there are rarely clear-cut answers and that many factors may need to be taken into consideration in reaching decisions and solutions.)

In small groups the students discuss one or more of these statements and decide whether they think they are true or false, or 'it depends', giving their reasons for their answer to the group:

- getting low marks is always terrible

- anger can be good

- if I don't join in with bullying, it might be my turn next

- change is inevitable

- the most important thing in life is to have lots of money

- a good friend should always agree with you

- most of what we worry about doesn't happen

- stuff happens — it's how you deal with it that matters

- boys should never cry

- we are more afraid of what we don't know than what we do know.

CHALLENGING ISSUES

Bullying

No student should have to deal with bullying of any kind on their own, including racial and sexual taunts. The policies of the school on social justice, equal opportunities and safety should be clear and effective.

There is increasing recognition that the continued existence of bullying depends on whether it is condoned by others. The following activities are designed to support the development of a safe classroom in which everyone takes responsibility for what happens. The focus is on what students feel and what they want to feel. (Other activities in Chapter 7 on belonging and Chapter 8 on friendship are also relevant, especially for younger students.)

Silent Statements

Stand up and change places if:

- you know that there is bullying in this school

- you have seen bullying in this class

- you have heard put-downs in this class

- you have felt sorry for someone who was bullied

- you want to feel safe in school

- you have ever been sorry for something you have said or done

- you have been able to acknowledge that you regret something.

Sentence Completions

- Bullying is when ...

- I would feel bullied if ...

- Watching someone being bullied would make me feel ...

- A person who bullies others might feel ...

- Bullying affects everyone because ...

- People bully others because ...

Taking care of Teddy

Y

Each small group is given a soft toy, such as a teddy. They are told what the toy's name is and that he or she is a bit scared of coming to school because people might be unkind. The group talk about what they could do to make sure that the teddy was safe and happy. Feedback to the Circle.

Recipe for a Safe and Happy Class

YM

(Recipes are made up of amounts of ingredients, mixed together in a certain way.)

Small groups decide how much of what would go into their recipe. They ask the teacher to write the ingredients down for them. You may wish to divide these up into things that you would see, things you would hear and things you could feel. For very young children you might tell them that what you have in your store-cupboard.

- smiles

- friends

- playing together

- kindness

- helping

- saying hello

- quiet voices

- laughing

- talking

- making a space to let someone in.

Extensive Discussions

■ What things might spoil your recipe for a safe and happy class?

■ How could you stop this getting into the mix?

P-Charts

MS

(Bullying is picking on someone (or deliberately ignoring them), in a situation in which there is a power imbalance. The behaviour is persistent (happens regularly) and prolonged (goes on over time).)

The groups are given a piece of paper divided into four, with a heading in each square:

■ Picking on

■ Power Imbalance

■ Persistent

■ Prolonged.

They are given one of the scenarios below (or others devised for the class) and in each square fill in the details of what this would mean in the situation. Everyone needs to be discussing the same scenario. When they have done this, they take a second piece of paper divided up into squares with the words 'Prevent', 'Protect', 'Plan of Action' and 'Appraise' in each quadrant. They brainstorm ideas about how this situation might be prevented in the first place and what might be done to protect the person being bullied. In 'Plan of Action' they decide on the best options and who will do what. The final square outlines how they would evaluate how well the plan is working.

■ On the school bus one student with learning difficulties is made the target of 'fun' by two or three others. At first he thinks they are being friendly. He is encouraged to do silly things such as call out of the window to other passengers.

■ A new girl is deliberately ignored. No one sits next to her and she is rejected if she tries to join in with anything. She is increasingly miserable at school.

■ One boy has a condition that gives him a bald spot on the top of his head. He wears a cap to cover it up. One boy in particular gives him a hard time, teasing him, taking off his cap and throwing it around. Others think it's a laugh.

■ One girl is particularly good at maths. A small group want her to help them do their homework. At first they are really nice to her, but when she becomes reluctant to do their work they begin to intimidate and threaten her.

■ A teacher has developed a difficult relationship with a student. This has resulted in the student not being asked when they are ready to give an answer, sarcastic remarks being made and belittling comments. The student does not receive any positive comment on their work or effort.

■ A boy is having a hard time at home. He gets upset easily and can lose his temper. One fellow student has worked out ways to wind him up, and does so regularly. The boy then gets into trouble from teachers.

Extension Activity

- In the centre of the Circle, role-play the characters in the scenario:

    - the person being bullied

    - the person leading the bullying

    - those joining in

    - bystanders who watch

    - those who defend.

The first time, play the scene as described; the second time, intervene to support the person being bullied. Debrief by talking about the feelings of each character, both at the time of the 'incident' and afterwards.

All for One and One for All

(Small group discussions followed by circle discussion)

- What feelings do we want in this class? Decide on the three most important.

- What can each of us as individuals do to create feelings of safety here? Choose three actions.

- What can our class do to make this a safe place for everyone? Decide on three things.

- What should our school be doing? Give three suggestions.

Extension Activities

- Design an anti-bullying T-shirt for this class.

- Design an anti-bullying poster for this class.

Doing Sorry

MS

Small groups make a list of things together that someone might be sorry for doing, saying or not doing. Why would someone be sorry? Talk about how easy or difficult it is to admit that someone has done or said something that they wished afterwards that they hadn't. They then make a list of things that someone could say or do (not just saying sorry) to make it up to the person who was hurt.

MS

Washing Line of Insults

(This game is intended to take the heat out of verbal abuse, to reduce its incidence and give those on the receiving end some strategies to deal with it.)

Each person in the circle writes down something that someone might find hurtful (no swear words allowed). Each statement is collected by the teacher and read out anonymously. Then it is pegged up onto a 'washing line' of insults. This is a string that is strung across the circle or held up by two people at either end.

Discussions

This can be in pairs, small groups or the Circle, depending on what suits the class best.

■ What are these insults intended to do?

■ What does the person doing the insulting want to feel?

■ How do insults get to be powerful?

■ What can we do to put them back in their place and without power to hurt?

■ For insults against family and 'race', what are better ways of being loyal than rising to the bait?

■ Does it help to become defensive and try and deny what is being said?

■ What might you do if you hear someone insulting a classmate?

Extension Activities

■ Washing out — Use water-soluble pens and put the 'insults' into water at the end of the activity so that they 'disappear'.

■ Go with the flow — the worst thing someone can do when they are insulted is to be defensive, as it often encourages the person who is taunting. This activity looks at alternative 'come-backs'.

The insults are taken down from the 'washing line' and divided between small groups. Each group creates a statement that someone could use to undermine each insult. Examples:

■ 'fatty' — be careful I don't sit on you

■ 'skinny' — they will never keep me behind bars

■ 'stupid' — better than being clever at being nasty

■ 'racial insults' — yes and proud!

■ 'all insults' — take out a notebook and pencil, saying: 'Can you say that again?' and prepare to write it down. It may be a good idea to have someone else close by when you do this.

The 'washing line' is then re-erected with the responses on the other side of the paper.

(This strategy is not the answer for everyone — some students will not have the confidence to use a 'go with the flow' response; some may benefit from practice, encouragement and class support.)

Belief in a Just World

S

(Sometimes, people say that the victims of bullying deserve what they get. This activity challenges this. It is recommended for a group experienced in using Circle Time.)

The Circle is divided into small groups. The facilitator has a round, flat cake. The cake is divided up into as many pieces as there are groups but these portions are not equal: some are large and others very small. Each group is given a piece according to spurious reasons for what they 'deserve', e.g:

■ you deserve a large piece because you live in a nice area

■ you deserve a smaller piece because you didn't have the money to go to school

■ you deserve a tiny piece because people in your street fight with each other.

Discussions

Take these topics one at a time.

■ How do you feel about the size of the piece of cake that your group has been given?

■ Some people believe that everyone gets what they deserve. This is called 'belief in a just world'. Why is there a problem with this belief?

■ In what ways might you see this belief being demonstrated? Do people sometimes get blamed for being poor, living in a war zone, being mugged?

■ What might this mean for someone who tries to be a good person, but something terrible happens to them?

■ What does this mean for the statement that some people 'deserve' to be bullied?

■ Is there a problem with the belief that everything happens by chance?

■ What might be alternative ways of thinking?

Circles of Restoration

S

This is a role-play about bullying which follows a restorative justice model. The players are the accused (someone who is accused of bullying), the co-accused (two people who joined in), the prosecuting witness (the person who is bullied), someone who represents the law (prosecutor), someone who speaks up for the accused (the defence) and members of the community (the Circle). The facilitator invites people to speak in turn. You could use the scenarios provided in the P-Chart activity.

The role play takes 20–30 minutes and takes place in the Circle. The rest of the Circle has a chance to say how this behaviour has affected the community and what should happen now.

Loss

Loss is a serious issue for many young people and is at the root of many strong emotions. These activities address the universality of this experience and encourage discussion about what helps. There are some excellent programs now available to help students with loss.

Silent Statements

Stand up and change places if:

■ you have ever moved house

■ have lived in another country

■ the team you support has ever lost a match

■ someone has taken something that belonged to you or your family

■ a family pet has died

■ you know someone who has lost an important person in their lives.

Winners and Losers

It is a common insult to be called a 'loser' but everyone has experiences of both winning and losing. In pairs, students interview each other about something that has made them a winner. This can be something that they have done, something that turned out well or getting something they really wanted.

Loss and Losing

In small groups, students make a list of everything that people might lose, from losing a game, losing a possession to losing an important person. Loss is not only about death but someone disappearing from your life in other ways.

■ What are all the feelings you might experience when this happens?

■ Do the circumstances of the loss make a difference to your feelings?

■ What has helped people come to terms with a loss? Make a list.

Celebrating a Life

How might you celebrate someone's life, or an animal you had loved and lost? Make a poster with drawings and words.

Memory Box

Individuals write down a positive and special memory of a person that they have lost and put it in a memory box. Each person takes out a memory and reads it to the Circle before putting it back in the box. This means that the memories are anonymous.

Losing Someone at School

This sometimes happens and affects everyone. Circle Time can help. Without going into details or breaching confidentiality, the facilitator speaks to the Circle about what happened. Facts are easier to deal with than imaginings. It is useful to acknowledge the range of emotions that may accompany this announcement. These include:

- shock

- sadness

- emptiness

- anger

- numbness

- confusion

- fear

- indifference.

Not everyone will feel the same. How individuals feel depends on many things, including how well they knew the person, the circumstances of the death and what else is happening in their own life.

- Ask students to talk to each other in pairs about what support people might need at this time. What, if anything, do they need for themselves and what could they do for others? The facilitator might then choose one or more of the following activities, perhaps leaving this for later Circle Time sessions.

- In pairs, talk about the person and in what ways they might be missed.

- In small groups plan a memorial Circle for the person. Each group decides what they will do for this.

Loss of Trust

This happens when someone lies, breaks confidences, talks behind your back, takes things belonging to someone or lets them down badly. This is not only interpersonal but can be a class concern and difficult to address. These activities help to do so without accusation and blame.

Sentence Completions

■ Trusting someone means ...

■ Keeping confidences means ...

■ Being honest means ...

■ I am able to trust someone who ...

■ I would feel let down by someone if ...

■ I need to trust people in this class because ...

Pair Shares

Trust means different things to different people. Interview each other and find out what it means for them. How important is trust in a friendship?

What happens to friendships when trust is broken? Can it be mended? How might trust be restored?

A Tick for Trust

MS

Each group has two pieces of paper. Each represents the same classroom. In one trust is present, and in the other it is absent. Draw and write in what happens in both.

Discussions

■ What feelings are present in both?

■ What can we do to encourage trust in this class?

Conflict

Conflict is an inevitable part of life: people see things differently, want different things and have different priorities. It is how it is managed that matters. Conflict that is not managed well can lead to feelings of hate, revenge and violence.

Silent Statements

Stand up and change places if:

■ you have ever felt that something was very unfair

■ you have argued over who was right about something

■ you thought you had a right to something and so did someone else

- you have felt that your viewpoint was not listened to or respected

- someone has wanted you to do something you did not want to do

- you have ever regretted something you said or did

- you have felt stuck in a conflict situation.

Swapping Sides

MS

Each pair is given a conflict situation such as:

- someone accusing another of cheating in a game

- one person deriding the religion of the other

- two people wanting the same thing

- someone labelling the other person in a negative way.

They each take up one role and begin a conversation. After two minutes the facilitator stops the conversation and asks the pair to swap seats. They then start arguing from the other person's position.

Discussions

- How did they feel in the different roles?

- Did they begin to understand that there were two sides to a conflict?

- What happened that made the conflict worse? Was anything said that made it better?

Conflict Conversations

MS

(This activity gives the bare bones of a conflict resolution framework.)

Each pair is given a conflict situation or agrees an alternative one. An example could be:

A young person queues up to get an ice cream. As they are leaving with the ice-cream in their hand another person runs into them, not looking where they are going. The ice cream is knocked to the ground. The first person screams abuse at the first and the second takes offence and starts to threaten violence.

Each person takes one of the roles and is given one minute without the other interrupting to give their view of the situation and what they think happened. Then each person is given 30 seconds to say what they feel but does not blame the other. This means a sentence beginning 'I felt ... when you ... ', rather than 'You made me ... ' Each person says what they would want as an outcome. Both partners brainstorm solutions and choose one.

Flight, Fight or Doing it Right?

(There are three responses to challenging situations: aggressive, in which you stand up for your rights at all costs; passive, in which you let other people walk over you; and appropriately assertive, where you state what you want as objectively as possible.)

Give small groups these actions and statements and ask them to divide them into three piles: one a passive flight response, one an aggressive fight response and the other assertive:

- 'You made me do that'

- complain about someone behind their back

- walk a different way home to avoid someone

- 'I feel it's unfair when you ask me for help when I'm watching my favourite TV programme'

- 'You have no idea what you're talking about'

- shout and scream

- go silent

- 'When you yell at me, it's hard to listen to what you're saying'

- agree with someone for the sake of peace and quiet

- ask someone to let you know the day before when plans have been changed

- 'I'm just telling you …'

- 'When I have something important to tell you, I feel upset if you don't listen to me'.

Extension Discussions

- What actions/statements are more likely to resolve a conflict? Which will add to the conflict?

- What feelings are likely for each of these actions/statements for both parties?

Responsibility Circles: Peace and Violence

Give each small group a piece of paper with five concentric circles and a line across the middle so there is a top and bottom half (see Appendix 4). The innermost circle represents the individual person. The next circle represents the class or school. The next circle represents the community including the media. The outermost circle represents society, including culture, politics and the law. In the top half of each circle, write down the ways that violence is created. In the bottom half of each circle, write down the ways in which each level has a responsibility for reducing violence and creating a safe and civil society. Feedback: what needs to happen at each level to reduce violence?

Extension Discussions

■ How does each level affect the others?

■ How might someone intervene at each level?

■ There is a phrase: 'If you think you are too small to make a difference, try sleeping with a mosquito!' Which people do you know who have made or are making a difference to reduce conflict and violence in our society?

■ Every time you don't taunt someone else or lash out in anger, you are making a difference. What other differences can each of us make?

Variation

■ You can also do this activity with feelings and values such as fear, respect, racism and tolerance and so on.

FEELINGS THAT CHALLENGE

The main aim of the following activities is to reflect on ways to limit the damage that negative feelings can do to individuals and to others.

Anger

Anger can be related to many things including loss, attacks on self-esteem and injustice. These activities help students to understand the many roots of anger and ways of expressing their anger safely.

Silent Statements

Stand up and change places if:

■ you have seen someone be angry because of something someone said

■ you have seen someone be angry because they jumped to the worst conclusion

■ you have seen someone be angry because they have been left out of something

■ you have seen someone be angry because they felt they were hurt or treated badly

■ you have been angry because things didn't go the way you wanted

■ you have been angry because you saw other people being treated badly

■ you have been angry and not really known why

■ there have been times in your life when you have felt like crying with frustration

- you have been angry because you have lost something or someone

- you have been angry at the 'wrong person'

- you have been able to keep in control of your anger

- sometimes your anger has been in control of you

- you are angry about some of the things that are happening in your world.

Pair Shares

What things make you both angry?
What have you done with those angry feelings?
In which ways can anger be useful?

Ready, Steady, Stop

Give each small group three body outlines. The first is headed 'Green — all calm'. The second is headed 'Orange — on the alert'. The third is headed 'Red — danger zone'. Write the bodily responses for each level: calm is when things are going your way, orange is when a potential threat appears and red is when the body is fired up to respond. Threats to a sense of self mean that the body gets ready for either flight or fight. Anger is likely to lead to a fight response.

Discussion

- What can you do and when is a good time to do it when you feel yourself getting angry?

- What can you do to show that you are angry that does not get you into trouble or make things worse?

Blow Up

(To think about how anger is increased or released.)

The leader has a balloon and begins a story about anger. Each person takes a turn to add something to the story. If they want to, they can say something that either will increase or release anger. Each time something is said that increases anger, the leader blows air into the balloon; each time something is said that releases anger, air is let out of the balloon. When everyone has had a turn the leader finishes the story. Either the situation has become explosive and the leader bursts the balloon, or anger has been defeated and the balloon is released to whizz round the Circle.

Four Corners

(Exploring alternative reactions to challenging situations.)

The four corners of the room are given these labels:

- Bottle it up

- Fight and hit

- Yell and scream

- Do something else.

Students are given a scenario and go to the corner that shows what they would do. The following are examples, but students could come up with many others:

- someone pushing in front of them in a queue

- being mildly insulted/teased

- being rejected/told to '... off'

- their family is insulted

- someone not looking where they are going and barging into them

- someone taking something without asking.

Discussions

- Does it matter who was doing these things?

- What about the circumstances?

- What are the 'other things' that people might do?

- Do you think about your reactions or just react?

- What might this mean in the future for you?

Worry

Worry Warts

Some worries get bigger if you keep picking at them but fade away if you deal with them effectively. Discuss in pairs what you might do to 'grow' worries and what you might do to shrink them. Here are some examples:

- there's something nasty under the bed!

- you will forget something important

- you will fail an exam

- you will lose something

- you will do something foolish

- you might have upset a friend.

Feedback one thing each that helps worries to get smaller. (Checking the facts, putting things into perspective, checking if you can do anything or not and whose responsibility it is, affirmations, relaxation exercises, working out why this is a particular worry, focusing on what you do well and preparing are all useful strategies that students may suggest.)

Stress

The Last Straw

MS

(Sometimes it is the last thing that happens that causes you to crash.)

Give students a pile of thin coloured sticks (straws) about six inches long (these are available commercially). Ask them to pile these into a heap. Each person takes one stick from the pile in turn. The aim is to do this without all the other sticks collapsing. How many sticks can they get out before this happens?

Discussions

- Often many negative or difficult things happen before you get to that 'last straw', when you feel that you can no longer 'hold it all together'.

- Can you give examples of how things pile up?

- How can you tell that you or someone else is getting very stressed? What are the signs?

- What might be done to stop stress building up or to increase the resources to cope?

- The group feeds back their ideas to the Circle.

Variation

- Building a house of cards in a group has the same message.

Feeling Blue

These activities are intended to stop misery sliding into depression. If you do identify students who are seriously depressed, action needs to be taken.

Silent Statements

Stand up and change places if:

- you have ever had a day in which nothing seemed to go right

- you have ever felt like staying in bed all day

- you know someone who is sad and upset about something that is going on in their life

- you know someone who has managed to get over some really difficult times and is now doing well.

Managing Mountains

MS

(Looking at competencies in coping.)

In pairs, each student draws a mountain and a small person at the bottom of it. This mountain represents the biggest challenge that the student has faced. Each student talks to the other about the qualities that help them to manage the mountains in their life. Do they see themselves as getting through it, over it or around it?

Feedback to the group. Each student says one quality that helped the other person. They do not report back on the 'mountain'.

Half-Full or Half-Empty?

MS

Each group is given a bottle that is filled with water to the halfway mark.

Discussion and activities

- Is the bottle half-full or half-empty?

- Life can be like this — you can focus either on things that are going well or things that are going badly.

- Make a list of 'half-full' statements and thoughts.

- Make a list of 'half-empty' statements and thoughts.

- Think about using the words 'always', 'never' and 'yes but ... ' to yourself. What does this do to how you feel?

- Make a list of 10 'blessings' — things you are grateful for.

- Write a thank-you letter to someone for something they did or said that was important to you.

Bottling Bad Feelings

MS

(This helps with understanding that repressing bad feelings is not necessarily a good idea — it is how they are expressed that matters.)

Each person in the Circle thinks of situation in which they experienced a bad feeling. Did they:

A.   Bottle it up – not say anything to anyone?

B.   Blow it up – express it in ways that made things worse?

C.   Be brave with it – express the feeling in ways which helped?

They write A, B or C or a piece of paper and put this into a bottle. The facilitator counts out how many in each category. The facilitator asks the group what happens if you bottle up or bury bad feelings. This can be a sentence completion or comments from the Circle.

Affirmations

(Affirmations are statements that can help people to think more positively. Like strength cards, these can be bought commercially or made.)

Affirmations are statements such as:

- I am getting better/smarter/wiser every day
- I am able to learn from everything that happens
- I am a survivor
- Today I will find something to smile about
- I am a good friend
- I am special and unique in the world
- I have many strengths to help me in my life
- I can rise to challenges
- Opportunities will be there for me.

Many activities can take place with affirmations both in small groups and the whole circle. Here are some ideas.

- Spread affirmation cards in the centre of the Circle. Each person chooses one for the week. The following week they give feedback.
- In pairs, students choose a card for their partner and tell them why they have made this choice.
- Students are given cards by the facilitator and talk in pairs about what this card might mean for them.
- Each person illustrates their affirmation for themselves to place in their Circle Time file.

Resources

 ## Internet Resources for Circle Time Games

- www.aidsmap.com – Aidsmap

- www.childfun.com – Child fun

- users.stargate.net/~cokids/Circle.html – Circle Time activities

- www.dennydavis.net – Denny's Poems and Quotes (lots of useful alphabet lists for strengths, qualities, etc.).

- www.earlychildhood.com – Early Childhood

- iteslj.org/games – Internet TESL Journal (has activities for students with English as a second language)

- www.wilderdom.com/games – Wilderdom (this also leads to other sites)

Other Useful Websites

- www.authentichappiness.org – Authentic Happiness; this is Martin Seligman's positive psychology website. Here you can identify your 'signature strengths'.

- www.adl.org/education/curriculum_connections – Anti-Defamation League. This US website has ideas for promoting respect for diversity, including multiculturalism and additional needs inclusion. There is a page of basic signs in American Sign Language and an annotated bibliography on children's literature dealing with bullying and building empathy.

- www.livingvalues.net – Living Values is a program supported by the United Nations Educational, Scientific and Cultural Organization (Unesco) and the United Nations Children's Fund (Unicef). On this site you can download posters for a wide range of values for children aged three to seven and eight to 14. This site also has information about Living Values Activities books for purchase.

- www.antidote.org.uk – Campaign for Emotional Literacy (UK)

- www.casel.org – Collaborative for Academic, Social and Emotional Learning (USA)

- www.wellbeingaustralia.com.au – this is the organisation promoting social and emotional literacy in Australia and the Pacific Region.

- www.ncab.org.au – National Coalition Against Bullying (Australia)

- www.rootsofempathy.org – Roots of Empathy (Canada)

- www.safersanerschools.org – Safer Saner Schools; restorative practices in schools

- www.ethosnet.co.uk – Scottish Schools Ethos Network; anti-bullying network (UK)

- www.circlespeak.com.au – restorative practices in schools (Australia)

- www.bounceback.com.au – resilience

Organizations Running Circle Time Training

1. ELECT: Emotional Literacy in Education Consultancy and Training (including Australia and the Pacific Region). Contact: Sue Roffey, enquiries@elect-consultants.com
2. Jenny Mosley Consultancies – www.circle-time.co.uk

Meditation and Relaxation Resources

Garth, M. (1991) *Starbright.* San Francisco, CA: Harper Collins.
Garth, M. (1993) *Moonbeam.* San Francisco, CA: Harper Collins.
Garth, M. (1997) *Earthlight.* San Francisco, CA: Harper Collins.
Massage in Schools (www.massageinschools.com) – training organization promoting the use of safe massage for children by children.
Peace Foundation Network (www.peacefoundationnetwork.org) *Chill Out and Feel Good* CDs. This organization also produces affirmation cards.
Weatherhead, Y. (2004) *Enriching Circle Time: Dream Journeys and Positive Thoughts.* London: Lucky Duck Publishing. (The book comes with a CD.)
White, M. (1999) *Picture This: Guided Imagery for Circle Time.* London: Lucky Duck Publishing.

Strength Cards and Other Useful Materials

Innovative Resources – www.innovativeresources.org

Good Stimulus Stories

Books

Angus, R. (2003) *The Giant Child*. Trowbridge: Positive Press.

Angus, R. (2004) *The Turning Cloth*. Trowbridge: Positive Press.

(Both deal with the same character, Olaf, and how he learns to value his special talents. For primary students.)

Bornman, J., Collins, M. and Maines, B. (2004) *Just the Same on the Inside*. London: Paul Chapman Publishing. (Includes activities to support inclusion and diversity in Circle Time for six to 11-year-olds.)

Brown, T. (1993) *Broken Toy*. London: Paul Chapman Publishing. (Book with accompanying video about bullying for nine to 12-year-olds. Video from America.)

Brown, T. (2000) *Joey*. London: Paul Chapman Publishing. (Story for 13 to 18-year-olds. Video from America.)

Collins, M. (2005) *It's OK to Be Sad*. London: Paul Chapman Publishing. (Book containing 20 stories about different and difficult life events. For four to nine-year-olds.)

Ingouville, F. (2005) *On the Same Side: 133 Stories to Help Resolve Conflict*. London: Paul Chapman Publishing. (For all ages.)

Ironside. V. (1996) *The Huge Bag of Worries*. London: Hodder Children's Books. (For primary students.)

Leicester, M. (2005) *Stories for Circle Time and Assembly: Developing Literacy Skills and Classroom Values*. London: Routledge Falmer. (For younger students.)

Mathr, M. and Yeowart, E. (2004) *The Crescent: Stories to Introduce the Concept of Moral Values for Children aged 5–7*. London: Paul Chapman Publishing.

Moses, B. (1994–2001) *Your Emotions*. London: Hodder Wayland. (Series of books for young children including suggestions for coping with difficult feelings.)

Paul, K., and Thomas. V. (1987) *Winnie the Witch*. Oxford: Oxford University Press.

Petty, K. and Firmin C. (1993) *Playgrounds*. New York: Barron's Educational Hauppauge. (Series on issues such as being left out. For young children.)

Rae, T. (1998) *Dealing with Feelings*. London: Lucky Duck Publishing.

Rae, T. (2003) *Dealing with Some More Feelings*. London: Lucky Duck Publishing.

Videos

Firth, S. (2005) *Outside the Circle*. London: Paul Chapman Publishing. (Video story and activities to combat racism and prejudice. For primary students.)

Firth. S. (2005) *Staying In or Standing Out*. London: Paul Chapman Publishing. (Video and activities to address peer pressure for eight to 12-year-olds.)

Books with even more ideas for developing emotional literacy in Circle Time

(Many of these are photocopiable.)

Bowkett, S. (1999) *Self-Intelligence: A Handbook for Developing Confidence, Self-esteem and Interpersonal Skills.* Stafford: Network Educational Press. (A wealth of activities for working with individual students.)

Cornelius, S. and Faire, S. (1989) *Everyone Can Win: How to Resolve Conflict.* Roseville, NSW: Simon & Schuster. (Still one of the best texts on all aspects of conflict.)

Field, E.M. (1999) *Bully Busting: How to Help Children Deal with Teasing and Bullying.* Sydney, NSW: Finch Publishing.

Fuller, A., Bellhouse, B. and Johnston, G. (2001) *The Heart Masters: A Program for the Promotion of Emotional Intelligence and Resilience.* Queenscliff, Victoria: Inyahead Press. (Three books for lower primary, middle and upper primary and junior secondary.)

Greef, A. (2005) *Resilience, Vol. 1: Personal skills for Effective Learning.* Carmarthen: Crown House Publishing.

Hromek, R. (2004) *Game Time: Games to Promote Social and Emotional Resilience for Children Aged 4 to 14.* London: Lucky Duck Publishing. (Board games suitable for small groups. There are resources adaptable for Circle Time included on a CD.)

McGrath, H. and Noble, T. (2003) *Bounce Back: A Classroom Resiliency Program.* Melbourne: Pearson Education. (Teachers Resource Books have many excellent ideas and activities based in the multiple intelligences model. For lower primary, middle primary, upper primary and junior secondary levels.)

Moore, C. and Rae, T. (2000) *Positive People: A Self-Esteem Building Course for Young Children.* London: Lucky Duck Publishing (Contains role-play cards, certificates and shields.)

Rae, T. (2000) *Purr-fect Skills: A Social and Emotional Skills Program for 5–8-year-olds.* London: Paul Chapman Publishing.

Rae, T. (2004) *Emotional Survival: An Emotional Literacy Course for High School Students.* London: Paul Chapman Publishing.

Schilling, D. (1996) *50 Activities for Teaching Emotional Intelligence.* Austin, TX: Pro-Ed Inc. (For elementary students.)

Southampton Psychology Service (A. Faupel, ed.) (2003) *Emotional Literacy: Assessment and Intervention* (2 vols: 7–11 and 11–16). London: NFER Nelson.

Warden, D. and Christe, D (1999) *Teaching Social Behaviour: Classroom Activities to Teach Social Awareness.* London: David Fulton Publishers. (Cartoon scenarios for discussion. For all ages.)

Western Australian Centre for Health Promotion Research (2000–2) *Friendly Schools: Bullying Intervention Project.* Perth, WA: Curtin University. (Available at: http://wachpr.curtin-edu.au/ htmlprojects/project_detail_FSBIP.html)

Whitehouse, E. and Pudney, W. (1996) *A Volcano in My Tummy: Helping Children to handle anger.* Auckland, NZ and Gabriola Island, Canada: Foundation for Peace Studies and New Society Publishers.

APPENDICES

Appendix 1: Circle Time Plan

Class/teacher/other participants		
Date		
Aims of this Circle		
Rules statement		
ACTIVITIES		Time
Greeting		
Mixing up		
Whole Circle game		
Small group activity		
Any other game of activity		
Closing		
Resources needed		
Notes and follow-up		

Appendix 2: Proforma Letter to Parents/Carers About Circle Time

Dear

This is to let you know that Class   will be doing Circle Time from

Circle Time is a structured framework for group interaction that is intended to support communication skills, personal and social development, resilience and a supportive class atmosphere. It meets a number of curriculum targets.

Circle Time uses individual, paired, small group and whole class activities. Many of these activities are presented as games. Students usually find Circle Time very enjoyable and no doubt will want to tell you about the fun things that they have been doing. However, it does have a very serious intent in providing a space for reflection and discussion on important issues. It enhances the skills needed in healthy relationships, addresses bullying and increases confidence in communication. It also helps students to learn what is involved in creative problem-solving. Positive feelings promote self-esteem, reduce stress and also increase engagement with learning.

If you would like any further information about Circle Time, please contact

Yours sincerely,

Appendix 3: Social Bingo

Find someone different for each category, write down the answer and their name.

Appendix 4: Responsibility Circles

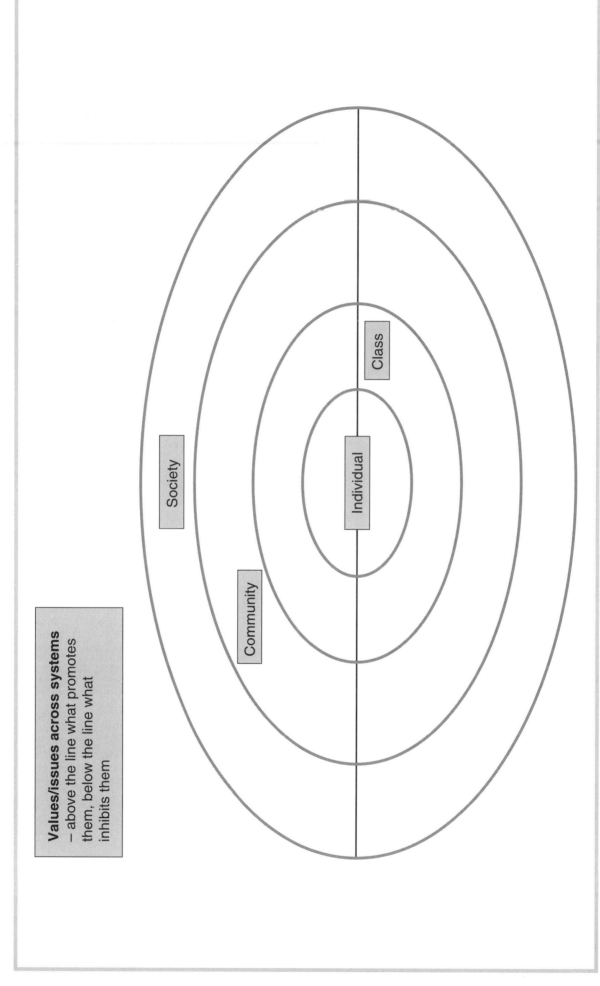

Values/issues across systems
– above the line what promotes
them, below the line what
inhibits them

Society

Community

Class

Individual

Photocopiable: Circle Time for Emotional Literacy
Paul Chapman Publishing 2006 © Sue Roffey

REFERENCES

Bandura, A. (1986) *Social Foundations of Thought and Action.* Englewood Cliffs, NJ: Prentice-Hall.

Bowlby, J. (1982 [1969]) *Attachment.* New York: Basic Books.

Cohen, J. (ed.) (2001) *Caring Classrooms, Intelligent Schools: The Social Emotional Education of Young Children.* Columbia, NY: Teachers College Press.

Commonwealth of Australia (2005) *The National Framework for Values Education.* Canberra: Department of Education, Science and Training.

Department for Education and Skills (DfES) (2005) *Excellence and Enjoyment: Social and Emotional Aspects of Learning.* London: DfES. (Available at: http://www.publications.teachernet.gov.uk)

Fredrickson, B.L., Mancuso, R.A., Branigan, C. and Tugade, M.M. (2000) 'The Undoing Effect of Positive Emotions', *Motivation and Emotion* 24(4): 237–56.

Gable, S.L., Reis, H.T. and Downey, G. (2003) 'He Said, She said: A Quasi-signal Detection Analysis of Spouses' Perceptions of Everyday Interactions', *Psychological Science* 14: 100–5.

Gilligan, C. (1982) *In a Different Voice: Psychological Theory and Women's Development.* Cambridge, MA: Harvard University Press.

Glasser, W. (1997). '"Choice theory" and Student Success', *Education Digest* 63(3): 16–21.

Ishikawa, K. (1985) *What Is Total Quality Control?* (trans. D.J. Lu) Englewood Cliffs, NJ: Prentice-Hall.

Kohlberg, L. and Turiel, E. (1971) 'Moral Development and Moral Education', in G. Lesser (ed.) *Psychology and Educational Practice.* Glenview, II: Scott, Foresman.

Moen, P., Elder, G.H. and Luscher, K. (1995) *Examining Lives in Context: Perspectives on the Ecology of Human Development.* Washington, DC: American Psychological Association.

Murray, J. (2004) 'Making Sense of Resilience: A Useful Step on the Road to Creating and Maintaining Resilient Students and School Communities', *Australian Guidance and Counselling* 14(1): 1–15.

Phillips, B. (2002) *An Evaluation of AVP Workshops in Aotearoa/New Zealand.* Wellington: Alternatives to Violence Project Aotearoa.

Potter, J. (1996) *Representing Reality: Discourse, Rhetoric and Social Construction.* London: Sage.

Rigby, K. and Bagshaw, D. (2006) 'Using Educational Drama and Bystander Training to Counteract Bullying', in H. McGrath and T. Noble (eds) *Bullying Solutions: Evidence-based Approaches to Bullying in Australian Schools,* pp. 133–45. Melbourne: Pearson Education.

Roffey, S. (2004) *The New Teacher's Survival Guide to Behaviour.* London: Sage.

Roffey, S. (2005a) 'Promoting Relationships and Resilience: Effective Processes for the Implementation of Circle Time' unpublished paper (available from the author).

Roffey, S. (2005b) 'Respect in Practice: The Challenge of Emotional Literacy in Education', Australian Association for Research in Education Conference Papers, Paramatta, Australia, 30 November. (Available at: http://www.aare.edu.au/05pap/abs05.html)

Seligman, M., Steen, T., Park, N. and Peterson, C. (2005) 'Positive Psychology Progress: Empirical Validation of Interventions', *American Psychologist, CO:* 410–21.

Stanley, F., Richardson, S. and Prior, M. (2005) *Children of the Lucky Country? How Australia Has Turned its Back on Children and Why Children Matter.* Sydney: Macmillan.

Taylor, M. (2003) *Going Round in Circles: Implementing and Learning from Circle Time.* Slough: NFER.

Vygotsky, L. (1978). *Mind in Society.* Cambridge, MA: Harvard University Press.

Zins, J.E., Weissberg, R.P., Wang, M.C. and Walber, H. (2004) *Building Academic Success on Social and Emotional Learning: What Does the Research Say?* Columbia, NY: Teachers College Press.

INDEX